```
IIIIIIIIIIIIIIIIIIIIIIIIIII
    I0126107
```

VOLUME

2

MORTGAGE LENDING

Loan Processing Level 2

ISBN-13: 978-1-933039-23-7

Library of Congress in Publication Data

November 03, 2003

Mortgage Loan Processor Advancement Training

10 9 8 7 6 5 4 3 2 1

The enclosed material is designed for educational purposes only. Each State may have different certification and specific guidelines. Please refer to your State for additional and future information. The information contained herein is considered correct at the time of creation but laws and regulations are updated frequently and the reader assumes the responsibility for confirming current regulations and applicable data. The publisher and author make no warranty as to the success of the individuals using the training material contained herein. The publisher and author make no warranty as to any action taken by any individual completing this program. The reader is responsible for the appropriate use of the materials and information provided. This publication is designed to provide accurate and authoritative information concerning the subject matter. All material is sold with the understanding that neither the author nor the publisher guarantees the actions of any individual making use of the inclusions. Neither the author nor the publisher is rendering a legal opinion, accounting recommendation or other professional service. If legal advice or other expert assistance is desired, the services of a legal professional or other individual should be sought. The applicable federally released forms, disclosures, and notices are generated from public domain. Copyright law does apply to all intellectual materials and all rights under said law are reserved b y the copyright owner.

Coursework is available at special quantity discounts to use as premiums and sales promotions within corporate or private training programs. To obtain information or inquire about availability please write to Director, PO Box 1, Hollidaysburg, PA 16648.

NOTICE

MORTGAGE LENDING

Loan Processing Level 2

Benefits-Enhanced Skill Base

Congratulations on your decision to improve your skills and knowledge base to increase your career potential. Your position carries a tremendous workload and incredible responsibilities that encompass a wide range of projects, tasks, strengths, and talents.

The breadth of skills you have mastered to reach a level of competence where you feel secure in stating that you are ready for an advanced degree of training is enormous.

Throughout this course, you will obtain information to assist you in progressing in your career path. You have mastered a certain level of competence, ingenuity, and drive to obtain a level of competence that allows you to feel secure that you are ready for advanced education and skills.

This course is an advanced education program for professional Mortgage Loan Processors who have the experience and skills in place that allow them to perform their job efficiently. What we will do in the coming days is fine-tune your advanced practices to incorporate new, upper level skills into your workday. These new practices and skills will assist you in understanding the advanced practices your packages undergo as they move through the loan strategy planning, underwriting, and approval processes. This new understanding will assist you in gaining the ability to qualify your packages before they reach the desk of the underwriter.

You will learn to assess each item that may create an additional stipulation or slow the loan process before you submit the package to the underwriter. This ability will enable you to address many of these issues before it even becomes an issue. Competently handling potential problems before they develop into a true roadblock in the path to closing the loan will dramatically smooth your processes. You will decrease the time from loan submittal to loan closing and promote a higher level of satisfaction within each individual involved in the loan process.

The materials in this course are applicable for all levels within the mortgage office structure. The materials you will review in the following days are materials that cross over every position within the system and lead to the path to success.

When you have completed the course inclusions, you will know that you are walking into your office better skilled and with more promotion potential than those who have not taken the initiative to improve their career building skills. Moreover, you will know that you obtained this advanced degree of knowledge and skill because you have a special spark and forward moving potential that made you a candidate for enrollment.

You have shown that you have excellent tools and proven techniques you use on a daily basis to ensure you perform your duties in a professional and efficient manner. This course will not attempt to alter your excellent performance but rather will fine-tune certain aspects of your professional skills to lead you to greater success both on a daily basis and throughout your career.

Today's competitive work environment increases the demands and responsibilities that fall upon you each day. Your position has grown to encompass more responsibility and challenges then ever before.

This course design provides you with the tools and information necessary to develop the best possible processing skills. Your success in your present and future responsibilities is dependent on your ability to master the advanced understanding to competently assess the entire loan file, locate potential roadblocks that exist and solve problems before they become an issue.

The course includes many skill-building exercises designed to assist you in gaining a competitive edge. You will implement some essential techniques that will create an aura of efficiency and power around your performance. You will find that the integration of these techniques will make yours the most desirable service within the office structure.

Once you have mastered the skills included, you will find that your workday progresses more smoothly. There will be enough time in the day to complete each task on your desk. Best of all your potential will increase with each Chapter you master.

CHAPTER 1

THE LENDING PROCESS

Gaining a comprehensive understanding of the lending arena and the processes that occur between the application by a borrower and the purchase of packaged closed loans on the secondary market is the first step you must take on the path to career success.

The mortgage market is divided into two classifications.

- The primary mortgage market

- The secondary mortgage market

The primary mortgage market is the area where lenders work directly with borrowers to originate, document and close loans. Examples of entities within the primary mortgage market are

- Mortgage Brokerage Office
- Savings Banks
- Commercial Banks
- Mutual Savings Bank
- Credit Union

These lending institutions work directly with borrowers who need funding to purchase real estate.

The employees who work within the mortgage department at these locations are known as loan processors, loan originators, mortgage brokers, and loan officers.

COMMON TITLES

A **Loan Originator** is someone who spends a great part of the workday on the streets soliciting borrower referrals from affinity groups. They bring these borrower referrals back to their office, structure the loan package that meets the borrowers needs, and document a package that will enable the lending institution to fund a solid loan. The act of being an originator means that your primary focus is to originate loans.

A **Loan Officer** is someone who spends a great deal of his or her time in the office, interviewing potential borrowers and structuring the available loan products to meet the needs and specific situation of the borrower. The primary goal of the loan officer is to ensure that each loan closed provides all of the parties involved with the best possible loan package.

A **Mortgage Broker** is someone who uses their vast knowledge of the mortgage industry to bring potential borrower packages to the right lending institution and obtain the loan program that meets the needs of both the borrower and lender. The broker acts as a liaison bringing the potential borrowers together with the right lender and loan program to ensure that the borrower achieves their dreams of homeownership.

A **Loan Processor** assists the borrower in obtaining all of the documents and services that are required to complete the loan process and purchase transaction. The essential element of the loan-processing career is to act as a liaison between the borrower and all other individuals whose assistance is required to achieve a closed loan. The loan processor's primary focus during the loan process is to ensure all tasks are completed in a timely manner and that all items incorporated into the closing package are correct and free of errors.

Each of these individuals will work directly with the borrower to accomplish the tasks that lead to a home loan funding.

- Complete the mortgage loan application or 1003.
- Obtain loan stipulations or documentation required by the stipulations list or sales agreement.
- Order affiliate services such as Title Searches and Appraisals.
- Generate the borrower's good faith estimate.
- Provide all required disclosures and notifications to the borrower.
- Structure the mortgage loan funding and borrower down payment to meet the parameters of the loan approval.
- Arrange and oversee the borrowers closing on the property.

Many borrowers assume that the bank where they make the loan application funds the mortgage loans through available cash resulting from the deposits of the individuals who conduct their banking activity at that bank. In some cases, this is exactly where the funds required to provide a mortgage loan originate. However, these depository funds are often inadequate to meet the borrowing needs of all of the individuals who obtain loan proceeds from the local institution.

SECONDARY MORTGAGE MARKET

Lenders within the primary mortgage market will underwrite and fund mortgage loans that the borrower applies for with the cash that they have on hand. Once the lender has a group of funded loan packages, they will combine the many funded loan packages into one large package and offer it for sale to the secondary mortgage market.

The secondary mortgage market includes entities such as

- Insurance Companies
- Primary Lenders with excess deposits
- Pension Funds
- Individual Investors

The secondary mortgage market purchases funded and closed loans from the direct lender in the primary mortgage market.

- This purchase of the closed loans enables the banks and institutions within the primary market to fund more loans than would be possible if they had to fund and service all of the debt load within their portfolio themselves.

- This funding enables the entities on the secondary market to obtain the return on their investment generated through the interest and penalty figures applied to the borrowed funds.

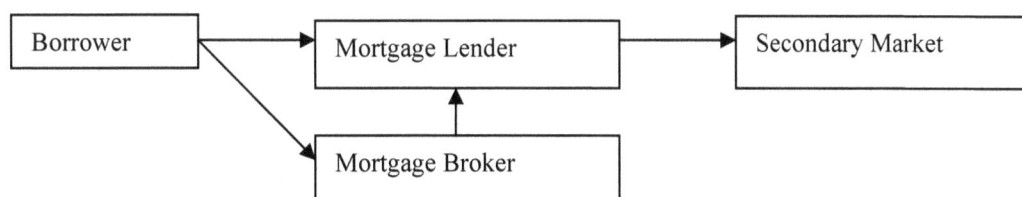

Figure 1:1 Mortgage Market Flow

How it works:

1. The borrower makes a mortgage application with mortgage loan officer or mortgage loan processor who works in a Mortgage Bank that funds its own loans or in a Mortgage Brokerage that works with multiple funding sources.

2. The mortgage lender provides the borrower with the funds to purchase the home.

3. The mortgage bank or loan funding institution completes this process as many times as possible with the funds that they have available.

4. The mortgage bank or loan funding institution then packages the loan with other loans that have been funded with their capital.

   - If the overall loan package is large enough (worth enough money), the funding institution offers that package for sale to investors within the secondary mortgage market.

   - If the mortgage-funding source does not have enough loan products to package into large enough groups to meet the needs of the secondary mortgage market, they will package them into a smaller grouping and offer the package to another lending institution or a smaller investing group.

     This smaller group of investors forms what is termed an investing pool. An investing pool can include anyone who is seeking a low risk, long-term investment and has the capital available to purchase the packaged loan products.

     This investing pool will then collect the interest on the loans that they have purchased and achieve the return on their capital investment that meets their needs.

- If the loans are packaged and sold to another lending institution, that institution will package the purchased loans with their own funded loan packages and create an overall offering large enough to be offered to the secondary mortgage market.

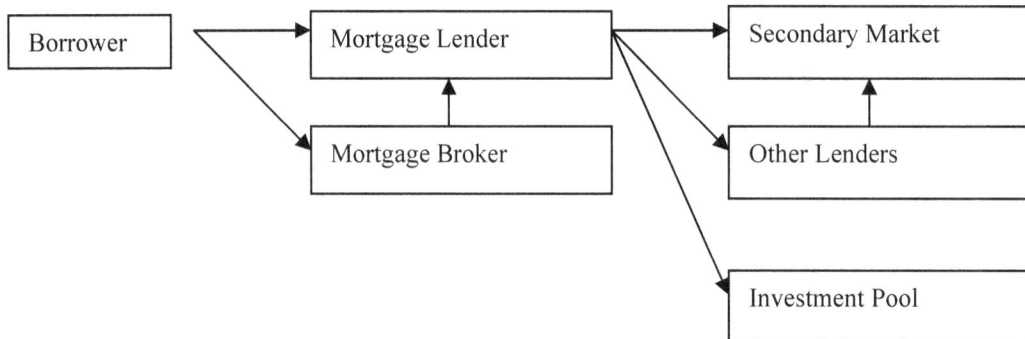

```
 ┌──────────┐        ┌─────────────────┐        ┌──────────────────┐
 │ Borrower │ ─────▶ │ Mortgage Lender │ ─────▶ │ Secondary Market │
 └──────────┘   ╲    └─────────────────┘   ╲    └──────────────────┘
                 ╲            ▲              ╲            ▲
                  ▼           │               ▼          │
            ┌─────────────────┐         ┌──────────────────┐
            │ Mortgage Broker │         │  Other Lenders   │
            └─────────────────┘         └──────────────────┘
                                        ┌──────────────────┐
                                        │ Investment Pool  │
                                        └──────────────────┘
```

Figure 1:1 Mortgage Market Expanded Flow

As a loan processor, you will play a critical part in the success of all of these entities. The fundamental beginning that enables all of the described processes to function will rest on the work you will complete in assisting borrowers in fulfilling all of the stipulations required to obtain loan approval and close the loan package. You will complete these tasks for either a mortgage bank or a mortgage brokerage.

BANKING VS BROKERING

The first decision you will make as a loan processor is whether you will choose to create your business within the structure of a traditional banking institution or within a mortgage brokerage. Included within this decision is whether you will base your office out of a home office or within the conventional environment of the mortgage bank or brokerage.

Working in a Bank

A bank is a lending institution that typically underwrites, processes, and funds mortgage loans with their own money. The benefits of working with a traditional banking environment are obvious.

- Traditional banking institutions are typically located within the community that they serve. Working within a recognized community institution will provide you with name recognition that gives your borrowers an immediate sense of reliability.

- Traditional lenders often retain their own team of loan underwriters, processors, closers, and post-closers that will enable you to create a "team" atmosphere that may assist in smoother loan processes and closings.

- The loans that you originate and process will be funded by the bank for which you work. This in-house funding typically creates a smoother loan process in that the underwriters will usually not change the loan terms, stipulations, or requirements after you have obtained an initial approval of the application.

Working for a bank also has its downside.

- A bank will have a limited number of products available and these will have very specific guidelines.

The limited program availability from a bank means, if your borrower does not fit within those guidelines, they will be declined.

Since you will only have access to the products or loan types offered by the bank for which you work, a borrower who is declined for your loan products will need to "shop" other lenders to obtain their mortgage loan.

- Banks are more likely to have only "A" paper product available. This limited product availability limits your borrowers to those who have "A" credit. Most banks do have additional programs for those B/C borrowers who fall just below the A Paper criteria but the programs are typically not as competitive as the products your Brokering competition can locate.

  This lack of product availability will place limitations on how large your personal business is able to grow because you will only be able to work with those borrowers in your region who meet the specified guidelines of your bank. The remaining borrowers will work with another loan processor.

Working in a Brokerage

A Mortgage Broker acts as a liaison between the borrower seeking mortgage funds and multiple funding sources. The mortgage brokerage will typically not fund any loans but will fulfills the task of shopping for the perfect loan to meet each borrowers specific situation and mortgage needs.

- A Broker typically works with multiple lenders enabling them to offer a variety of loan programs. You will find most Brokerages have contracted to write loans for between 40 and 200 different lenders. This variety allows you to shop many programs making it relatively easy to find an approval program for more of the loan applications that you originate.

- As a loan processor with a mortgage brokerage, you will have the ability to obtain competing approvals for the funding of each loan application that you process. Rather than one cut and dried approval that may kill your deal at the time of loan application, you should be able to find options that allow you to customize the loan program to suit your borrower's needs.

Example:	Lender 1 approves the borrower's application with a low interest rate but requires that the borrower place a large amount of money down as a contingency of the approval.
Issue:	Your borrowers are cash poor but are willing to make a higher monthly payment.
Solution:	You locate another lender within your contracts that is willing to fund the loan at a slightly higher interest rate in exchange for the borrower's ability to place less money down.

Working at a mortgage brokerage also has some inherent disadvantages that you would need to overcome.

- You are not on the same "team" as your underwriters, closers and post-closers but you will find that if you build respectful rapport with these individuals your goals are the same – closed loans.

- Mortgage Brokerage offices are typically not as recognizable within the community. Banking institutions offer many services to their customers beyond the mortgage loan service enabling the loan officer within the bank to originate more borrowers from the customer base of the bank. A mortgage brokerage typically offers only loan services. This will limit the name recognition of the company within the community and the available customer pool will be related only to the mortgage processes rather than a diverse group of customer offerings.

Regardless of the employment method you choose, there are as many ways to put a loan package together as there are borrowers in your town. It will be up to you to combine your knowledge of the industry and the products available to you with the essential drive and creativity that led you to the lending arena.

Working from Home

Many banks and brokerages are now hiring loan processors as full W-2 employees and enabling them to base their business out of their own home. These loan processors process and document loan packages in the same manner as the more conventional specialists working out of an office.

Some banks and brokerages will hire a loan processor who will e-commute and blend the two location options to customize their business around their lifestyle. A loan processor working in this manner will spend a portion of their time in the office and the remainder of their time working from home.

- Through e-commuting or setting your office up entirely out of your home, you will be able to customize your career around your lifestyle and family to create the career option that will enable you to excel within the industry.

- You will be able to use the resources of the bank or brokerage for which you work during your in-office time but service your customers from your home office enabling you to build a customer base that depends entirely on you. If you transfer positions or companies, you will retain the customer base you have built providing you with a solid foundation upon which to build your career.

- You are considered an employee with all of the benefits of W-2 employment while you retain the freedom and independence of being your own boss.

There are varieties of positions available within the Mortgage Lending arena to suit your personal goals, needs and personalized career path. You will customize your career path around your situation, desired level of managerial input, and the freedom you need to build your career successfully.

Upon completion of this coursework, you will be better trained than 90% of the loan processors currently employed within the mortgage industry. You will be an asset in the industry with the ability to build your career to suit your needs and desired level of success.

We will review materials concerning charting your career and negotiating a position in the Career Tools segment. Throughout your training you should continue to consider what environment would most benefit you and we will provide the foundation of knowledge, industry skills, and tools you need to achieve success in that environment.

Chapter

2

BORROWER PRE-QUALIFICATION

From the moment you first speak with a prospective borrower, you should be gathering information and planning how you will process the loan. Many mortgage professionals fail to achieve their goals for the simple reason that they are afraid to ask for information.

Information is your most valuable tool in planning a loan strategy. Obtaining information is quite simple if you just get over the natural shyness of asking strangers for personal information. You will find that, as a professional, people will answer almost any question you ask. However, you must ask!

On the next page, you will find a "Pre-approval Questionnaire" that we recommend using for each prospective borrower. Most of your initial contacts will be over the telephone. If you have this form handy, preferably bound in a notebook, you will always be able to lead the conversation exactly where you, as the professional, need it to go.

The pre-approval questionnaire is your most important ally. Most of the information required when pre-certifying a loan package is included in the questionnaire. In fact, much of the basic information that will be required for the residential mortgage application is included. This allows you to pre-fill some information, subject to verification during the application interview.

Pre-filling saves time and allows you and the borrower to focus on the loan process requirements.

Kenney

Pre-Qualification Questionnaire Date: _____

Referral: _____ Phone: _____

Borrower Name: _____ Co-Borrower Name: _____

Home Phone: _____ Other Phone: _____ Best time(s) to call: _____

DOB: _____ SSN: _____ DOB: _____ SSN: _____

May I run a credit report?___ Yes ___ No   May I run a credit report? ___ Yes ___ No

Employer: _____ Employer: _____

Address: _____ Address: _____

Phone: _____ No yrs. ___ Position: _____ Phone: _____ No yrs. ___ Position: _____

Current Address: _____ Check? ___ Yes ___ No

Landlord/Mortgage Holder: _____ Phone: _____

Rent ____ Own ___ No. Yrs: ___ Have you chosen a home to purchase? ___ Yes ___ No Value$_____

___ 1st ___2nd ___Rate/Term Refi ___ C/O Refi ___ Special: _____

Gross Income   Debt

Borrowers Mthly $_____   Mortgage/Rental Payment $_____

    Prev Year $_____   Auto Payment $_____

Co-Borrowers Mthly $_____   Auto Payment #2 $_____

    Prev Year $_____   Installment Debt / Type _____ $_____

Other Income _____ $_____   Installment Debt / Type _____ $_____

Other Income _____ $_____   Other _____ $_____

    Total Income $_____   Total Debt $_____

DTI _____%

Explanation of Credit Situation/Notes: _____
_____
_____
_____

Outcome:

Taken By: _____

L/P: _____

10

Pre-qualification Questionnaire Key

Date You will always want to date the query.

You may need to 'shelve' a query until an issue has seasoned.

It is our recommendation that you bind each month's questionnaires in a master folder for tracking of referral sources, inquiries vs. applications and other numbers that will affect your career.

You will want to keep a copy of any query that does not lead to a full application for follow-up marketing.

Referral You will want to have referral information available so you may provide follow-up information.

Tracking referral source information will allow you to assess your branches marketing and advertising effort effectiveness.

Telephone Number You will want to have the referral partner's telephone number handy to assist you in maintaining communication.

Look these up yourself, DO **NOT** require your borrower to find the number for you.

Keeping referral partners informed of the progress of a package is one of your greatest assets.

These updates provide a fabulous reason for a face-to-face 'call' on a referral partner and their office.

Referral partners appreciate frequent updates. Referral partners are reluctant to work with a loan processor who does not consistently provide status information concerning the status of a borrower's application.

Borrower Name You will need the full name including middle initial and any additional information Jr., Sr., II

Do not use nicknames.

Note any aliases that the borrower commonly uses.

Names, especially among family, can be very similar.

The more identifying information you can acquire the more pure your credit report will be.

Co-Borrower Name Some applications will not have a co-borrower.

When a co-borrower exists, it is important to acquire correct identifying information for this person to ensure sufficient pre-qualification data is available.

If the co-borrower information is not readily available at the time of the call, complete the primary borrower information and request the applicant telephone you later the same day with the co-borrower information.

Date of Birth/Social Security Number etc	This information is important for the loan application and vital when you are pulling a credit report.
	Always pull credit reports separately.
	Even if the borrower and co-borrower are married, you will want to have separate reports.
	There are times you will want to drop one borrower in an effort to improve loan grades.
May I run a credit report?	It is imperative that you obtain permission to pull a borrower's credit report.
	You will have the borrower sign the credit consent forms later in the loan process.
	Consent must be available before you may run the report.
	You may not run a credit report on any individual without their consent.
Employer	This information aids you in determining some of the issues that may arise during the course of the loan.
	If there is a history of job changes or there is not a 2-year employment history a problem may exist during documentation. Issues such as these are red flags.
Number of years at present employment	You are looking for a minimum of two years employment history.
	If the borrower/co-borrower has not been in their current employment two years, you will need to trace back under comments until you acquire a complete two-year history.
	This is an excellent reference when you have an application that requires an exception. A common compensating factor is 'at current employment more than 5 years.
Current Address	This is identifying information you will want to have to clarify identity on the credit report.
Do you rent or own?	This allows you to determine potential source of funds, loan product possibilities and additional documentation that you may require from the borrower.
Landlord/Mortgage Holder	It is important to determine from the start if the borrower pays an entity or an individual for their housing expense.
	You can verify payments to an entity via VOR/VOM but an individual will typically require checks for verification of payment history.
Do you pay by check?	This question is important if the borrower or co-borrower rents or is purchasing from an individual.
	If your borrower or co-borrower rents or is buying from an individual and does not pay by check, you will typically need to acquire alternate documentation as proof of rental/mortgage payment history.

Number of years at Present address?

You will need a two-year residence history for each borrower on the application.

If the borrower has been at the current residence less than two years, you will need to add in comments any additional residence history until you obtain two full years.

This is an excellent reference when you have an application that requires an exception. A common compensating factor is 'at current residence more than 5 years.

Have you chosen a home to purchase?

You will want to determine the urgency of the query and if the borrower is currently working with an Agent.

If no Agent is working with the borrower, you will want to take the opportunity to refer the borrower to an affinity member with whom you would like to establish a referral relationship.

Perform all referrals after you have the borrower commitment to your programs. Since you do not have a referring relationship built with the referral partner, they may refer these borrowers to another lender if you do not obtain the commitment before sending the borrower to the partner.

Value

This question pertains to the package even if they have not chosen a home to purchase.

You will want to get an idea of their expectations and the price range they are considering.

The loan officer will need to take this figure and determine if their expectations are reasonable and fit into their DTI.

Often borrowers are very high or very low in their estimate of what they are able to afford.

The loan officer will want to pre-qualify the borrower for the highest amount they feel comfortably fits their budget.

Type of Loan

1st Mortgage, 2nd Mortgage, Rate or Term Refinance, Cash-out Refinance.

Knowing the type of loan the borrower or co-borrower believes they desire, allows the loan officer to begin planning the loan structure and matrix placement from the moment of query.

You will find some product approvals vary greatly depending on the type of loan.

Income Information

In order to pre-qualify a package you must have complete income information.

Many loan denials occur due to excessive DTI Ratios.

All income should be entered even if the borrower does not wish to use all income as qualifying income or if not all the income can be used as qualifying income. This is an excellent reference when you have an application that requires an exception. Income is a part of many compensating factors.

Debt Information

Debt load will be visible on the Credit Report but it is important to ask a borrower this information. There may be new debt, which is not yet showing on the report but may crop up before closing the loan.

Child support and alimony payments do affect the debt load.

**Explanation of
credit situation?**   This is the opportunity for notes.

Your borrowers will usually explain any information that is present on their credit report.

Gathering this information now allows you to pre-plan the loan package, request any additional documentation that you may need and is an excellent reference if problems appear later in the loan process.

Outcome   You will want to note what happened with the query.

Some queries will lead to an application.

You will file other queries for follow-up when an issue is resolved.

Keeping a file of this information allows you to track your numbers in future months.

Outcome is important if the borrower's are working with an agent.

You will want immediate documentation if the package dies at query so your agent is not spending valuable time working with borrower's who you cannot qualify at this time.

Lending is a service business. The final analysis shows that our most important "product" is our professionalism, attentiveness, and responsiveness to our borrowers. Much of our communication is on the telephone.

Whether you are communicating with a borrower, prospect, or others on the telephone or in person, the impression that you convey creates an image in the person's mind. This image will affect your future relationship with that person. For those reasons, it is important that your conversations are controlled and concise. A complete course on telephone and conversational control is available in our advanced program offerings. For now, you must focus on learning career basics. To assist you we have provided a script to allow you to flow smoothly through the pre-qualification process.

The pre-approval questionnaire offers an excellent tool for structuring your first contact.

The proper way to use the questionnaire is as follows:

L/P: Good morning/afternoon/evening, Your Company Name this is Your Name, may I help you?

Borrower: They will state the reason for there call and very likely explain their situation.

L/P: Do you have a few minutes to answer a couple of questions?

Borrower: Since they made the call to you, they will typically have a few minutes to spare while they determine if you have a program to fit their situation.

L/P: Could you tell me how you were referred to us? (DO NOT ask for details such as telephone number of referral source – you can look this information up yourself).

L/P: What is your name?

L/P: Will you be on loan alone or with someone else? (Keep in mind that it is occasionally prudent to cut either the borrower or co-borrower from the loan later in the process. This is a decision will be made based on credit scores and/or income and debt ratios.

L/P: What is your Date of Birth?

L/P: What is your Social Security Number?

L/P: May I run a credit report?

You are looking for a yes. None of the other information you acquire will aid you in any way if you cannot see what type of credit situation you are dealing with. The approval to run a credit report signifies a commitment on the part of the borrower to your loan program.

L/P: Where are you employed?

L/P: How long have you been there?

If they have been at their current employment less than two years, you will need to acquire two full years' employment history before completing the application.

L/P: What is your position?

L/P: Ask for the same information for the co-borrower.

L/P: What is your current address?

L/P: How long have you lived there?

L/P: Do you rent or own the home?

L/P: Who is your landlord or mortgage holder?

If the landlord or lender is a company there is no need for further documentation, it will typically appear on the credit report. However, if the landlord/mortgage holder is an individual, more documentation will be required to prove a mortgage/rental history.

L/P: Do you pay by cash or check?

This question only applies in the event that their landlord/mortgage holder is an individual.

L/P: Have you chosen a home to purchase?

This will allow you to rate the urgency of the file. A borrower who has not begun the home search process will be less urgent than a borrower with a sales contract in hand.

L/P: Do you know the amount you are looking to spend?

This question allows the loan officer to determine from the start if their spending expectations are set too high for some of the loan products and place them accordingly.

L/P: What is your monthly income?

You will frequently need to do the math yourself. Accept the income they give you whether they provide yearly, monthly, or weekly income figures.

L/P: Do you have income you wish use from any other source: rental property, alimony, child support etc?

A borrower is not required to use additional income as part of the approval criteria. If the borrower wishes to use other income, it is allowable.

L/P: Obtain the same information for the co-borrower.

L/P: What is your monthly rent/mortgage payment?

L/P: What is your car payment?

L/P: Do you have a second car?

L/P: Do you have any credit cards or personal loans?

L/P   What are the monthly payments?

A borrower's debt load will be visible on the credit report but it is advisable to review the debts with the borrower to limit surprises later in the process.

Throughout the questionnaire, the borrower will be giving you information that you will want to note in the explanation of credit situation section. This aids you in determining the special circumstances surrounding this loan package.

Upon completion of the questionnaire, you will want to assure the borrower that they ARE your borrower, plan to pre-qualify their questionnaire and set an appointment to meet face-to-face, verify their information, and discuss their loan options. A sample of how to do this smoothly is as follows:

L/P: Ok, I plan to pass this information over to _____. They will be working with us to during the early stages of your loan. We will review your information tonight to see what programs will work best for your situation. Are you available date not more than two days away?

Borrower: Answers positive or negative

L/P: Set up an appointment.

L/P: Ok, when you come I will need you to bring a few things. I will need (below are the most common items to request – you will need to refer to documenting a loan package for detailed information):

- W-2's from the last two years

- Proof of any additional income you want me to consider – child support order, divorce decree

- Any proof you have concerning (whatever their special credit situation BK, Divorce Decree, etc.)

- 12 months cancelled rent checks (if paying an individual)

L/P: Ok then, I will see you on date at time if there are any problems, please give me a call.

Upon completion of the questionnaire, you will be able to pre-qualify a borrower. Providing you obtained their permission, your next step is to pull a credit report and provide the entire pre-qualification package to the loan officer so they may determine initial purchase levels and possible loan programs.

Chapter 3

TELEPHONE AND TIME MANAGEMENT

Before moving on to assessing a credit report there is a vital skill you must obtain that will assist you with the implementation of each facet of your advanced training skills. Learning professional skills is as important to your career success as gaining the core industry.

Today you make most of your contacts with people over the telephone. If you review your list of tasks and the times per day, you complete each task, the telephone contacts will no doubt outnumber any other task on the listing.

One capability you must obtain is the ability to maintain control of conversations either on the telephone or in person.

The ability to maintain control of each conversation provides many vital benefits.

- You communicate more effectively.

- You will obtain and relay the required information in a more time efficient manner.

- You will quickly move on to the next important task on your list.

- You will gain control of your workday ensuring you allocate enough time in your schedule to complete each task on your task list in a time efficient manner.

In today's high pressure, fast-paced business world time is a commodity we cannot afford to waste. Many of us spend hours a week in one of the biggest time consumers in an average workday. We make telephone calls that aimlessly wander from subject to subject with no apparent core purpose.

Outgoing Calls

When you are preparing to make a telephone call, you will have specific goals in place that generate the need for the call. You must be able to:

- Clearly and concisely, control the call.

- Convey the information necessary.

- End the call.

You must do all of these tasks with professionalism and the customer service oriented personality that makes it a pleasure to receive a call from you.

Before making any call, ask yourself some important questions.

1. Why am I making this call?

2. What information do I need to obtain from this call?

3. What information must I convey with this call?

4. Is the information I must convey vital enough that I must speak directly with the person?

5. Can I include the necessary information in a message?

This may look like an inefficient list of questions to take time answering before each call but it is not. The time saved by minimizing aimless conversation and return calls will have a dramatic impact on the overall time you have invested in telephone calls each day.

You will soon be in the habit of knowing these answers before you make any call.

Until you have retrained, your habits to incorporate this list of questions into each telephone call efficiently and without conscious thought you will want to:

- Keep this list of questions taped under your telephone area.

- Generate a list of answers to each question for each contact on your task list or in the contact journal entries.

This reminder system will soon become an unnecessary function for you, but initially it will be vital in training your mind and habits to control conversational flow.

SKILL BUILDER HABIT:

Organize your call to obtain control.

1. Make a listing of the essential items that you need to discuss with the person.

2. Prioritize that list so that you introduce the most important items into the conversation early.

3. Have the journal, files and documents that pertain to that contact available for reference before you place the call.

4. Prepare to enter information into the journal entry of the contact so that you can later reference the conversation and quickly determine any essential factors discussed during the conversation.

Many of us interject social niceties into the conversation when we place a business call. These social graces have a huge place in today's workplace and assist you in conveying a professional, customer service oriented persona to each contact.

There are simple methods of smoothly accomplishing your goals with a telephone call. You can convey and obtain all of the required information while maintaining a short conversational flow and incorporating social pleasantries that makes the contact feel pleased to have you call.

A point to remember is that by taking control of the conversational flow and ensuring the conveyance of all vital information you are not creating an abrupt telephone personality.

You are accomplishing a vital task that will save you hours during the course of a regular workweek and save your contacts vital time as well. The people you are calling are under the same time sensitive pressures as you and you will quickly become their favorite telephone contact. If you are efficient at accomplishing all of the vital tasks required from a telephone call in a smooth and efficient manner. You are saving time on both sides of the handset.

Incoming Calls

The previous pages explained to you how to prepare for and control the flow of outgoing calls. Your workday will also contain a number of incoming calls that equal or even exceed your outgoing calls. You must become proficient at controlling the flow of incoming calls just as you would an outgoing call.

The people you come in contact with during an incoming call have probably not completed a course such as this one. They may not have the training or skill to conduct an efficient telephone call and to maximize both their time and yours. Because you are completing this course and have shown the capability of taking control of your workplace, you must also take control of incoming calls.

Earlier we suggested you place the list of conversational control questions right in front of your telephone. You must train yourself to greet your incoming caller and then guide the conversation along the course that you know is the most time efficient method.

Conversational Control Questions

1. Why am I making this call?

2. What information do I need to obtain from this call?

3. What information must I convey with this call?

Allowing your incoming calls to wander until the caller reaches the point of their call is not a time efficient activity. You will often end the call without obtaining or conveying the essential information that stimulated the contact to place the call in the first place. Aimless conversational flow often causes both parties to forget the points of discussion.

The pre-qualification questionnaire included in the previous Chapter will assist you with maintaining control of the call when the purpose is a pre-qualification inquiry but you will receive other incoming calls throughout the day. It is these other calls that this section will assist you in completing efficiently and professionally.

Incoming Call Control Process

1. Access the caller's records in your borrower management program during the greeting portion of the call.

2. Skim the last two or three entries to refocus the vital facts and business of that contact to the front of your thoughts.

> This access will provide you with clues as to the callers needs with the telephone call.

> Example: If your last contact with the borrower was to schedule an appointment for a future date, the contact will likely be calling to confirm the appointment.

> Example: If your last contact with the borrower was to request information, the borrower is likely calling to confirm you received the requested documentation.

> Having clues that point you toward the purpose of the call allows you to address each question on your control question list.

3. Ask yourself the essential questions learned during incoming call-control training.

> Why am I receiving this call?

> What information do I need to obtain from this call?

> What information must I convey with this call?

4. Control the flow of the conversation, leading the caller to complete the call in an efficient, time effective manner.

5. Make notes in the caller's journal entry database during the call to ensure proper documentation.

> You should note the answers to each question listed above so that you can control the course of the next contact in an efficient manner.

6. Learn the techniques of necessary to smoothly end a call and use them.

Voice Mail

Technological advancements have provided us with voice mail. Voice mail can be your greatest frustration or your biggest asset. You must determine the best methods to make voice mail benefit you and your time management strategy.

Because most of the people on your call list are busy, it is often difficult to make direct contact with the person you are trying to reach. You call and reach their assistant or voice mail. You leave a message for them to return your call. They reach your voice mail. This cycle can go on and on until you finally manage to be in contact. Often, when you do finally manage to speak to the person you have forgotten the point of your initial call and wasted valuable time in the voice mail cycle. Sometimes they will forget to return your call and you will forget that you were waiting for a call and you never relay the vital information you need or want to convey.

There are methods to minimize the time waste within the voice mail system and returning returned calls.

Voice mail systems are in place to simplify your life not to increase the obstacles to the completion of your task list.

The list of questions you should ask yourself before placing the call contained one question that applies strictly to handling the situation when the contact is unavailable.

> Is the information I must convey vital enough that I must speak directly with the person? Could I include the necessary information in a message?

This is an easy question to answer.

> If you are the only participant in the call who must convey information then you can do so in a voice mail message.

Voice Mail Message Composition

- Voice mail messages should be succinct and to the point.

- Incorporate your conversational control skills into the message.

- Keep your message to the point.

    > Succinct messages enable the recipient to note vital information the first time they play your message and make decisions or take action based upon the information included in the message.

- You should always repeat vital information twice in the message.

    > Repeating vital information allows the recipient to revisit the important components of your message during their note taking without replaying the entire message.

SKILL BUILDER HABIT:

The proper method of leaving a voice mail that incorporates all of your conversational control techniques is included in the following example:

Good Morning, CONTACTS NAME. This is YOUR NAME from YOUR OFFICE. I am calling to CONFIRM YOUR APPOINTMENT for DAY AND DATE, AT TIME. Please return my call at YOUR NUMBER to confirm that you are able to attend DATE AND TIME. Again, my number is YOUR NUMBER. Thank you and have a nice day

You will note that:

- Your message incorporated each piece of vital information into the call two different times.

- You include the social graces in an efficient and pleasing manner.

- You complete the task on your list of being in contact with the individual to confirm the appointment.

- You request that the contact return your call to confirm that they are able to attend.

This request carries with it two needs that you should immediately address.

1. Note the voice mail message in the contact journal log.

   This note will allow you to access the reason for the return call from this contact. In other words, when they call you and you access their journal you can immediately take control of the conversation because you are aware that the next contact with this person is the confirmation of an appointment.

2. Generate a medium priority follow-up.

   You will want to note a follow-up task on your master task list. This follow-up task reminds you to place another confirmation call if the contact does not return your call within a reasonable period.

   You will define a reasonable period on a case-by-case basis.

   If the appointment is set one week away, it is feasible that you may not hear from the contact until the day before the appointment. You should create a follow-up task to call the contact again the day before the appointment if they have not called you.

   If the appointment you were confirming were set for the following afternoon, you would want to create a higher priority follow-up for early the next day. This reminds you to attempt to call the individual to confirm the appointment.

Most times the contact will return your call and you may remove the follow up task from your schedule. In the event that your voice mail and the need to return your call slips through the cracks at the contacts office you have the situation under control.

Incoming Voice Mail

A vital factor that many people fail to note is that voice mail works in both directions. Your particular office may require you to answer each call whenever possible, if not you can maximize your time through the efficient use of voice mail.

You would not answer the telephone during a meeting that is scheduled on your task list.

You should schedule major projects and tasks on a time basis exactly as you would a meeting.

The reason you schedule these tasks in this manner is to ensure you have sufficient time, with few interruptions, for high-priority task completion.

This scheduling method ensures that you complete all projects of high priority in a timely manner and that they are professionally executed.

Just as you would not answer the telephone during a meeting, you should not answer the telephone during a vital, scheduled task or project.

When the telephone rings, it is an interruption in the flow of your careful scheduling and prioritization of your day. The use of voice mail is a time management tool in which all business people must become proficient. Allowing the voice mail to assist in the control of incoming telephone calls may frustrate the caller or it may cause them to adopt time management skills much like the ones you are incorporating.

Leaving vital information you must obtain in your voice mail maximizes the caller's time as well as yours.

The outgoing message should clearly state the expectations you have for a voice mail message.

When a person calls you, there are certain essential pieces of information you must obtain:

1. Who is calling?

2. What does the caller need to convey to me?

3. What does the caller need from me?

4. How does the caller want the return information?

Your outgoing greeting should explain concisely what you expect the caller to provide in their message. Your voice mail greeting should format something like this:

Example: Thank you for calling YOUR COMPANY. You have reached the desk of YOUR NAME. I am currently unavailable or away from my desk, but your call is very important to me. Please leave your name, number and the purpose of your call and I will get back to you as soon as possible.

You have now incorporated a request for the answer to each of your questions into a smooth voicemail message that allows the caller to maximize their time as well as yours.

Your outgoing greeting should present the caller with the impression that while they have reached voice mail you are a pleasant and professional individual.

The caller should feel you are pleased that they called and will handle their needs efficiently and in a pro-active manner.

We have just told you that the voice mail greeting your callers hear should be concise and to the point. Now we are telling you the message should convey enthusiasm, professionalism, and a personable image. To incorporate these impressions while keeping your voice mail greeting concise does not require you to change the words of your greeting it simply requires you change the way you say the words.

Recording Your Greeting

1. Take a deep breath before you start speaking.

    Deep breathing allows you to leave a message with few pauses and enhances the depth and power of your voice.

2. Speak slowly and clearly.

    Speaking slowly and distinctly allows your caller to understand each word you include in your message. You carefully construct the outgoing greeting to convey a specific message and request each piece of information you desire from the caller. If the message is hurried and difficult to understand, the caller will have difficulty meeting your needs.

3. Smile before you begin speaking.

    You convey the expression on your face in your voice. If you take a moment, you can think of calls you have made where the person answering the telephone was smiling with their face and voice. People respond positively to smiles. Smiling during your greeting presents a friendlier image that encourages the caller to leave their message rather than hanging up and trying to call back later.

4. Review your message.
    You must review the message you have recorded to ensure it conveys the proper information and reflects the correct impression to your callers. Many times, we do not realize how we sound until we hear our voices recorded.

5. Record the message again.

Today's busy offices rely heavily on voice mail and often the outgoing greeting your callers receive dramatically influences their opinion of both you and your office. If there is any flaw, no matter how small, take the time to record your message again. You want to be certain that you have adequately represented yourself no matter who is calling.

Another benefit of using voice mail and then returning telephone calls in groups is that it allows you to time block return calls and to be fully prepared with all of the time management techniques you are integrating into your daily telephone protocols. By returning the call, rather than receiving it, you have the opportunity to review the contact journal entries, clearly define the purpose of the call and plan your strategy for maintaining control of the conversational flow.

Professional Distance

One of the final keys to telephone contact management is to keep it pleasant but professional. You want each contact to feel important and to enjoy telephone conversations with you but they will view you more positively and more eagerly accept your calls if they know that you are both pleasant and efficient in your calling. What this means is that you must limit the socialization that occurs during your call.

If you socialize for only two or three minutes with each caller throughout the day it is very easy to lose one, two or even three hours of your workday to non-vital socialization.

It is important to maintain proper telephone etiquette and to make each caller feel important but you do not need to discuss multiple personal factors with each caller. Remember that two or three minutes lost per call adds up to one to one and a half-hours lost per day if you only make thirty telephone contacts per day.

| 2 minutes non-vital conversation | x 30 calls per day = 60 minutes lost time |

| 3 minutes non-vital conversation | x 30 calls per day = 90 minutes lost time |

One to one and half-hours per day will add up to five to seven and half-hours lost per average workweek.

| 1 hour lost time per day | x 5 days per week = 5 lost hours per week |

| 1 ½ hours lost time per day | x 5 days per week = 7 ½ lost hours per week |

By limiting the social content of each telephone call, you can add up to one entire working day worth of timesaving to your time budget.

While you cannot buy more time, you can generate more time for task management through efficiency.

Add the time you save through minimizing social conversation to the time you save through conversational control and the effectiveness of voice mail and you will find you have up to two extra working days per week. This time is time you will have available to accomplish other vital tasks and make your work time run more smoothly and lead you to additional closing opportunities. Additional closing opportunities lead to more money earned for your branch. One of the most dramatic factors in your performance review and promotional considerations will be your overall value to the branch and company. By increasing your time efficiency, you increase overall profit. Increasing overall profit is the ultimate goal of any business.

How do others hear you?

While addressing time management there are a few simple actions you can take to make your messages and calls more pleasing to the other party allowing you to project a professional and positive persona to each contact. The bulk of your daily contacts will be via the telephone. When speaking on the telephone, whether in person or via voice mail, you always want to be aware of the impression you are making on the other party. There are some simple steps you can take to ensure you convey your professionalism and enthusiasm.

1. **Plan your calls**

   Following the guidelines outlined in this Chapter will allow you to plan each call before you begin dialing. Whether you speak with the person you are calling or reach their voice mail, forethought and planning allow you to speak clearly and concisely. Speaking clearly and concisely projects an impression that you are a truly efficient professional.

2. **Take a deep breath**

   Before you begin leaving a message, take a deep breath so that your message contains limited interruptions and flows smoothly. Taking a deep breath also strengthens your voice giving your message more depth and power.

3. **Smile before you speak**

   A smile on your face will transmit to your voice. A smile in your voice projects a positive attitude, which will cause the person you are calling to view you, your message and the requests you are making in your message in a more positive frame of mind.

4. **Speak slowly, clearly and concisely**

   Exceptional diction is an essential element in effective messages. The person you are calling should be able to understand each word of your message the first time that they listen. Speaking clearly and concisely makes the task of voice mail transcription easier for your contact and shows a professional attitude.

5. **Repeat the focus points of your call**

   Repeating vital information allows the other to obtain the necessary information in one playing of the voice mail rather than requiring another playing. This shows a respect for the time of your contact.

6. **Use proper telephone etiquette such as greetings and closings**

Chapter 4

READING THE CREDIT REPORT

Every action that a consumer takes affects their credit report. These actions can have a negative or a positive effect.

Credit reports are an overview of a person's entire history of spending and payment habits. Almost everything that a person does financially is collected, reported, and stored in the credit profile. The primary concern of during the mortgage process is any action that had a negative or derogatory impact on a borrower's credit history.

Debt is the term describing any situation in which funds are borrowed under an agreement to make repayment.

Debt Load is the amount of debt an individual is carrying or the amount that the individual owes to another.

Debt load may include many items. The most common being:

- Credit card debt
- Department store debt
- Charge accounts
- Auto loans
- Student loans
- Mortgages

The ability to borrow more money or to have additional credit extended is affected by how much debt a potential borrower currently carries.

You will be concerned with the debt-to-income ratio of the borrower.

Debt-to-Income Ratio's are the amount of open debt a borrower has available weighed against the borrower's monthly income.

The higher the DTI the greater the potential risk of a borrower default on the loan.

The credit report will provide a relatively accurate view of the borrowers current debt load. You must document the borrower's income in order to have the information necessary to calculate the debt-to-income ratio.

Late payments: Any payments that have been paid more than 30-days past the due date are considered to be late payments.

Late payments can be a severe blemish on the credit report.

You will need to rate late payments based on how late the payment was made and the frequency with which the late payments occurred.

- Prime lenders are typically reviewing the previous two-year payment history.

- Sub-prime matrixes will typically assess the preceding 12-month payment history.

A late payment will appear on the credit report for two years, though credit bureaus may keep them in the credit file for up to seven years.

Bankruptcy actions can remain on the credit report for as long as 10 years.

A bankruptcy is a significant factor the must be considered when choosing a loan program for a borrower.

A borrower in the prime market may have to wait up to four years to attempt to qualify for some prime loans after completing a bankruptcy process. The borrower must re-establish a credit history during that time. This re-establishment of credit will aid in showing that the borrower is no longer a credit risk.

The sub-prime market is more lenient as to time that must elapse after a bankruptcy. The sub-prime market is also more lenient concerning the amount credit the borrower must establish before seeking mortgage financing. The sub-prime market gains their security in the borrower through higher interest rates and fees.

Collection accounts are accounts that a borrower has failed to pay as agreed.

These accounts are turned over to a collection department within the structure of the original creditor, a collection agency, or another service in the attempt to collect the payments owed. The initial creditor and the collection agencies report these accounts to the bureaus.

At times, you may find collection accounts, or other accounts, entered more than one time on a borrower's credit profile. You should remit a credit supplement request to

27

the credit bureau asking that these duplicate entries be condensed to reflect that the entries all refer to one account. This may assist in raising the credit score of the borrower and helps to minimize issues during underwriting.

If your borrower has paid these debts in full, have them obtain a letter from the creditor stating that the debt has been satisfied and no further action on their part is necessary.

Loan program guidelines handle collection accounts differently. Some will allow a certain dollar amount of collections to remain open while others will require all of the collection accounts to be paid in full before the loan can close. Some underwriting guidelines will handle medical collection accounts differently than other accounts.

You will want to consider the type and amount of collections that your borrower has open and place the loan with the program that has the most beneficial guidelines for your borrower's profile.

Medical collections are accounts owed to medical service providers that the borrower has failed to pay.

Medical Collection Accounts are often treated differently than other collection accounts.

You will need to consider the type of collection accounts in the profile and review the underwriting guidelines to determine how to handle each type of account.

Credit inquiries are accesses to a borrower's credit profile.

These inquiries are visible on the credit report.

Underwriter training teaches them to note if a borrower appears to be on a credit-gathering spree.

- A credit-gathering spree means that the borrower is out to expand their credit quickly for a specific purchase.

A series of inquiries could also indicate that new credit obligations are present but not visible on the report.

If you can illustrate that a number of recent inquiries on the credit report pertain to the search for a home mortgage, the underwriting team will consider that information.

Credit Bureau Scores are the scores generated based solely on the data contained within the credit report. A Fair, Isaac Credit Bureau Score, is sometimes referred to as a FICO score. The FICO Score is calculated using a system of scorecards.

Credit Bureau Scores are one of the many elements that are reshaping today's mortgage industry.

Credit scoring has been around since the 1950's and Credit Bureau Scores became widely available in the 1980's.

Credit Scores are now used extensively in such industries as mortgage lending, auto lending, and bankcards.

A Credit Bureau Score is a scientific way of assessing how likely a borrower is to pay back a loan.

Score Range: The approximate range of the Fair, Isaac Credit Bureau Scores range is between 450 to 850 points.

Repositories: Credit scores are available through three national repositories.

The scoring programs of these credit bureaus are called:

BEACON   at EQUIFAX (CBI)
EMPIRICA   at TRANS UNION
TRW/FAIR, ISAAC   at TRW

The credit score is calculated at the repository and is based on the data within that repositories credit file.

How is the CBS calculated?

A Credit Bureau Score is based on the data available with in the borrower's credit report.

The score measures the relative degree of risk a potential borrower represents to the lender or investor.

A credit bureau score is not a measure of a borrower's income, assets, or bank account.
- These factors are taken into consideration by lenders and investors independent of credit scores.

In developing the credit scorecards, Fair, Isaac uses actual credit data from millions of consumers. They apply complex mathematical methods and perform extensive research into credit patterns that enable them to forecast credit performance.

Through this process, the repository identifies distinctive credit patterns. Each pattern corresponds to a likelihood that a consumer will make his or her loan payments as agreed.

This score is based on all of the credit-related data in the credit bureau report, not just negative data such as a missed mortgage payment or a bankruptcy.

The score will consider the amount of credit a borrower has available, the amount of credit the borrower is using compared to these limits, the types of credit a borrower has available, and the borrowers payment performance on their credit obligations among other factors.

Score Data: The types of credit information used in the credit bureau scorecards are typically the same items that the underwriter will use to make a credit decision. These can include

- Payment history
- Public records and Collection Items
- Severity, recentness, and frequency of delinquencies noted in the trade line section

29

- Outstanding Debt
- Number of balances recently reported
- Average balance across all trade lines
- Relationship between total balances and total credit limits on revolving trade lines
- Credit History
- Age of oldest trade line
- Inquiries and new account openings
- Number of inquiries in the last year
- Number of new accounts opened in the last year
- Amount of time since the most recent inquiry
- Types of credit in use
- Number of trade lines for each type pf credit

> Bankcard
> Travel and Entertainment cards
> Department Store cards
> Personal Finance Company references
> Installment Loans
> Other credit

Fair, Isaac observes tens of thousands of credit report histories to determine which credit report items or combination of items are the most predictive of future risk. This data indicates the amount of weight each item should contribute to a credit decision.

THE FAIR ISAAC CREDIT BUREAU SCORES DO NOT USE RACE, COLOR, RELIGION, NATIONAL ORIGIN, SEX, MARITAL STATUS, OR AGE AS PREDICTIVE CHARACTERISTICS.

OCCUPATION AND LENGTH OF TIME IN PRESENT HOUSING ARE NOT USED IN THE SCORECARDS.

ANY INFORMATION THAT IS NOT PRESENT IN THE CREDIT FILE IS NOT USED IN CREATING A CREDIT BUREAU SCORECARD.

Understanding a score's impact

The credit report will contain one or multiple credit scores followed by a series of score factor reason codes. This numerical score is often termed a fair isaac credit bureau score and it is a means of rank ordering potential borrowers based on the likelihood that they will pay their credit obligations as agreed.

A higher score indicates a better credit quality. If all other things in the borrower profile were equal, a borrower with a credit score of 642 is more likely to pay their debts as agreed than a borrower with a score of 537.

The Fair Isaac Credit Bureau Score models at each credit repository are of similar design. The scores are scaled to indicate a similar level of risk across all three repositories. In other words, a score of 660 at one bureau will represent a similar level of risk as a score of 660 at another bureau.

The risk denoted by the credit score is defined as the number of accounts remaining in good standing compared to those accounts that contain derogatory data or that have gone into default.

Sample credit score ranges for new mortgage borrowers from a national sample	
Score Range	Number of good loans for each bad loan showing delinquency or foreclosure (# of good to 1 bad)
Below 600	8 to 1
700 – 719	123 to 1
Above 800	1,292 to 1

Figure 4:1 Sample Score Range

Credit bureau scores will rank order potential borrowers based on risk or the number of good loans to bad loans denoted by the score. This rank order is likely to fluctuate depending on changes in the economy, regional differences, changes in credit guidelines and other reasons.

A lender who uses scores for rank order potential borrower is basing their guideline tiers of risk on historical data related to the files that they have processed and closed in the past. The levels or approval tier that the lender uses is likely to fluctuate over time due to changes in the economy. The lender will create approval tiers and loan product offerings by comparing the performance of their loans over time. This enables them to determine the relationship of borrower performance by market environment, credit score, and other details.

Report Appearance

Credit reports can take multiple visual forms depending on the bureau that issued the report and the type of record being requested. Regardless of the initial visual variations, all credit reports contain the same basic elements. These include borrower details and data, a summary of all of the credit inclusions, and a detailed breakdown of the borrower's current and historical credit transactions. Each section of the report will contain details that will assist you in determining if the potential borrower will qualify for one of your loan programs.

The upper portion of credit report will typically include identifying information including your name or company name as the individual, who requested the report.

Report type will usually be included in the header. Report type may be individual or joint.

Information relating to the individual within the credit bureau who pulled the report and the internal case ID # assigned to the report will be defined in the header of the report. This information will be important if you must request updates to the report or address a discrepancy in the report with the credit bureau.

MERGED INFILE CREDIT REPORT

Prepared For:	Property Address:	Prepared By:	Date Rec:
Attention:	Loan Type: Purpose of Loan: Report Type:	Computer ID: Lender Case #:	Date Comp: Date Revised:

APPLICANT		CO-APPLICANT	
Name: SSN: Marital Status: :	DOB: Dependents:	Name: SSN: Marital Status: :	DOB: Dependents:
Home Phone:		Home Phone:	
Present Address:		Present Address:	
Since:	Own / Rent	Since:	Own / Rent
Previous Address:		Previous Address:	
From: To:	Own / Rent	From: To:	Own / Rent

Date data will be included within the report. Date data can include the date the request was received by the credit bureau, the date the credit bureau completed the report, and the date of any revisions created by the credit bureau in relationship to the report.

Date is important because underwriting typically stipulates that the report must be current, or within a certain date range, in order to be used for closing.

If the report is out of date, underwriting will request a new report in order to ensure that no changes have occurred in the borrower's credit profile during the processing stage of the loan. You should caution your borrower not to make any large purchases or take any action that may alter the contents of the report until after the loan has closed.

Figure 4:2 Example - Credit Report Extract / Explanation

Borrower Information

The credit report will contain details relating to the individual or individuals to whom the credit report applies.

This portion includes specifics such as full name, social security number, and date of birth. Information relating to the borrowers address and employment may be included in this segment of the report. It is important that you remember that information you have gained directly from the borrower may be more up-to-date than information contained within the credit report.

Variations in borrower address and employment are common within the report. You should note any discrepancy between the report and your file information and verify with the potential borrower to ensure that the report does not contain entries that relate to another individual with a similar name. If you note a discrepancy, you must address these differences before the package is submitted to underwriting.

MERGED INFILE CREDIT REPORT

Prepared For:	Property Address:	Prepared By:	Date Rec:
Attention:	Loan Type: Purpose of Loan: Report Type:	Computer ID: Lender Case #:	Date Comp: Date Revised:

APPLICANT		CO-APPLICANT	
Name: SSN: Marital Status: Home Phone: Present Address: Since: Previous Address: From: To:	 DOB: Dependents:: Own / Rent Own / Rent	Name: SSN: Marital Status: Home Phone: Present Address: Since: Previous Address: From: To:	 DOB: Dependents: Own / Rent Own / Rent

Borrower and Co-Borrower identifying information is entered in this section.

You should verify that all details entered match the information included on the loss mitigation summary.

Figure 4:3 Example - Credit Report Extract / Explanation

Credit Summary

The credit report will contain a segment that summarizes the details contained within the actual report. You should review this area to ensure that the inclusions do not bring to mind a red flag issue. You may need to question the homeowner more closely regarding these matters.

CREDIT SUMMARY

	PAYMENTS	BALANCES	LIMITS	TRADES	30+	60+	90+
REVOLVING	0	2061	2200	4	4	4	17
INSTALLMENT 1307	1307	79365	90610	25	34	8	27
REAL ESTATE	378	35384	36600	1	2	0	0
OPEN/OTHER	991	1041	1041	5	0	0	0
TOTAL	2676	117851	129451	38	40	12	44

# INQUIRIES	50	# PUBLIC RECORDS	0	# BANKRUPTCIES	0
WORST TRADE	9	OLDEST DATE	07/01/89	# SATISFACTORIES	17

The summary will contain details identifying the types of credit that the borrower has available. You wish to ensure that the types and amount of credit available to the homeowner is exported into the DTI Analysis Form.

If you are using a system that does not automatically export report data into the Analysis Forms, you will need to enter each credit account, payment, and status by hand.

Credit payment totals and current balances will appear within the credit summary portion of your report.

You will confirm the payment information when you review the report inclusions.

Then you will use this information to confirm the debt ratio information and begin isolating potential loss mitigation options for the homeowner.

A summary data analysis of the details of the report will be included within the summary. This analysis will assist you in completing the scoring key. Much of the data you will use during credit scoring and mitigation screening will be summarized within this section. Before you export the data into the credit-scoring key, debt-to-income ratio form, or loss mitigation application, you must review the report with the homeowner to ensure that all of the inclusions of the summary are correct and relate to active accounts. You will confirm the status of each account by reviewing the detail pages of the credit report.

Figure 4:4 Example - Credit Report Extract / Explanation

CREDIT SUMMARY

	PAYMENTS	BALANCES	LIMITS	TRADES	30+	60+	90+
REVOLVING	0	2061	2200	4	4	4	17
INSTALLMENT 1307	1307	79365	90610	25	34	8	27
REAL ESTATE	378	35384	36600	1	2	0	0
OPEN/OTHER	991	1041	1041	5	0	0	0
TOTAL	2676	117851	129451	38	40	12	44

# INQUIRIES 50	# PUBLIC RECORDS 0	# BANKRUPTCIES 0
WORST TRADE 9	OLDEST DATE 07/01/89	# SATISFACTORIES 17

The number of inquiries into credit profile will be totaled and entered into the summary.

A detailed breakdown of the companies that made credit inquiries will be included at the end of the report.

The homeowner may be required to provide an explanation for any excessive inquiries.

Credit inquiries may indicate that the homeowner has already attempted to remedy the delinquency through outside measures, such as a refinance.

You should review the data relating to these inquiries and discuss the results of any outside efforts the homeowner has made.

Specifics regarding public records, bankruptcy, and the worst trade payment history that you will encounter in the report will be included within the credit summary.

You should note these entries to ensure that you locate the applicable data within the report relating to any bankruptcy, late payment, or public record detailed within the summary.

Public records could relate to liens placed against the property not related to a mortgage or refinance. These liens could become a factor in loss mitigation negotiations where the surrender of the property is being considered.

If a judgment or public record exists in the borrower profile, the details of that record will be included within the report.

This data could include bankruptcy or foreclosure actions as well as judgments and other public records.

Figure 4:5 Example - Credit Report Extract / Explanation

CREDIT SUMMARY

	PAYMENTS	BALANCES	LIMITS	TRADES	30+	60+	90+
REVOLVING	0	2061	2200	4	4	4	17
INSTALLMENT 1307	1307	79365	90610	25	34	8	27
REAL ESTATE	378	35384	36600	1	2	0	0
OPEN/OTHER	991	1041	1041	5	0	0	0
TOTAL	2676	117851	129451	38	40	12	44

# INQUIRIES 50	# PUBLIC RECORDS 0	# BANKRUPTCIES	0
WORST TRADE 9	OLDEST DATE 07/01/89	# SATISFACTORIES	17

The oldest date field indicates the date that the borrower fist obtained credit.

This inclusion allows you to ensure that an adequate credit history is available to the borrower. Many underwriting guidelines will require the potential borrower have at least a two-year credit history with at least three open active trade lines. If your potential borrower does not have a sufficient credit history or quantity of accounts, you may need to take alternative actions to aid the borrower in creating a credit profile that meets the minimum requirements of the loan guidelines.

It is important to address any issues early in the prequalification process. Proactively addressing issues early in the process helps to minimize stipulation requests, speeds the loan process, and facilitates positive relationships with borrowers, referral partners, and affinity service providers. This positive relationship building activity helps to ensure that your office gains the reputation as the office that can get the job done.

If a judgment or public record exists in the borrower profile, the details of that record will be included within the report.

This data could include bankruptcy or foreclosure actions as well as judgments and other public records.

You should scrutinize any inclusion within this section thoroughly to determine the status of the public record, the age of the public record, and the manner that the record will affect your borrower's approval status.

Figure 4:6 Example - Credit Report Extract / Explanation

The type of public record will be named.

This typing will indicate to you the specific handling of the matter per the loss mitigation option that is being considered for the homeowner.

The report will include the dates pertaining to the specific public record.

The opened date will indicate the age of the judgment.

The last active date may affect the handling of the record depending upon the specific loss mitigation option being considered for the homeowner.

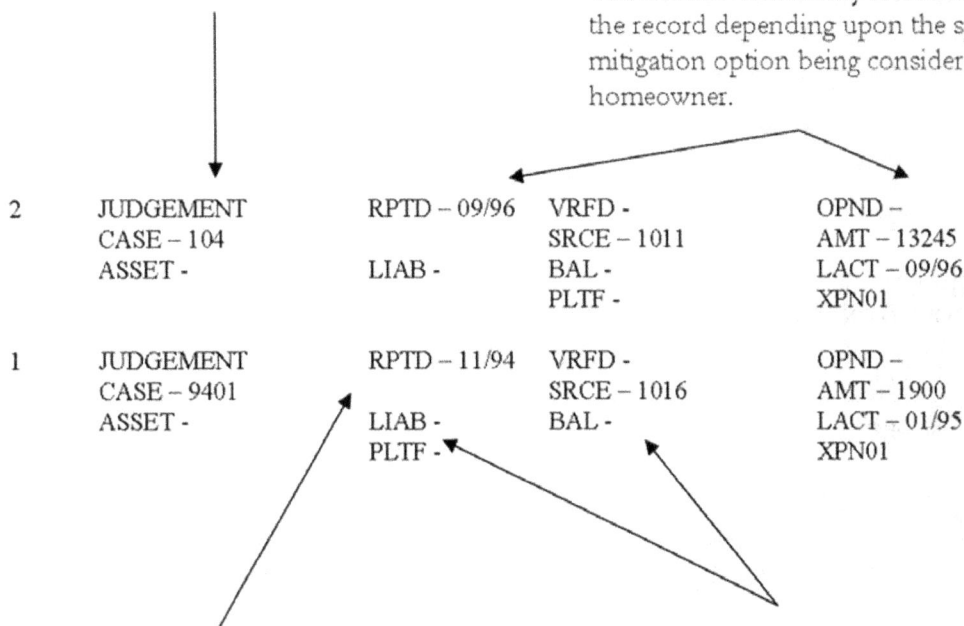

2	JUDGEMENT CASE – 104 ASSET -	RPTD – 09/96 LIAB -	VRFD - SRCE – 1011 BAL - PLTF -	OPND – AMT – 13245 LACT – 09/96 XPN01
1	JUDGEMENT CASE – 9401 ASSET -	RPTD – 11/94 LIAB - PLTF -	VRFD - SRCE – 1016 BAL -	OPND – AMT – 1900 LACT – 01/95 XPN01

Data regarding the status of the record will be included.

A satisfied judgment or closed bankruptcy will affect your file differently than an open or active record.

The liability or balance of the record will be included.

You will want to verify these figures and compare them to the specific
Underwriting Guidelines of the chosen loan program.

Underwriting guidelines will vary regarding the age requirements of a public record.

Figure 4:7 Example - Credit Report Extract / Explanation

Score Factors

The name of the repository issuing the credit score included with the report will be included.

The lender negotiating the loss mitigation workout will designate the repository score that will be used for the process.

This designation is a result of regional

The code of the applicable agency will be entered to confirm the source of the score.

EFX = Equifax

8	BEACON SCORE	EFX01

519
SERIOUS DELINQUENCY AND DEROGATORY PUBLIC RECORD OR COLLECTION FILED
AMOUNT OWED ON DELINQUENT ACCOUNTS
PROPORTION OF BALANCES TO CREDIT LIMITS TOO HIGH ON REVOLVING ACCOUNTS
LENGTH OF TIME ACCOUNTS HAVE BEEN ESTABLISHED

8	EMPIRICA SCORE	TRU01

493
SERIOUS DELINQUENCY, AND PUBLIC RECORD OR COLLECTION FILED
LEVEL OF DELINQUENCY ON ACCOUNTS
TIME SINCE DELINQUENCY IS TOO RECENT OR UNKNOWN
PROPORTION OF REVOLVING BALANCES TO REVOLVING CREDIT LIMITS IS TOO HIGH

8	FAIR ISAAC SCORE	XPN01

529
SERIOUS DELINQUENCY AND PUBLIC RECORD OR COLLECTION FILED
PROPORTION OF BALANCES TOO HIGH ON REVOLVING ACCOUNTS
NUMBER OF ACCOUNTS DELINQUENT
LENGTH OF TIME SINCE LEGAL ITEM FILED OR COLLECTION ITEM REPORTED

The factors that affect the score will be included on the report. This information is often referred to by a score factor code.

Figure 4:8 Example - Credit Report Extract / Explanation

Score Factors – Reason Codes

To understand why a credit report scored the way it did, you must review the reason codes given within each score. These reason codes provide the top reasons why a profile did not score higher. These codes only indicate the top reasons and other factors probably contribute to the overall score. You should review both the score and the reasons the score ranks where it does with your customer.

To find the scores you should locate a number or a letter followed by a brief description.

For example, a score of 540 may have the following factors

- 02 – Delinquency on accounts

- 01 – Amount owed on accounts is too high

- 09 – Too many accounts opened in the last 12 months

- 19 – Too few accounts currently paid as agreed

Score factors are less meaningful for higher scoring credit records as they merely point to the reasons why a very good credit report was not perfect.

Examples of adverse factors that may appear on the report as a consideration in the score calculation are

- Current outstanding balances on accounts

- Delinquency report on accounts

- Accounts not paid as agreed

- Too few open accounts

- Too many open accounts

- Too many bank accounts with outstanding balances

- Too many finance company accounts

- Payment history too new to rate

- Number of inquiries within the last 12 months

- Number of accounts opened within the last 12 months

- Balance too high

- Length of credit history

- No recent account information

- Too few accounts rate as current

- Amount past due on accounts

- No adverse factors

- Recent derogatory public record or collection

This is not an all-inclusive listing. The items listed are examples of issues you may find in the score coding section of a report. You should review each report carefully to determine the factors specific to that credit profile.

FRAUD ALERT

The fraud alert field is becoming increasingly filled field within today's environment. Any data that indicates possible fraud activity will be included with in this section. The information will often become a warning entry because of some action taken by the borrower but any entry other than *"available and clear"* should be reviewed and discussed with the potential borrower.

Basic information noted by the credit bureau as potential fraud will be flagged.

If the entry is not related to an action taken by the borrower, the borrower may be a victim of identity theft and all entries in the body of the report should be scrutinized to ensure that all of the accounts do belong to the borrower.

An example of a fraud alert entry would be the number of inquiries in the last 60 days.

Excessive inquiries may be a result of the mortgage shopping process. In this case, there is little cause for concern as the alert is related to an action taken by your borrower. However, excessive inquiries could indicate access to the credit profile by another party who is seeking to open fraudulent accounts in your borrower's name.

FRAUD ALERT

1	TRANS ALERT	TRU01
	# INQUIRIES IN LAST 60 DAYS: 04	
	RECORDED INQUIRIES ALTER	
1	HAWK ALERT	TRU 01
	HAWK AVAILABLE AND CLEAR	

Details regarding any activity that may indicate fraud will be included.

AVAILABLE AND CLEAR   =   No information found

inquiries in the last 60 days   =   potential credit gathering spree.

At times, this could indicate a stolen profile but more often, this insert is related to the search current loan search.

Figure 4:9 Example - Credit Report Extract / Explanation

CREDIT HISTORY DETAILS

The main body of the report will contain details of each account contained within the borrower's credit history. You will wish to scrutinize each entry within this section to determine the status of the borrower's credit, gain an understanding of the borrower payment and spending habits, and complete the credit history-scoring key.

The credit history-scoring key will be explained later and is included within the appendix section of your workbook. This key will assist you in extracting the necessary details from the credit profile.

CREDIT HISTORY

E C O A	CREDITOR ACCOUNT NO	DATE RPTED	DATE LAST ACT	DATE OPND	LIMIT / HIGHEST CREDIT	PRESENT STATUS		TERMS	PAY AMT	TYPE AND ACCT STATUS	HISTORICAL STATUS			
						BALANCE OWING	AMOUNT PAST DUE				NO MOS HIIST REV	30	60	90
8	AFM-BLOOM #APRINTLO COLLECTION	02/99	04/94		425	425				OPN05				

Figure 4:10 Example - Credit Report Extract / Explanation

The name of the creditor and the account number will be included within the report.

Account numbers are often shortened on the credit report and the full account number may not appear. You can obtain the full account number directly from your borrower if it is a necessary element of the loan process.

For example, a refinance transaction may require certain bills to be paid in full as part of the transaction. You will need to obtain the full account number for each account to confirm the pay off amount and to ensure that all payments are allocated correctly at the closing.

CREDIT HISTORY

E C O A	CREDITOR ACCOUNT NO	DATE RPTED	DATE LAST ACT	DATE OPND	LIMIT / HIGHEST CREDIT	PRESENT STATUS								
						BALANCE OWING	AMOUNT PAST DUE							
8	AFM- BLOOM #APRINTLO COLLEC- TION	02/99	04/94		425	425								

The date reported is the last reporting date for a particular account.

Not all creditors report on a monthly basis.

You may be required to bring the data pertaining to a specific account up to date to comply with specific underwriting requirements and to ensure that no derogatory data exists for the last months of the account.

The date last active provides you with information relating to the last date the account was in use.

Some accounts will be closed and will not effect of the transaction.

You should review the last active date before including the account in your history score.

The opening date of the account allows you to review the historical status with more accuracy.

The date opened may also help you to define when the homeowner began to have financial issues. This information is helpful when proving that the loss mitigation need is a result of a specific financial hardship and not an indication of poor planning or credit use on the part of the homeowner.

Figure 4:11 Example - Credit Report Extract / Explanation

The present status details the current balances and any amounts currently due or past due for each account.

You should scan this column to note any issues that may arise during qualification and workout processes.

Past due accounts may lead to a lien against the subject property and should be considered during the workout planning.

The terms field shows you the original and the current agreement relating to the payments and terms of the account.

A revolving account or credit card will typically not provide you with an end date for the payments as these amounts will fluctuate depending on the borrower's spending actions.

If the account is an installment note, the column will give you the payment terms agreed upon for the account.

Payment amount will provide you with the minimum payment that is due on the account.

You will export these payment amounts into the debt-to-income ratio calculation form.

If the account has no payment entered, it may be an inactive account or it may be a revolving account that does not currently have a balance.

Even if an account does not have a balance, if credit is available to the borrower you must factor a minimum payment into the debt ratio for that account.

The underwriting guidelines will define the payment amount you will use.

E C O A	CREDITOR ACCOUNT NO	DATE RPTED	DATE LAST ACT	DATE OPND	LIMIT / HIGHEST CREDIT	PRESENT STATUS		TERMS	PAY AMT	TYPE AND ACCT STATUS	HISTORICAL STATUS			
						BALANCE OWING	AMOUNT PAST DUE				NO MOS HIIST REV	3 0	6 0	9 0
8	AFM-BLOOM #APRINTLO COLLEC-TION	02/99	04/94		425	425				OPN05				

HISTORICAL STATUS details allow you to review the credit history as well as determine if a specific credit issues exists in relationship to a particular account.

NO MOS HIST REV indicates the number of months detailed within the historical data section.

The numerical entries indicate the status of the payments to be found within the report.

Each account history will contain numbers indicating the status of a particular month's payment.

1 = on time
2 = 30 days late
3 = 60 days late
X = same as previous month

Read the history from LEFT to RIGHT.

Type and account status will provide you with the type of account and its present status.

- Revolving REV
- Installment Ins
- Mortgage Mtg
- Consumer Cons

This field could also contain derogatory accounts such as collections, charge offs or judgments.

- The number of month's history shows the numbers of months reported on the history of the account.

  Underwriting guidelines will dictate the number of months that must be reviewed for each account.

- When you review the account, you will be seeking the status of the account.

  In other words, you will review the account to determine whether the payments were made on time or if any late payment exists within the history.

- You will also look for the date of each payment reference.

  Minimal account history requirements may also exist.

  This column will enable you to determine if the borrower can meet these minimum credit requirements of the loan program you are considering.

- The historical status and late payments section provides you with numerical entries that indicate any late payments that will be found within the report.

  Each account history will contain numbers indicating the status of a particular month's payment.

  1 = on time

  2 = 30 days late

  3 = 60 days late

  X = the same status as the previous month

  This section of the history summary will provide you with the number of times a borrower has been on time, 30 days, and 60 days late during the reported credit history.

  An account shows a 1 indicates that the account was paid on time within the history.

  ➢ When you note an account that contains derogatory information or a credit blemish, you should first confirm that the account is active and that the derogatory account is recent and the entry applies to the process.

  ➢ You will then determine the last date that the account is reported and begin counting backwards from the last entry.

    You will review account details by moving from left to right.

    Example: The reporting of this account begins in July.

The first entry is July. Moving backwards from Left to Right the next entries are

June	=	On Time
May	=	30 Days Late
April	=	On Time

and then backwards through time all of the payments were made on time.

Example: The next account was reported in June so the backwards counting will begin with the month of June.

You will need to obtain an update for this account that illustrates the payment in July to bring this account current with the other entries on the report.

When you locate an account that illustrates a late payment, you will enter a 1x30 day late into the status section of your credit history-scoring key.

You will complete this process for every account in the report that contains a derogatory entry. You will export any credit blemish or derogatory entry you find on the credit report into your credit history.

Many people find it helpful to note any derogatory or important data directly on the report prior to exporting this information onto the credit history-scoring key. This helps to ensure that you do not skip any important factors during the export processes.

Increasing the Score

Over time, a borrower can improve the information in his or her credit report by paying credit obligations as agreed and using credit wisely. As derogatory data in the credit report gets older, it affects the score less. A missed payment from four years ago will not count as much as a missed payment from six months ago. As the borrower uses their credit in a more controlled manner, keeping debt load well below their maximum credit limits, their score is also likely to increase.

A credit score, like a credit report, is a snapshot of an individual's changing credit record. If you make a request for a second repository report to get an updated score, the score is likely to change for many reasons.

The credit items on the report are updated often, so new items are likely to have been added since the previous report. Repeatedly requesting a borrower's credit report may substantially increase the number of inquiries on the repository report, which may affect the score adversely.

You can assist your borrower in understanding how they can improve their overall credit rating by reviewing the score factor reason codes with them an providing them with the direction that they need to use their credit wisely in the future.

The number of inquiries may or may not be a factor in the score. When inquiries are a factor, they are typically not a strong one. If a borrower is very close to the score threshold for a particular loan product, you may receive a score based exception from underwriting. To do this you must show that one or more inquiries appearing on the report are related to this particular loan process. You must also show that the number of inquiries appear as one of the score factor reason codes of the report.

The law requires the credit repository keep a record of all credit inquiries in the file. This means an inquiry cannot be removed from the credit report. Consumer disclosure inquiries are not used in determining score. It is up to the lender, as in all circumstances, to decide what constitutes a sufficient credit risk.

Removing Erroneous Information

Consumers who want to address what they believe is erroneous information on a credit report should contact the credit repository that developed the report.

The Fair Credit Reporting Act (FCRA) allows the credit-reporting agency a "reasonable period of time", generally not to exceed 30 days, to investigate consumer disputed items.

A significant number of credit grantors use an automated system for investigating the disputes and respond to the dispute within a few days. Most credit reporting agencies make a special effort to resolve disputed information affecting a mortgage decision. The lender can weigh these factors and documentation provided by the borrower when deciding whether a disputed item will be counted as a derogatory matter during the credit approval process.

** Special Note: As a Lender, you will have the ability to request a credit supplement. This is typically done by completing the last page of the credit report requesting further information. Most repositories will allow you to fax the supplement request, along with the Consent for Credit Check signed by the borrower, to the office creating the credit report.

Upon receipt of the supplement request, a staff member of the Credit Reporting Office will verify the validity and status of the debt. The staff member will issue a credit supplement. This supplement will show the true status of the account as of the date that the supplement was printed. The new data will often not show up on the borrower's credit report in time for loan closing, but this supplement will allow underwriting to underwrite the loan based on the supplemented information.

Because the score uses all of the credit-related data on the credit bureau report and takes into account all contributing factors, removing or changing one specific, derogatory item will not guarantee an increase in Credit Bureau Score. In some cases, a change in the credit bureau report will have little or no effect on the score. Because there are many scorecards and the score is calculated using a complex mathematical formula, it is not possible to estimate how much the score will change if specific derogatory information is removed.

MERGED INFILE CREDIT REPORT

Prepared For:	Property Address:	Prepared By:	Date Rec:
Attention:	Loan Type: Purpose of Loan: Report Type:	Computer ID: Lender Case #:	Date Comp: Date Revised:

APPLICANT		CO-APPLICANT	
Name: SSN: Marital Status: Home Phone:	DOB: Dependents:	Name: SSN: Marital Status: Home Phone:	DOB: Dependents:
Present Address:		Present Address:	
Since:	Own / Rent	Since:	Own / Rent
Previous Address:		Previous Address:	
From: To:	Own / Rent	From: To:	Own / Rent

CREDIT SUMMARY

	PAYMENTS	BALANCES	LIMITS	TRADES	30+	60+	90+
REVOLVING	0	2061	2200	4	4	4	17
INSTALLMENT 1307	1307	79365	90610	25	34	8	27
REAL ESTATE	378	35384	36600	1	2	0	0
OPEN/OTHER	991	1041	1041	5	0	0	0
TOTAL	2676	117851	129451	38	40	12	44

# INQUIRIES 50	# PUBLIC RECORDS 0	# BANKRUPTCIES	0
WORST TRADE 9	OLDEST DATE 07/01/89	# SATISFACTORIES	17

2	JUDGEMENT	RPTD – 09/96	VRFD -	OPND –
	CASE – 104		SRCE – 1011	AMT – 13245
	ASSET -	LIAB -	BAL -	LACT – 09/96
			PLTF -	XPN01

1	JUDGEMENT	RPTD – 11/94	VRFD -	OPND –
	CASE – 9401		SRCE – 1016	AMT – 1900
	ASSET -	LIAB -	BAL -	LACT – 01/95
		PLTF -		XPN01

8   BEACON SCORE   EFX01
519
SERIOUS DELINQUENCY AND DEROGATORY PUBLIC RECORD OR COLLECTION FILED
AMOUNT OWED ON DELINQUENT ACCOUNTS
PROPORTION OF BALANCES TO CREDIT LIMITS TOO HIGH ON REVOLVING ACCOUNTS
LENGTH OF TIME ACCOUNTS HAVE BEEN ESTABLISHED

8   EMPIRICA SCORE   TRU01
493
SERIOUS DELINQUENCY, AND PUBLIC RECORD OR COLLECTION FILED
LEVEL OF DELINQUENCY ON ACCOUNTS
TIME SINCE DELINQUENCY IS TOO RECENT OR UNKNOWN
PROPORTION OF REVOLVING BALANCES TO REVOLVING CREDIT LIMITS IS TOO HIGH

8   FAIR ISAAC SCORE   XPN01
529
SERIOUS DELINQUENCY AND PUBLIC RECORD OR COLLECTION FILED
PROPORTION OF BALANCES TOO HIGH ON REVOLVING ACCOUNTS
NUMBER OF ACCOUNTS DELINQUENT
LENGTH OF TIME SINCE LEGAL ITEM FILED OR COLLECTION ITEM REPORTED

CREDIT HISTORY

ECOA	CREDITOR ACCOUNT NO	DATE RPTED	DATE LAST ACT	DATE OPND	LIMIT / HIGHEST CREDIT	PRESENT STATUS		TERMS	PAY AMT	TYPE AND ACCT STATUS	HISTORICAL STATUS			
						BALANCE OWING	AMOUNT PAST DUE				NO MOS HIIST REV	30	60	90
8	AFM-BLOOM #APRINTLO COLLECTIO	02/99	04/94		425	425				OPN05	132111111 TRU01			
8	BENEFICL-HFC #7101702	07/00	04/00	03/97	0	0	0	39M 125		INS 01	37 XX1111111X1111111111X XXX111111111111111111 TRU01	0	0	0
8	CAPTIAL 1 BK 05291071382	04/00	01/00	06/96	592	0	0			REV01	41 111111111111111111111 111111111111111111111 TRU01	0	0	0
8	CCB 42270972 CREDIT CARD	07/00	02/00	07/98	950	0				REV01	24 EFX01	0	0	0
1	CITIBANK 54241800	06/00	06/00	12/99	3500	3516	0	72	72	REV01	8 11111111 TRU01	0	0	0
8	CORNER STONE S0000070010	09/00	06/96	09/94	4374	0	0	18M 223		INS00	1 TRU01	0	0	0
8	DIRECT MERCH BK 54580000114	07/00	07/00	11/95	2600	2496		83	83	REV01	25 111111111111111111111 111111111111111111111 XPN01	0	0	0
EC	CREDITOR ACCOUNT NO	DATE RPTED	DATE LAST	DATE OPND	LIMIT / HIGHEST	PRESENT STATUS		TERMS	PAY AMT	TYPE AND	HISTORICAL STATUS			

O A			ACT		CREDIT	BALANCE OWING	AMOUNT PAST DUE			ACCT STATUS	NO MOS HIIST REV	30	60	90
8	AFM-BLOOM #APRINTLO COLLEC CLOSED – CONS	02/99	04/94		425	425				OPN05	132111111 TRU01			
8	BENEFICL-HFC #7101702 CLOSED	07/00	04/00	03/97	0	0	0	39M 125		INS 01	37 XX1111111X1111111111X XXX11111111111111111111 TRU01	0	0	0
8	CAPTIAL 1 BK 05291071382 CLOSED – CONS	04/00	01/00	06/96	592	0	0			REV01	41 11111111111111111111 11111111111111111111 TRU01	0	0	0
8	CCB 42270972 CREDIT CARD CREDIT CARD	07/00	02/00	07/98	950	0				REV01	24 EFX01	0	0	0
1	CITIBANK 54241800 CREDIT CARD	06/00	06/00	12/99	3500	3516	0	72	72	REV01	8 11111111 TRU01	0	0	0
8	CORNER STONE S0000070010 CLOSED AUTO	09/00	06/96	09/94	4374	0	0	18M 223		INS00	1 TRU01	0	0	0
8	DIRECT MERCH BK 54580000114 CREDIT CARD	07/00	07/00	11/95	2600	2496		83	83	REV01	25 11111111111111111111 11111111111111111111 XPN01	0	0	0
1	FCNB/NEWP 4220507 CHARGE ACCOUNT	07/00	06/00	09/99	900	888		30	30	REV01	10 11111111111111111111 11111111111111111111 TRU01	0	0	0
3	FIRST USA BANK NA 5417623 CREDIT CARD	07/00	07/00	12/99	3000	2602	0	65	65	REV01	8 11111111 TRU01	0	0	0
2	FNANB 15230035125 CREDIT CARD	09/00	09/00	12/99	3000	1976		79	79	REV01	9 11111111111111111111 11111 EPN01	0	0	0
1	FNANB VISA 54063555013	06/00	06/00	06/98	700	0				REV01	27 X112111111111111111111 EFX01	1	0	0

FRAUD ALERT

1	TRANS ALERT # INQUIRIES IN LAST 60 DAYS: 04 RECORDED INQUIRIES ALTER	TRU01
1	HAWK ALERT HAWK AVAILABLE AND CLEAR	TRU 01

Kenney

Credit History (12 months)
Borrower

Mortgage Last 12 Months	Consumer Last 12 Months	Bankruptcy NOD/Foreclosure	Charge offs/Judgments
_____ X 30	_____ X 30	Chapter _____	# Filed _____
_____ X 60	_____ X 60	Discharge Date:	$ Amount _____
_____ X 90	_____ X 90	_____	$ to remain open _____
_____ X 120	_____ X 120	Balances: _____	$ to be paid _____
_____ Level	_____ Level	_____ Level	_____ Credit Score

Estimated Credit Level:_____

Credit History (12 months)
Co-Borrower

Mortgage Last 12 Months	Consumer Last 12 Months	Bankruptcy NOD/Foreclosure	Charge offs/Judgments
_____ X 30	_____ X 30	Chapter _____	# Filed _____
_____ X 60	_____ X 60	Discharge Date:	$ Amount _____
_____ X 90	_____ X 90	_____	$ to remain open _____
_____ X 120	_____ X 120	Balances: _____	$ to be paid _____
_____ Level	_____ Level	_____ Level	_____ Credit Score

Estimated Credit Level:_____

Figure 4:16 Sample Form – Credit History Grading

50

Credit History Scoring Key

You now have a better understanding of the inclusions of a credit report. You must learn to score each credit report to determine the loan availability for each barrower. The credit history-scoring key provides a simple method of extracting necessary information from the report and organizing the information for credit rating functions.

To begin the credit scoring process, you should locate the credit history-scoring key in the credit report section of your workbook. This key will assist you and organizing the information found in the credit report into a format that you can easily use when placing the loan.

  ➢ The first item of importance in the credit report is the mortgage history.

   Locate the mortgage for the borrower's primary residence on the report.

   Review the entries within the status segment to determine if any late payments exist over the last 12 to 24 months.

   Conforming or government loans typically use the last 24 months credit   history.

      Some programs will use the last 12 months.

      You should refer to the underwriting guidelines for specific loan program you are considering for the borrower to determine the time period that must be used for scoring purposes.

   Most product matrix are interested only the worst trading rating that exists during the specified time.

   Example: If the borrower was one time 60 days late then the quantity of payments that were 30 days late is unimportant.

   If the borrower does not have a mortgage or rental history showing on their credit report, you will need to acquire other documentation in order to determine the residence payment history.

   If the borrower has additional real estate beyond their primary residence, you will need to determine how the loan product guidelines require you to handle these housing payments. Most programs will define non-owner occupied mortgage payments as consumer credit rather than mortgage. A nonresident mortgage is often rated as consumer debt and you will need to rate the payments accordingly.

  ➢ Consumer history is the next field you will review.

   You will tally all of late payments falling into the consumer debt category. These will include personal loans, credit card debt, revolving lines of credit, nonresident mortgage loans, and any other report items that indicate the borrower makes monthly payments toward the payment of a debt.

   Consumer data typically tallied based on the worst piece of history over the last 12 to 24 months.

   The rating term you will use depends on the loan guidelines for the product you are considering.

   You will tally the worst consumer payment status that appears on the credit report. In other words if the borrower has paid a debt one time 60 days late, this payment makes any 30-day consumer late payments appearing on the report unimportant.

  ➢ In addition to reviewing the body of the report to determine the status of the payments on each account, you will need to review the section relating to public records.

The public records field will contain information relating to any bankruptcy, foreclosure, or judgment against the borrower.

You will typically become aware to look for these issues during the pre-qualification processes. The borrower will usually define any derogatory debt that exists.

You should review the dates of all derogatory entries to determine if it is within the review period of the credit report.

At times, a derogatory debt may be showing in the columns that has been discharges as part of a bankruptcy proceeding.

> If an item is showing on the report as an open account but has been discharged as part of a bankruptcy proceeding, you will need to obtain a credit supplement from the credit-reporting agency verifying that the debt is fully discharged.

> You may also be required to submit full bankruptcy discharge paperwork as supporting documentation.

➤ Each product matrix has different criteria concerning charge-offs.

You will need to have an idea of which loan product you will use for the borrower before determining what charge off accounts will need to be paid in order to close the loan.

For the present, you will include all charge off, judgment and collection history in the total number and total account balances in the credit history-scoring key.

Any account related to a bankruptcy should be noted as discharged and left off the form.

You will complete the section of the scoring key related to accounts to be left open and the amount to be paid prior to or at closing later in the process.

Some credit matrix allows certain charge off accounts to be left open. An example is an account that is less than $200 and over four-year old.

Early in your career, you may wish to complete a separate credit scoring form for each program until you become familiar with the requirements of each loan program and can determine the possible loan programs from a single form.

➤ The final element that you will export into the credit scoring history key is the credit score.

Some programs will use the middle of the three credit scores on a tri-merged report, while others will require you to use a specific repository score depending on which repository is considered the most complete for the borrower's particular area.

You should review the underwriting guideline manual for each loan program you have available to determine which credit score will be applicable for the borrower.

➤ Each piece of credit history will denote a level on the corresponding credit matrix.

A sample product matrix is included later in the course.

It is important for now that you understand that some programs will provide blending approvals while others will use the lowest level denoted by the credit history for approval. This is information you will obtain from the lender guidelines for the each program you have available.

Once you have completed all of the rating activity for the borrower, you will follow the same rating system for the co-borrower. You should score each credit report separately so that you can gain an approval level for each applicant. If you do complete a separate credit scoring history assessment for each applicant, you should be aware that joint accounts may be reported on both reports and be careful not to count these accounts twice during the scoring process.

If you tally an account twice, it will affect the debt to income ratio of the applicant, may affect the overall credit placement, and could alter the loan program you choose for the borrower.

It is sometimes beneficial to review the reports side by side and cross off any duplicate accounts on one of the reports, typically the co-borrower's report.

 If it becomes beneficial to remove one borrower later in the process, you should review the reports and ensure that you have counted these duplicate accounts for the applicant who will be obtaining the loan.

Once you have completed the credit history-scoring key, the elements of the key will be compared to the product matrix of the loan programs that are available for the borrower. Each lender's method of rating a potential borrower is different. You will wish to review multiple matrixes, compare the program requirements and approval levels to the borrower's profile, and choose the best product to suit your borrower's loan goals.

When reviewing the matrix, you will note that some lender's will use a blended approval process that takes every element of the credit and borrower profile into account, other lender's will issue an approval level based only on the credit score while still others will use the worst rating within the borrower profile to determine a loan offering.

Chapter 5

COMPENSATING FACTORS AND DEBT-TO-INCOME

You will occasionally come across borrowers that fall on the edge of a credit tier. In these cases, you can attempt to use compensating factors to request an exception from the underwriting team.

When a borrower's situation exceeds normal guidelines set forth by underwriting, the loan may obtain a higher approval or exception to the guideline with compensating factors.

It is your job to make a strong case for your borrower. You will base your case on any piece of information you gather that reflects favorably on your borrowers. Some compensating factors include:

- Less than 10% increase for old rent/housing payments, to the new housing expense.

- A decrease from the old rent/housing payments to the new housing expense

- A borrower's excellent savings ability (as shown by savings accounts, etc)

- 3 or more months cash reserves.

- Borrower has income that is not qualifying income.

- Larger than minimum down payment

- Residual income (excess after expense) of $500 per adult and $250 per child

- Time at current residence exceeds 5 years.

- Time at current employment exceeds 5 years.

- Debt-to-income ratios below maximum guideline as set forth for that approval level.

- Credit scores fall within a few points of next highest level.

- A perfect mortgage or rental history proven through the credit bureau

Figure 5:1 Example – Compensating Factors

These are only examples of the most commonly used factors. Each loan package has a different set of circumstances and it is up to you to make the best case to the underwriting team on behalf of your borrowers.

DEBT-TO-INCOME RATIO'S

The debt ratio is what will determine "how much" loan a borrower can afford.

You will use two types of debt ratios during the borrower qualification.

Front-End Ratio   The front-end ratio is the gross income divided by the new PITI mortgage payment.

This standard guideline is 29%.

Non-conforming loan programs often use only the back-end debt ratio.

Ratio guidelines will vary depending on the loan product.

Back-End Ratio   The back-end ratio is the gross income divided by the new PITI mortgage payment and the minimum monthly payments from all of the borrowers other liabilities.

The standard guideline is 41%.

The non-conforming guideline can be as high as 55%.

Following are the typical debts used to determine the qualifying ratios:

Front-End Ratios

- the current and or future house payment

Back-End Ratios

- the minimum required monthly payments on all of the following:

  Auto Loans (unless there is less than 10 months left to pay)

  Student Loans (unless there is less than 10 months left to pay)

  Personal Loans (unless there is less than 10 months left to pay)

  Charge Cards - minimum required payments only (all open credit accounts will be counted at the minimum payment even if there is no balance outstanding. The availability of the credit line requires a payment to be factored.)

  Child Support (unless if there is less than 10 months left to pay)

  Alimony (unless there is less than 10 months left to pay)

  Federal Tax Lien Repayment Schedules (unless there is less than 10 months left to pay)

  State Tax Lien Repayment Schedules (unless there is less than 10 months left to pay)

  Other open debt may be a consideration if it is an open line, with regular monthly payments and is not a part of housing or personal maintenance.

  Common monthly liabilities that you will not use to calculate debt ratios:

  Utility Bills

  Car & Health Insurance

  Cell Phone Bills

This is not to be considered an all-inclusive list. The lists included for review are for example purposes only. Other debt may exist in the borrower profile.

The percentage of debts to income is called the debt-to-income ratio. An example of the income to debt calculation is as follows:

Income			= $3,000	
New Mortgage Payment			= $900.	
Minimum Monthly Payments			= $300	

FRONT END CALCULATION:

Mortgage	/	Income	=	30%
900	/	3,000	=	30%

BACK END CALCULATION

Mortgage	+	Monthly Payments	=	Debt Load
900	+	300	=	1200

Debt Load	/	Income	=	40%
1200	/	3000	=	40%

In this scenario, your front-end is 30% and back-end is 40%, which is acceptable for many conforming loan programs.

These ratios can also be adjusted or exceeded if there are item(s) that can be paid-off, if you are able to lower the interest rate, or you can lower the loan amount for the borrower.

Additional debt ratio exercises are included in the Workbook.

DEBT TO INCOME RATIO (DTI%)

Monthly Income

Borrower
$_____ Base Pay/ _____
$_____ Commission/ _____
$_____ Other _____
$_____ Other _____
$_____ Total Monthly Income

Co-Borrower
$_____ Base Pay/ _____
$_____ Commission/ _____
$_____ Other _____
$_____ Other _____
$_____ Total Monthly Income

Combined Monthly Income $_____

Monthly Debt

Borrower
$_____ House/Rent Payment
Automobile Payment
$_____ Credit Card _____
$_____ Credit Card _____
$_____ Credit Card _____
$_____ Personal Loan _____
$_____ Other_____
$_____ Other_____
$_____ Total Monthly Debt

Co-Borrower
$_____ House/Rent Payment(factor once) $_____
$_____ Automobile Payment
$_____ Credit Card _____
$_____ Credit Card _____
$_____ Credit Card _____
$_____ Personal Loan _____
$_____ Other_____
$_____ Other_____
$_____ Total Monthly Debt

Combined Monthly Debt $_____

Take combined debt $_____ (factor each debt only once – if it is a joint debt list under the primary income earner only) and divide by the combined income $_____. The percentage _____% is your monthly debt-to-income ratio. This number should be below the maximum set forth in the loan matrix for the product level you have chosen for your borrowers. You can change the housing expense ratio to customize the ratios to fit your matrix. Just remember to alter the purchase price on your application to match or your underwriting team will decline the loan package for excessive ratios.

Figure 5:2 Sample – DTI Ratio Assessment Form

Chapter

6

THE LOAN APPLICATION

The proper completion of the loan application, or 1003, is a critical element in the creation of loan packages that will move smoothly to closing. The underwriting team will scrutinize each entry on the loan application and issue a loan approval based on these inclusions.

The documentation that you gather over the course of the loan process will support the entries on the loan application.

The completion of the loan application and obtainment of the necessary file documentation that will support these entries is critical to the structure, process, and closing of the loan.

You must gain a comprehensive understanding of each element on the loan application and of how each entry on the application will affect the loan approval terms.

Kenney

Uniform Residential Loan Application

This application is designed to be completed by the applicant(s) with the Lender's assistance. Applicants should complete this form as "Borrower" or "Co-Borrower", as applicable. Co-Borrower information must also be provided (and the appropriate box checked) when ___ the income or assets of a person other than the "Borrower" (Including Borrower's spouse) will be used as a basis for loan qualification or ___ the income or assets of the Borrower's spouse will not be used as a basis for loan qualification, but his or her liabilities must be considered because the Borrower resides in a community property state, the security property is located in a community property state or the borrower is relying on other property located in a community property state for repayment of the loan.

I. TYPE OF MORTGAGE AND TERMS OF LOAN

Mortgage Applied for:	__ VA __ Conventional __ Other __ FHA __ FmHA	Agency Case Number	Lender Case Number
Amount $	Interest Rate %	No of Months	Amortization Type __ Fixed Rate __ GPM	__ Other (explain) __ ARM (type)

II. PROPERTY INFORMATION AND PURPOSE OF LOAN

Subject Property Address (street, city, state, & zip code)	No Of Units
Legal Description of Subject Property (attach description if necessary)	Year Built

Purpose of Loan __ Purchase __ Construction __ Other (explain) __ Refinance __ Construction-Permanent	Property will be: __ Primary Residence __ Secondary Residence __ Investment

Complete this line if construction or construction-permanent loan

Year Lot Acquired	Original Cost $	Amount Existing Liens $	(a) Present Value of Lot	(b) Cost of Improvements	Total (a-b)

Complete this line if this is a refinance loan

Year Acquired	Original Cost $	Amount Existing Liens $	Purpose of Refinance	Describe Improvements __ made __ to be made Cost $

Title will be held in what Name(s)	Manner in which Title will be held	Estate will be held in __ Fee Simple
Source of Down Payment, Settlement Charges, and / or Subordinate Financing (explain)		__ Leasehold (show expiration date)

III BORROWER INFORMATION

Borrower	Co-Borrower
Borrowers Name (include Jr or Sr if applicable)	Co-Borrowers Name (include Jr or Sr if applicable)

Social Security Number	Home Phone	Age	Yrs School	Social Security Number	Home Phone	Age	Yrs School

__ Married __ Unmarried (include single __ Separated divorced, widowed)	Dependents (not listed by co-borrower) No / Ages	__ Married __ Unmarried (include single __ Separated divorced, widowed)	Dependents (not listed by borrower) No / Ages
Present Address (street, city, state, zip code) __ Own __ Rent No Yrs		Present Address (street, city, state, zip code) __ Own __ Rent No Yrs	

If residing at present address less than two years, complete the following

Former Address (street, city, state, zip code) __ Own __ Rent No Yrs	Former Address (street, city, state, zip code) __ Own __ Rent No Yrs
Former Address (street, city, state, zip code) __ Own __ Rent No Yrs	Former Address (street, city, state, zip code) __ Own __ Rent No Yrs

IV EMPLOYMENT INFORMATION

Borrower	Co-Borrower
Name & Address of Employer __ Self Employed	Years on this Job / Years employed in this line of work or profession	Name & Address of Employer __ Self Employed	Years on this Job / Years employed in this line of work or profession
Position/Title/Type of Business	Business Phone	Position/Title/Type of Business	Business Phone

If employed in current position less than two years or if currently employed in more than position, complete the following:

Name & Address of Employer __ Self Employed	Dates (from-to) Monthly Income $	Name & Address of Employer __ Self Employed	Dates (from-to) Monthly Income $
Position/Title/Type of Business	Business Phone	Position/Title/Type of Business	Business Phone
Name & Address of Employer __ Self Employed	Dates (from-to) Monthly Income $	Name & Address of Employer __ Self Employed	Dates (from-to) Monthly Income $
Position/Title/Type of Business	Business Phone	Position/Title/Type of Business	Business Phone

Figure 6:1 1003 – HUD RELEASE

I. TYPE OF MORTGAGE AND TERMS OF LOAN				
Mortgage __ VA __ Conventional __ Other Applied for: __ FHA __ FmHA			Agency Case Number	Lender Case Number
Amount $	Interest Rate %	No of Months	Amortization __ Fixed Rate __ Other (explain) Type __ GPM ___ ARM (type)	

Figure 6:2 1003 Extract – HUD RELEASE

The upper portion of the 1003, *Type of Mortgage and Terms of Loan*, contains file copy data and details relating to type of loan that you have chosen for the borrower.

Type of Mortgage	You will need to check the box for the loan type that you have chosen for your borrower.
	This ensures that the proper guidelines are applied to the prequalification and approval processes.
Agency Case Number	The agency case number is the file tracking number assigned by the individuals who underwrite, pre-qualify, and approve the loan package.
Lender Case Number	The lender case number is the internal case number that you office assigns to the file.
Terms of Loan	The terms of loan section of the 1003 refers to the type of mortgage that you are requesting.
	These numbers are based on the calculation that you perform using the product matrix charts and borrower needs assessment.
	When you submit an application for a pre-approval, you will enter the highest loan amount you and the borrower feel comfortable with given the borrower's specific situation and needs. This will be the pre-approval number and may be subject to a change when the borrower has chosen a home to purchase.
	You should ensure that the amount you enter under loan amount is the highest loan the borrower will require to complete the purchasing process.
	It is easier to request a loan reduction from underwriting than to request a loan increase later in the process.
	If you need to return the file to underwriting to obtain an increase in the loan amount qualification, underwriting will review the entire file and issue a new pre-approval.
Interest Rate	The information you enter relating to interest rate is also preliminary unless your borrower has locked the offered interest rate.
	You should ensure that you obtain a completed rate lock/float option form before submitting an application to underwriting for pre-approval or final approval.
Number of Months	The number of months refers to the amortization term of the loan.
	You should enter the amortization term agreed to with the borrowers. The amortization term will effect the monthly payments and loan approval. The amortization term should match the current interest rate sheet for the loan program.

Amortization Type
The amortization type is the method that will be applied to the loan. The amortization type is a vital part of the application because the method and term of amortization dictates the monthly payment. You should also remember that certain amortization methods would require additional disclosures to the borrower.

II. PROPERTY INFORMATION AND PURPOSE OF LOAN					
Subject Property Address (street, city, state, & zip code)					No Of Units
Legal Description of Subject Property (attach description if necessary)					Year Built
Purpose of Loan __ Purchase __ Construction __ Other (explain) __ Refinance __ Construction-Permanent				Property will be: __ Primary __ Secondary __ Investment Residence Residence	
Complete this line if construction or construction-permanent loan					
Year Lot Acquired	Original Cost $	Amount Existing Liens $	(a) Present Value of Lot	(b) Cost of Improvements	Total (a-b)
Complete this line if this is a refinance loan					
Year Acquired	Original Cost $	Amount Existing Liens $	Purpose of Refinance	Describe Improvements __ made __ to be made Cost $	
Title will be held in what Name(s)		Manner in which Title will be held			Estate will be held in __ Fee Simple
Source of Down Payment, Settlement Charges, and / or Subordinate Financing (explain)					__ Leasehold (show expiration date)

Figure 6:3 1003 Extract – HUD RELEASE

Section 3 of the 1003 provides details relating to the *property* that is to be financed and the *purpose of the loan.*

Subject Property
If the borrower has a sales agreement or knows the address of the subject property, you will enter the applicable details into the loan application.

You will extract the information for this section from the sales agreement or property listing form.

If the borrower is requesting a pre-approval, with no property in mind, you will write, "to be decided" on the property address section.

All of the other information concerning the property will be determined once the borrower has chosen a property and the application moves from a pre-approval to an actual loan package.

Number of Units
Federal Housing Acts and Loan Matrix treat properties differently based on the number of units in the property.

Example: You will enter a single-family property as 1.

Example: You will enter a duplex as 2.

Legal Description
The loan package documents will use the legal description of the property. You can obtain the legal description from the sales agreement, public records system, previous title work, or other documentation provided to you by the borrower or real estate agent.

If the legal description information is too long to fit within the space provided, you will enter "*See Attached Legal Description*" and then attach an addendum page to the application that includes the full legal description of the property.

Year Built

The age of a property will affect various factors ranging from approval status to property valuation. You can obtain information about the age of the property from the Real Estate Agent, the Appraiser, or other sources.

Purpose of Loan

You will always include information about the purpose of the loan.

Understanding the purpose of the loan aids the underwriter in applying the correct underwriting standards to the loan package.

A purchase, refinance, construction, construction to perm, and other types of loan will be handled differently during the underwriting processes.

Property Use/Occupancy

You must include information relating to how the borrower intends to use the property.

- Primary residence
- A vacation home
- Secondary residence
- Investment property

Loan guidelines will vary depending on the use of the property. Owner occupied properties typically obtain a higher LTV status and lower interest rates.

Construction and Construction to Permanent

loans require different processing, approvals, and closing activities.

If the loan is a construction loan, you will incorporate information within the segment that relates to the construction status and costs.

This includes

- The year the borrower obtained the building lot
- The original cost of the lot
- Any existing liens on the property
- The current value of the lot

The details of the building lot added to the costs of the improvements planned using the loan funds enables underwriting to calculate a total property cost and value.

Refinance

transactions will require additional information that pertains to the borrower's history with the property.

If the loan is a refinance transaction, you must enter

- The year the property was acquired
- The original cost of the property

- Current liens against the property
- The purpose of the refinance:
  - Cash Out
  - Interest Rate Reduction
  - Other
- You should provide a brief description of any improvements relating to the property.

  Improvements are typically current improvements that are being made or improvements that will be made using the loan funds.

  Many times when individuals apply for a property refinance, they will use some of the funds received during the refinance to complete improvement, renovations, or upgrades to the property.

  These actions will typically improve the property condition or value and should be described within the loan submittal package.

Title

You should include information relating to the title of the property.

The manner that title will be held and the names of the individuals on the property will affect the security of the loan and may alter the individuals who must be included on the loan application.

Most loan guidelines require that any individual who will hold title as an owner of the property also be included on the mortgage loan application.

Source of Funds

The final entry in this section of the application pertains to the source of the down payment, settlement charges, or other financial matters relating to loan.

You should enter the manner that the borrower intends to supply the funds necessary to close.

You may change the source funds details as you move through the loan process.

Example: If the down payment relates to the equity from the sale of a prior property, you will enter that information.

You will include a copy of a Preliminary HUD 1 or other documentation that illustrates the amount of money that will be received from the sale of the other property.

Example: Some loan programs will allow a certain amount of subordinate financing.

Subordinate financing may be a personal loan or a 2nd mortgage held by the seller or other entity.

- Remember that the payments for this financing must fit within the DTI guidelines set by the lender.

If the borrower intends to subordinate financing from the seller or an outside source, you will provide the details of this arrangement within the application package.

All funds that will be used by the borrower to build the amount that they are required to bring to settlement should be defined.

Other common examples of borrower funds to close include

- Seller concessions toward closing costs

- Savings

- 401(k) withdrawals

- A gift from a friend or family member

You should ensure that the information entered in this section matches the funds defined in page two of the 1003, meets the underwriting standards for the loan being requested, and that all sources of funds can be documented.

The underwriter will screen the entries to ensure that the source of funds used matches the guidelines of the particular loan product being obtained.

If you do not document the source of funds inclusions at the time of the initial application, the documentation necessary for each entry will become part of the stipulation list.

It is a part of your job to help the borrower determine the best source of funds to use for their transaction. You must also assist the borrower by telling them what sources are allowed under the guidelines.

Borrower				III BORROWER INFORMATION		Co-Borrower	
Borrowers Name (include Jr or Sr if applicable)				Co-Borrowers Name (include Jr or Sr if applicable)			
Social Security Number	Home Phone	Age	Yrs School	Social Security Number	Home Phone	Age	Yrs School
__ Married __ Unmarried (include single __ Separated divorced, widowed)	Dependents (not listed by co- borrower) No / Ages			__ Married __ Unmarried (include single __ Separated divorced, widowed)	Dependents (not listed by borrower) No / Ages		
Present Address (street, city, state, zip code) __ Own __ Rent No Yrs				Present Address (street, city, state, zip code) __ Own __ Rent No Yrs			
If residing at present address less than two years, complete the following							
Former Address (street, city, state, zip code) __ Own __ Rent No Yrs				Former Address (street, city, state, zip code) __ Own __ Rent No Yrs			
Former Address (street, city, state, zip code) __ Own __ Rent No Yrs				Former Address (street, city, state, zip code) __ Own __ Rent No Yrs			

Figure 6:4 1003 Extract – HUD RELEASE

Much of the borrower information entered into the 1003 will mirror the data you acquired during the completion of the prequalification questionnaire.

You must verify and document this information before submitting the completed application to the underwriter.

Residence History

The borrower should include a residence history that extends back 2 years. If additional space is necessary, they may include the information on the final page of the application.

Employment History

The borrower will enter their employment information into the 1003.

You should verify and document this information through pay stubs, W-2's, and other documentation provided by the borrower during the application meeting.

Employment information must extend back 2-years.
The borrower may use the final page of the application to enter any employment details that do not fit within the designated space.

Additional Income

If the borrower has income that does not relate to direct employment such as disability, child support, or other income, and they wish to use this income for qualifying purposes; they should enter it within the employment history field.

Additional income entries may cause multiple income sources to be entered for the same time period.

You should note this entry on the cover sheet before submitting the application to underwriting.

If the borrower does not wish to use additional or other income for qualifying purposes but still wishes to disclose it on the application as a compensating factor, they should enter the applicable details within the field labeled *"income not to be used for qualifying proposes"*.

The borrower is not required to disclose this income if they do not wish to do so.

Continuation Period

Certain types of income will require a continuation period in order to be considered as qualifying income. This type of income requires that the borrower prove that the income will continue into the future.

Example: Child support income requires documentation proving that the child support payments will continue for two years into the future in order for it to qualify as income used for loan qualification.

Each loan program will have a specified continuation period that they require.

Uniform Residential Loan Application

V. MOTHLY INCOME AND COMBINED EXPENSE INFORMATION						
Gross Monthly Income	Borrower	Co-Borrower	Total	Combined Monthly Housing Expenses	Present	Proposed
Self Empl Income *	$	$	$	Rent	$	
Overtime				First Mortgage (P&I)		$
Bonuses				Other Financing (P&I)		
Commissions				Hazard Insurance		
Dividends/Interest				Real Estate Taxes		
Net Rental Income				Mortgage Insurance		
Other (before completing see the notice in describe other income below)				Homeowner Assn Dues		
				Other		
Total	$	$	$	Total	$	$

* Self Employed Borrower(s) maybe be required to provide additional documentation such as tax returns and financial statements.

B/C	Describe Other Income Notice Alimony, child support or separate maintenance income need not be revealed if the Borrower (B) or Co-Borrower (C) doesn't choose to have it considered for repaying this loan.	Monthly Amount
		$
		$
		$

VI. ASSETS AND LIABILITIES

This Statement and any applicable supporting schedule may be completed jointly by both married and unmarried Co-Borrowers if their assets and liabilities are sufficiently joined so that the Statement can be meaningfully and fairly presented on a combined basis; otherwise separate Statements and Schedules are required. If the Co-Borrower section was completed about a spouse, this Statement; and supporting schedules must be completed about that spouse also.

ASSETS	Cash or Market Value	Liabilities and Pledged Assets List the creditors name, address and account numbers for outstanding debts including automobile loans, revolving charge accounts, real estate loans, alimony, child support, stock pledges, etc. Use continuation sheet if necessary. Indicate by (*) those liabilities which will be satisfied upon sale of real estate owned or upon refinancing of the subject property.		
Description		LIABILITIES	Monthly Pmt & Mos Left To Pay	Unpaid Balance
Cash deposit toward purchase held by	$			
List checking and savings accounts below		Name and Address of Company	$ Payt / Mos	$
Name and address of Bank, S&L, or Credit Union				
Acct no.	$	Acct No		
Name and address of Bank, S&L, or Credit Union		Name and Address of Company	$ Payt / Mos	$
Acct no.		Acct No		
Name and address of Bank, S&L, or Credit Union		Name and Address of Company	$ Payt / Mos	$
Acct no.	$	Acct No		
Name and address of Bank, S&L, or Credit Union		Name and Address of Company	$ Payt / Mos	$
Acct no.	$	Acct No		
Stocks & Bonds (company name/number & description)	$	Name and Address of Company	$ Payt / Mos	$
Life insurance net cash value Face amount: $	$			
Subtotal Liquid Assets	$	Acct No		
Real estate owned (enter market value) from schedule of real estate owned)	$	Name and Address of Company	$ Payt / Mos	$
Vested interest in retirement fund	$	Acct No		
Net worth of business(es) owned (attach financial statement)	$	Name and Address of Company	$ Payt / Mos	$
		Acct No		
Automobiles owned (make and year)	$	Alimony/Child Support / Separate Maintenance Pmst)	$	
Other Assets	$	Job Related Expense (child care, union dues, etc.)	$	
		Total Monthly Payments	Total Liabilities b	
Total Assets	$	Net Worth (a minus b) $		$

Figure 6:5 1003– HUD RELEASE

Gross Monthly Income	Borrower	Co-Borrower	Total	Combined Monthly Housing Expenses	Present	Proposed
Self Empl Income *	$	$	$	Rent	$	
Overtime				First Mortgage (P&I)		$
Bonuses				Other Financing (P&I)		
Commissions				Hazard Insurance		
Dividends/Interest				Real Estate Taxes		
Net Rental Income				Mortgage Insurance		
Other (before completing see the notice in describe other income below)				Homeowner Assn Dues		
				Other		
Total	$	$	$	Total	$	$

Figure 6:6 1003 Extract – HUD RELEASE

Page 3 of the 1003 will deal with *income, housing expense and credit related* matters.

Income and Expense

The basic income overtime income, bonus income, commission income, or other income should mirror the income related to the job information that the borrower included on page one of the application.

You must verify and document all of this income before you submit the final application package.

All documentation should be included with the loan package at the time of submittal. This enables underwriting to consider this income as part of the approval process. All of the income that is documented and verified will be totaled and used as a baseline for the DTI ratio calculations and loan approval figures completed by the underwriting department.

B/C	Describe Other Income Notice Alimony, child support or separate maintenance income need not be revealed if the Borrower (B) or Co-Borrower (C) doesn't choose to have it considered for repaying this loan.	Monthly Amount
		$
		$
		$

Figure 6:7 1003 Extract – HUD RELEASE

Additional Income

At times, there may be income that cannot be used as qualifying income. This income will not be entered into the regular income and employment section.

Example: Child support payments that will only continue for 1 ½ years

This income cannot be considered as part of the base DTI income but by including it within the 1003; you strengthen the loan file and set the stage if you must request an exception later in the loan process.

In addition to income and assets, page 3 of the 1003 will address *present rent or mortgage payments* and the *proposed mortgage payment* that will exist after the loan is completed.

You may verify current rent or mortgage payments form the credit report or send a VOR/VOM form to the current property owner or mortgage holder.

Combined Monthly Housing Expenses	Present	Proposed
Rent	$	
First Mortgage (P&I)		$
Other Financing (P&I)		
Hazard Insurance		
Real Estate Taxes		
Mortgage Insurance		
Homeowner Assn Dues		
Other		
Total	$	$

Figure 6:8 1003 Extract – HUD RELEASE

You should enter the

- monthly housing expense
- any housing insurance payments
- the amount of real estate taxes the borrower pays for the present property
- any mortgage insurance premium
- homeowner's association dues
- any other fixed housing expenses related to the property the borrower and co borrower use as their primary residence

The total of all of these figures will be the current housing expense information.

You will enter the proposed mortgage payment based on the

- loan amount
- amortization term
- interest rate

that the borrower is requesting.

You will also calculate

- Insurance
- real estate taxes
- other expenses related to the home

You will total these, and this figure will act as the baseline for the housing expense ratio.

ASSETS Description	Cash or Market Value
Cash deposit toward purchase held by	$
List checking and savings accounts below	
Name and address of Bank, S&L, or Credit Union	
Acct no.	$
Name and address of Bank, S&L, or Credit Union	
Acct no.	
Name and address of Bank, S&L, or Credit Union	
Acct no.	$
Name and address of Bank, S&L, or Credit Union	
Acct no.	$
Stocks & Bonds (company name/number & description)	$
Life insurance net cash value Face amount: $	$
Subtotal Liquid Assets	$
Real estate owned (enter market value) from schedule of real estate owned)	$
Vested interest in retirement fund	$
Net worth of business(es) owned (attach financial statement)	$
Automobiles owned (make and year)	$
Other Assets	$
Total Assets	$

Figure 6:9 1003 Extract – HUD RELEASE

Assets

In addition to income, assets will be considered as part of the approval process.

The borrower and co-borrower will need to inform you of all assets they have available.

The underwriter will often refer to the assets section of the 1003 to verify the availability of the funds that you have indicated will be used as the source of funds to close.

The loan program in which you are placing your borrower will dictate the asset documentation requirements.

Example: Bank accounts and other savings will typically require the use of the VOD form.

VOD forms are included within the documentation section of the coursework.

You should review the use and completion of these forms as well as the other documentation requirements to ensure that you have an understanding of how loan funds and assets will be verified.

Liabilities and Pledged Assets List the creditors name, address and account numbers for outstanding debts including automobile loans, revolving charge accounts, real estate loans, alimony, child support, stock pledges, etc. Use continuation sheet if necessary. Indicate by (*) those liabilities which will be satisfied upon sale of real estate owned or upon refinancing of the subject property.

LIABILITIES	Monthly Pmt & Mos Left To Pay	Unpaid Balance
Name and Address of Company	$ Payt / Mos	$
Acct No		
Name and Address of Company	$ Payt / Mos	$
Acct No		
Name and Address of Company	$ Payt / Mos	$
Acct No		
Name and Address of Company	$ Payt / Mos	$
Acct No		
Name and Address of Company	$ Payt / Mos	$
Acct No		
Name and Address of Company	$ Payt / Mos	$
Acct No		
Name and Address of Company	$ Payt / Mos	
Acct No		
Alimony/Child Support / Separate Maintenance Pmst)	$	
Job Related Expense (child care, union dues, etc.)	$	
Total Monthly Payments	Total Liabilities b	
Net Worth (a minus b) $		

Figure 6:10 1003 Extract – HUD RELEASE

Liabilities

The segment relating to recurring debts will often be exported directly from the credit report. You may be required to enter the data regarding debts from the credit report by hand if your company does not use an automated program to conduct this function.

You will verify that all of the debt exported to the liability section of the 1003 is accurate.

If you are aware of any debt that is not included on the credit report, you must enter the information by hand to ensure that underwriting has a clear understanding of the borrower's monthly liabilities.

Example: If child support is paid out to another individual by your borrower or co-borrower, you should attach documentation showing how much the payments are on a monthly basis and how long the payments will continue.

You will then enter this information into the 1003 liability section.

You may be able to discount some of the debt included within the credit report.

You will wish to refer to the guidelines for the loan program for which you are submitting the application.

Example: An installment note with less than 10 payments may often be discounted because the term of the note illustrates that these payments are nearly complete

You should enter all liabilities including those accounts that do not currently have a balance.

Example: A credit card or revolving account that is open enables access to credit by the borrower or co-borrower.

Since these accounts do not have a balance, they will not show a monthly payment.

Since this credit line is available for use, a monthly payment must be factored into the debt ratio even though the account is not presently in use.

Each loan program will set the standards for the amount of payment that will be entered on an open revolving account with a zero balance.

71

Example: A common practice is to factor a 15-dollar minimum monthly payment for each open revolving account available to the borrower or co-borrower. This ensures that a payment for this account will fit into the debt ratio if the borrower chooses to use this available credit over the life of the loan

VI ASSETS AND LIABILITIES (cont)							
Schedule of Real Estate Owned (if additional properties are owned use continuation sheet)							
Property Address (enter S if sold, PS if pending sale or r if a rental being held for income)		Type of Property	Present Market Value	Amount of Mortgage/Liens	Gross Rental Income	Mortgage Payments	Insurance Maintenance & Taxes	Net Rental Income
			$	$	$	$	$	$
	Total		$	$	$	$	$	$

Figure 6:11 1003 Extract – HUD RELEASE

Real Estate   Any additional real estate that the borrower owns but is not selling during this transaction should be defined within the application.

The assets and history from this real estate may be considered a compensating factor.

Underwriting grading processes relating to the mortgage history from non-owner occupied real estate will vary and including the details of this other real estate enables the underwriter to differentiate the entries on the credit report.

List any additional names under which credit has previously been received and indicate appropriate creditor name(s) and account number(s)		
Alternative Name	Creditor Name	Account Number

Figure 6:12 1003 Extract – HUD RELEASE

Aliases   At times, a borrower may have used a different name or a variation of their full name when applying for credit.

Example: A married woman will often establish credit under her maiden name. The name change upon marriage could confuse her credit history report unless you report the maiden name.

Alias information is important to the underwriting team for verification of additional debt and as a combat against fraud.

VII DETAILS OF TRANSACTION		
a. Purchase Price	$	
b. Alterations, improvements, repairs		
c. Land (if acquired separately)		
d. Refinance (incl items to be paid off)		
e. Estimated prepaid items		
g. PMI, MIP, Funding Fee paid in cash		
h. Discount (if Borrower will pay)		
i. Total costs (add a through h)		
j. Subordinate Financing		
k. Borrower's closing costs paid by seller	(	)
l. Other credits (explain)		
m. Loan amount (exclude PMI, MIP, Funding Fee financed)		
n. PMI, MIP, Funding Fee financed		
o. Loan Amount (add m & n)		
p. Cash from/to Borrower (j, k, l & o from i)		

Figure 6:13 1003 Extract – HUD RELEASE

The *details of transaction* section of the 1003 will summarize all of the mathematical and structural planning that you have completed as part of the application process.

The details of the transaction numbers will automatically export as part of the application process in applications that are computer generated. Hand calculated applications require that you enter these figures manually

Regardless of the method of entry, you should review the details of the transaction carefully to ensure that all entries match the

- structure

- source of funds

- other details you have planned for your borrowers

The underwriter will use this section of the 1003 to gain an understanding of the loan that you are planning for your borrowers and to issue all approval figures. The approval information provided to the borrower from the underwriting team will base all of its inclusions on the entries within the details of the transaction summary.

- You will enter the purchase price of the property or the refinance amount being requested into the 1003.

  If there is no property attached to the loan, and the package is being submitted for a pre-approval, you will want to ask for the highest loan amount your borrowers are eligible to receive based on ratios.

  The loan amount request can be lowered later in the process, however, a higher loan request will require that the underwriting department recalculate all numbers and issue an entirely new approval. New approval documents and disclosures will be issued on a lowered loan amount, but the approval will not need to be re-underwritten to determine if the borrower can afford a higher loan amount.

- Once the borrower has obtained a sales agreement, you will want to verify other details beyond just the purchase price.

  The sales agreement can include any item negotiated between the buyer and the seller.

  A commonly negotiated matter is seller concession toward the buyers closing costs. You will want to ensure that any negotiated financial matter incorporated into the sales agreement is entered into the financial details section of the 1003 AND meets the guideline standards of the loan program.

- Some loan guidelines will require that the borrower pay certain items in advance.

  Any item that will be pre-paid before the date of closing should be entered into the details of transaction.

+ You will enter the closing costs figures directly from the good faith estimate that you provided to the borrower.

  The good faith estimate may need to be revised at the time that the borrower chooses a property. If the good faith estimate is revised, you should ensure that you change the closing costs estimate within the 1003.

+ If the loan program applicable to the transaction requires that the borrower obtain PMI, any cash premium associated with the insurance should be entered into the details of the transaction.

+ At times, the borrower may pay discount points as part of the transaction.

  If the funds are available to pay discount points and the borrower chooses to use this option, you should ensure that the quoted interest rate evident on the 1003 and applicable monthly payment reflects these discount points.

  You should enter the total amount paid toward discount into the details of the transaction.

= All costs related tog the loan will be totaled.

- Subordinate financing or second loans will be added into the details of the transaction.

  You should ensure that the terms of the subordinate financing meet the underwriting guidelines and that they payment for this financing falls within the DTI Ratio of the borrower.

+ Any closing costs that the seller has agreed to pay on behalf of the borrower must be documented on the sales agreement and entered as a credit on the details of the transaction.

+ If the are additional credits allocated to the borrower as a part of the process, you should include the amounts within the details of the transaction summary and then provide an explanation for any unusual credit.

- The loan amount that the borrower will receive because of the transaction should be entered. This loan amount entry should not include any PMI premium that is financed as part of the agreed upon loan terms. You will enter financed PMI premiums under the designated field.

= All of the figures will then be totaled and a final figure for cash from OR to the borrower will be included within the details of the transaction. Cash to the borrower typically results from a refinance transaction but may result from a higher loan amount and higher up-front payments by the borrower.

- Cash from the borrower will usually be an included figure in a purchase transaction.

The cash from the borrower is the amount of funds that you must source, usually as the borrowers own money, in order to meet the source of funds guidelines.

- Cash to the borrower will usually be an included figure in a refinance transaction or in a high LTV transaction if the borrower has placed a higher earnest money deposit or paid a substantial amount of money toward pre-paid items. At times, cash to the borrower might be due to a repair negotiation or other matter negotiated between the seller and the buyer.

  You should provide the borrower with a copy of the 1003 and ensure that they understand how the cash from or to the borrower figures were calculated. You should also ensure that they understand that the final figure is the amount of money that they are required to bring to the closing or will receive at the closing.

CREDIT REPORT AUTHORIZATION AND RELEASE

Authorization is hereby granted to _____ to obtain a standard factual data credit report through a credit-reporting agency chosen by _____
_____.

My signature below authorizes the release to the credit-reporting agency a copy of my credit application, and authorizes the credit-reporting agency to obtain information regarding my employment, savings accounts, and outstanding credit accounts (mortgages, auto loans, personal loans, charge cards, credit unions, etc.) Authorization is further granted to the reporting agency to use a Photostatted reproduction of this authorization if necessary to obtain any information regarding the above-mentioned information.

Applicants hereby request a copy of the credit report with any possible derogatory information be sent to the address of present residence, and holds _____
_____ and any credit reporting organization harmless in so mailing the copy requested.

Any reproduction of this credit authorization and release made by reliable means (for example, photocopy, or facsimile is considered an original.

_____   _____
Borrower's Signature   Borrower's Signature
Date: Date:
SSN: SSN:

Figure 6:14 – Sample Form – Credit Authorization and Release

CREDIT DENIAL LETTER

Dear Applicant:

Thank you for your recent mortgage application. Your request for a loan was carefully considered, and we regret that we are unable to approve your application at this time.

This decision is based on the following factor(s):

__ Insufficient income to meet our minimum requirements
__ Insufficient income to sustain payments on the amount of credit requested
__ Income could not be verified
__ Employment history is not of sufficient length to qualify
__ Employment history could not be verified
__ Credit history of timely payments is unsatisfactory
__ Credit history could not be verified
__ Lack of sufficient credit references
__ Lack of acceptable types of credit references
__ Current obligations are excessive in relationship to income
__ Other _____

We will keep your application on file and look forward to working with you in the near future when your situation has changed.

The consumer-reporting agency that provided information that influenced our decision in whole or in part was (*Name, Address, and Telephone Number of Reporting Agency*). The reporting agency is unable to provide specific reasons why we have denied credit to you. You have the right to know the information contained in your credit file under the Fair Credit Reporting Act. Any questions regarding such information should be directed to (Credit Reporting Agency).

Figure 7:15 Credit Denial Letter

CHAPTER 8

THE SALES CONTRACT

A sales agreement that is correctly prepared and endorsed is a binding contract that holds each signing party responsible for the terms negotiated within that contract. Once the sales agreement is written and signed, all of the parties are obligated to complete the transaction providing the terms of the contract can be met legally. An essential element of the sales contract and one of the reasons that a sales agreement may become null and void are the clauses relevant to the mortgage-financing portion of the transaction.

The sales agreement will dictate the handling of many matters with regard to both the pre-close activities that you must facilitate to ensure a timely closing and the type and terms of the mortgage loan that are acceptable under the contract. It is critical that you become familiar with all entries on a real estate sales contract and the proper action dictated by each item included within the contract.

A sales agreement may take many forms and include all of the entries on the example included for your review, additional entries created by the parties involved in the transaction or just some of the entries. If a sales agreement is created privately between the buyer and the seller, some information essential to the loan process may not be included. It is up to you to confirm that all of the required details are included in the sales contract or to gain the necessary information from the buyer and the seller prior to proceeding with the loan structure, order of affinity services, or closing processes.

This segment will assist you in understanding the clauses within the standard real estate sales contract that are most critical to the process from your perspective. Additional sections and clauses are included for your review. You should gain a basic familiarity with all areas of a standard residential sales agreement and focus more intensely on those sections that apply directly to the mortgage finance details of the transaction.

It is important to remember that a sales agreement may take many forms and that addenda can be created to the sales agreement. Addenda will typically address items of specific importance to the parties involved and will often create additional requirements or negotiations that will bind the parties. These clauses, requirements, and negotiation elements will alter the handling of the transaction and should be reviewed with care. Any alteration to the sales agreement should be scrutinized to ensure that the applicable party completes each action required according to the expectations of the involved parties.

STANDARD AGREEMENT FOR THE SALE OF REAL ESTATE

SELLERS BUISNES RELATIONSHIP WITH LICENSED BROKER
Broker (company) _____ Phone _____
Address _____ Fax _____
Licensee(s) _____Designated Agent __ Yes __ No
BROKER IS THE AGNET FOR THE SELLER   OR (if checked below):
Broker is NOT the Agent for the seller and is a/an: __ AGENT FOR BUYER __ Transaction Licensee

BUYERS BUISNES RELATIONSHIP WITH LICENSED BROKER
Broker (company) _____ Phone _____
Address _____ Fax _____
Licensee(s) _____ Designated Agent __ Yes __ No
BROKER IS THE AGNET FOR THE BUYER   OR (if checked below):
Broker is NOT the Agent for the seller and is a/an: __ AGENT FOR SELLER __ Transaction Licensee

When the same Broker is Agent for Buyer, Broker is a Dual Agent. All of Broker's licensees are also Dual Agents UNLESS there is a separate Designated Agents for Buyer and Seller. If the same Licensee is designated for Seller and Buyer, the Licensee is a Dual Agent.

1. *This Agreement*, dated _____ is between SELLER(S):
   _____, called Seller, and
   BUYER(S): _____ , called Buyer.

2. PROPERTY Seller herby agrees to sell and convey to Buyer, who hereby agrees to purchase:
   ALL THAT CERTAIN lot or piece of ground with buildings and improvements thereon erected, if any, known as:
   _____
   _____

   In the _____ of _____ County of _____ in the State of
   _____. Identification (e.g., Tax ID#, Parcel #; Lot, Block; Deed Book, Page,
   Recording Date): _____
3. TERMS
   (A) Purchase Price _____
   _____ U.S. Dollars
   which will be paid to the Seller by the Buyer as follows:
      1. Cash or check at the signing of this Agreement_____ $ _____
      2. Cash or check within ____ days of the execution of this agreement_____ $ _____
      3. _____ _____ $ _____
      4. Cash or cashiers check at the time of settlement_____ $ _____
                              TOTAL $ _____
   (B) Deposits paid by Buyer within ____ DAYS of settlement will be by cash or cashiers check. Deposits, regardless of the form of payment and the person designated as payee, will be paid in U.S. Dollars to Broker for Seller (unless otherwise stated here) _____
   _____ who will retain deposits in an escrow account until consummation or termination of this Agreement in conformity with all applicable laws and regulations. Any check tendered as deposit monies may be held uncashed pending the acceptance of this agreement.

Figure 7:1 – Sample Real Estate Sales Contract – Page 1

(C) Seller's written approval to be on or before _____

(D) Settlement to be on _____ or before if Buyer and Seller agree

(E) Settlement will occur in the county where the Property is located or in an adjacent county, during normal business hours, unless Buyer and Seller agree otherwise.

(F) Conveyance from Seller will be by fee simple deed of Special Warranty unless otherwise stated here _____
_____

(G) Payment of transfer taxes will be divided equally between Buyer and Seller unless otherwise stated here _____
_____

(H) At the time of settlement, the following will be adjusted pro-rata on a daily basis between Buyer and Seller, reimbursing where applicable current taxes (see Information regarding Real Estate Taxes), rents, interest on mortgage assumptions, condominium fees, and home owners association fees, water and or sewer fees together with any other lienable municipal services.

Figure 7:2 – Sample Real Estate Sales Contract – Page 1

---

1. ***This Agreement***, dated _____ is between SELLER(S):

_____ , called Seller, and

BUYER(S): _____ , called Buyer.

Figure 7:3 – Sample Real Estate Sales Contract Extract– Page 1

The full names of the buyers and the sellers of the transaction should be included within the sales agreement.

If the individuals named as buyers on the sales contract are different from the name of the borrower on your loan package, you must discuss this matter with the borrower. The underwriter will wish to have every individual named on the sales agreement placed on the application and loan.

If any individual is named on the sales agreement but is not included within the application, you must have the name of the extra party removed before the sales agreement is remitted to the underwriting team or add the second borrower to the loan application and remit all of the necessary supporting documentation for the added individual.

All documents pertinent to the transaction should match in all ways. If there is a discrepancy, you must request correction of the document that contains the error.

---

2. PROPERTY Seller herby agrees to sell and convey to Buyer, who hereby agrees to purchase:
    ALL THAT CERTAIN lot or piece of ground with buildings and improvements thereon erected, if any, known as:

    _____
    _____
    In the _____ of _____ County of _____ in the State of
    _____ . Identification (e.g., Tax ID#, Parcel #; Lot, Block; Deed Book, Page,
    Recording Date): _____

Figure 7:4 – Sample Real Estate Sales Contract Extract– Page 1

The property information should be included on the sales contract.

The description of the property including physical address, city name, county name, and deed information should match all of the other documents in the transaction. If there is a discrepancy, you must request correction of the document that contains the error.

Kenney

The individual overseeing the file and preparing the documents for closing will use the information entered on these forms to complete the closing package and to generate the signature pages that will close the transaction.

---

3. TERMS
   (A) Purchase Price _____
   _____ U.S. Dollars
   which will be paid to the Seller by the Buyer as follows:
   1. Cash or check at the signing of this Agreement_____ $ _____
   2. Cash or check within ____ days of the execution of this agreement_____ $ _____
   3. _____ _____ $ _____
   4. Cash or cashiers check at the time of settlement_____ $ _____
                                                        TOTAL $ _____

Figure 7:5 – Sample Real Estate Sales Contract Extract– Page 1

Purchase Price

The financial details that have been agreed to between the borrower and seller as the basis of the agreement for the sale should appear on the sales agreement.

The purchase entry details the final sales price agreed upon for the transaction.

This figure will act as the basis for all other transaction calculations during the process.

Cash or check at Signing

The area defined as cash or check at the signing of the agreement is termed the earnest money deposit on your worksheet.

It is important that you review the handling of the earnest money deposit.

The earnest money deposit is often used as a source of borrower funds to close and should be reflected on both the mortgage application.

If these details are not included, you must request that the information be included on the sales agreement or within an addendum to the sales agreement in order to have the funds applied correctly as the transaction progresses.

Additional Funds

At times, the buyer and seller may negotiate a transaction in which the buyer pays more than one deposit. If this is the case, the details of these additional payments should be outlined within the contract and the application of the funds should be defined. If these funds are to be allocated to the buyer as part of the process, you will include them in the details of transaction section of your loan package.

Signing Funds

The amount of money that remains due to the seller after the application of all deposit money will be defined on the sales agreement. You should review these numbers to confirm that all of the funds listed add up to the sales price detailed on the contract. If there is a discrepancy, you should contact the Real Estate Agent if one is being used, or the buyer and seller to have the discrepancy corrected prior to proceeding.

The financial figures entered into the sales agreement will be the ones that you use as the basis for all of the calculations applicable to the transaction. It is essential that the financial basis you use match the sales agreement, as even a slight variation in figures will alter the borrower's debt-to-income ratio, down payment requirements, loan amount, and all other financial estimates.

80

You should note that these figures only pertain to the actual sales price money for the property. Details pertaining to the closing costs and other financial matters will usually not appear within this section of the sales agreement. The calculation of the remaining costs will be based upon the completion of the good faith estimate and loan structure that your office creates for the borrower.

(B) Deposits paid by Buyer within ____ DAYS of settlement will be by cash or cashiers check. Deposits, regardless of the form of payment and the person designated as payee, will be paid in U.S. Dollars to Broker for Seller (unless otherwise stated here) _____
_____ who will retain deposits in an escrow account until consummation or termination of this Agreement in conformity with all applicable laws and regulations. Any check tendered as deposit monies may be held uncashed pending the acceptance of this agreement.

Figure 7:6 – Sample Real Estate Sales Contract Extract– Page 1

The method of payment, term for payment, and handling of the deposit money, both before and after the offer is accepted will be detailed here.

The contingencies pertaining to the application and or the return of the earnest money deposit were explained earlier.

(C) Seller's written approval to be on or before _____
(D) Settlement to be on _____ or before if Buyer and Seller agree
(E) Settlement will occur in the county where the Property is located or in an adjacent county, during normal business hours, unless Buyer and Seller agree otherwise.

The dates pertinent to the transaction will be included within this section.

The most important date from your prospective will be

"Settlement to be on 'preferred closing date' or before if buyer or seller agree"

The date entered on this line is the date that you will use to manage the flow of the transaction. All applicable actions and documentation should be completed on or before this date so that the transaction can close in compliance with the agreement. If not all of the required items can be completed by this date, an extension agreement will need to be made between the buyer and the seller.

(F) Conveyance from Seller will be by fee simple deed of Special Warranty unless otherwise stated here _____

Figure 7:7 – Sample Real Estate Sales Contract Extract– Page 1

The specific type of deed that the seller agrees to provide and the buyer agrees to accept will be detailed within the sales agreement.

You should confirm that the type of deed and warranties contained within the deed match the requirements set forth by the underwriting guidelines. The decision to lend money for a specific transaction is contingent on the property specifics as well as the borrower specifics. Any deed limitations could affect the value of the property and would affect the approval terms and loan parameters.

(G) Payment of transfer taxes will be divided equally between Buyer and Seller unless otherwise stated here _____
_____

(H) At the time of settlement, the following will be adjusted pro-rata on a daily basis between Buyer and Seller, reimbursing where applicable current taxes (see Information regarding Real Estate Taxes), rents, interest on mortgage assumptions, condominium fees, and home owners association fees, water and or sewer fees together with any other lienable municipal services.

Figure 7:7 – Sample Real Estate Sales Contract Extract– Page 1

The payment of transfer taxes and the pro-rata calculations of other costs related to the transaction will be detailed within the sales agreement.

You should note

- The division of transaction expenses outlined within the sales contract.

- The date set for the division of fixed expense.

The individual responsible for the preparation of the HUD 1 will calculate and verify the payments incorporated into this clause before finalizing the closing package.

A rough estimate of the calculations should be incorporated into the financial details of the 1003 and disclosed on the good faith estimate.

STANDARD AGREEMENT FOR THE SALE OF REAL ESTATE
(Continued)

4. **FIXTURES & PERSONAL PROPERTY**
    (A) INCLUDED in this sale are all existing items, permanently installed in the Property, free of liens, including plumbing, heating, lighting fixtures (including chandeliers and ceiling fans); water treatment systems; pool and spa equipment; garage door openers and transmitters; television antennas; unspotted shrubbery, plantings and trees; any remaining heating and cooking fuels stored on the Property at the time of settlement; sump pumps; storage sheds; mailboxes; wall to wall carpeting; existing window screens, storm windows and screen storm doors, window covering hardware, shades and blinds; awnings; built-in air conditioners, built in appliances; and the range unless otherwise stated. Also included: _____

    (B) LEASED items (not owned by Seller): _____
    _____
    (C) EXCLUDED fixtures and items: _____
    _____

5. **DATES / TIME IS OF THE ESSENCE**
    (A) The settlement date and all other dates and times referred to for the performance of the obligations of this Agreement are of the essence and are binding.
    (B) For purposes of this Agreement, the number of days will be counted from the date of execution, excluding the day this Agreement was executed and including the last day of the time period. The Execution Date of this Agreement is the date when Buyer and Seller have indicated full acceptance of this Agreement by signing and/or initialing it. All changes to this Agreement should be initialed and dated.
    (C) The settlement date is not extended by any other provision of this Agreement and may only be extended by mutual written Agreement of the parties.
    (D) Certain time periods are pre-printed in this Agreement as a convenience to the Buyer and Seller. All pre-printed time periods are negotiable and may be changed by striking out the pre-printed text and inserting a different time period acceptable to all parties.

Figure 7:8 – Sample Real Estate Sales Contract – Page 2

6. **MORTGAGE CONTINGENCY**
   __ WAIVED This sales is NOT contingent on mortgage financing, although Buyer may still obtain mortgage financing.
   __ ELECTED
   (A) The sale is contingent on Buyer obtaining mortgage financing as follows:

First Mortgage on the Property	Second Mortgage on the Property
Loan Amount $_____	Loan Amount $_____
Minimum Term _____ years	Minimum Term _____ years
Type of Mortgage _____	Type of Mortgage _____
_____	_____
Mortgage Lender _____	Mortgage Lender _____
Interest Rate _____% however, Buyer agrees to accept the interest rate as may be committed by the mortgage lender, not to exceed a maximum interest rate of _____%. Discount points, loan origination, loan placement, and other fees charged by the lender as a percentage of the mortgage loan (excluding any mortgage insurance premiums or VA funding fee) not to exceed _____% (1% if not specified)	Interest Rate _____% however, Buyer agrees to accept the interest rate as may be committed by the mortgage lender, not to exceed a maximum interest rate of _____%. Discount points, loan origination, loan placement, and other fees charged by the lender as a percentage of the mortgage loan (excluding any mortgage insurance premiums or VA funding fee) not to exceed _____% (1% if not specified)

The interest rate(s) and fee(s) provisions in paragraph 6(A) are satisfied if the mortgage lender(s) gives Buyer the right to guarantee the interest rate(s) and fee(s) at or before the maximum levels stated. Buyer gives Seller the right at Seller's sole option and as permitted by law and the mortgage lender(s) to contribute financially, without promise of reimbursement to the buyer and or the mortgage lender(s) to make the above mortgage terms available to the Buyer.

   (B) Within _____ days (10 if not specified) from the Execution Date of this Agreement, Buyer will make a completed, written mortgage application for the mortgage terms stated above to the mortgage lender(s) defined in paragraph 6(A), if any, otherwise to a responsible mortgage lender(s) of Buyer's choice. Broker for Buyer, if any, otherwise Broker for Seller, is authorized to communicate with the mortgage lender(s) to assist in the mortgage loan process.

   (C) Should Buyer furnish false or incomplete information to Seller, Broker(s), or the mortgage lender(s) concerning Buyer's legal or financial status, or fail to cooperate in good faith in processing the mortgage loan application, which results in the mortgage lender(s) refusing to approve a mortgage loan commitment, Buyer will be in default of this Agreement.

   (D) 1. Mortgage commitment date: _____ if Seller does not receive a copy of Buyer's mortgage commitment by this date, Buyer and Seller agree to extend the mortgage commitment date until the Seller terminated this Agreement buy written notice to the Buyer
   2. Upon receiving a mortgage commitment, Buyer will promptly deliver a copy of the commitment to the Seller.
   3. Seller may terminate this Agreement, in writing, after the mortgage commitment date, if the mortgage commitment
      a. is not valid until the date of settlement , OR
      b. is conditional upon the sale and settlement of any other property, OR
      c. does not satisfy all the mortgage terms as stated in paragraph 6(A), OR
      d. Contains any other conditions not specified in this Agreement that is not satisfied and or removed in writing by the mortgage lender(s)
   4. If this Agreement is terminated pursuant to paragraph 6(D)(1) or (3), or the mortgage loan(s) is not obtained for settlement, all deposit monies will be returned to Buyer according to the terms of paragraph 30 and this Agreement will be VOID. Buyer will be responsible for any costs incurred by Buyer for any inspections or certifications obtained according to the terms of this Agreement and any costs incurred by Buyer for (1) Title search, title insurance and or mechanics' lien insurance, or any fee for cancellation. (2) Flood insurance and or fire insurance with extended coverage, mine subsidence insurance or any fee for cancellation (3) Appraisal fee and charges paid in advance to mortgage lender(s)

Figure 7:8 – Sample Real Estate Sales Contract – Page 2 – Continued

---

4. **FIXTURES & PERSONAL PROPERTY**

   (A) INCLUDED in this sale are all existing items, permanently installed in the Property, free of liens, including plumbing, heating, lighting fixtures (including chandeliers and ceiling fans); water treatment systems; pool and spa equipment; garage door openers and transmitters; television antennas; unspotted shrubbery, plantings and trees; any remaining heating and cooking fuels stored on the Property at the time of settlement; sump pumps; storage sheds; mailboxes; wall to wall carpeting; existing window screens, storm windows and screen storm doors, window covering hardware, shades and blinds; awnings; built-in air conditioners, built in appliances; and the range unless otherwise stated. Also included: _____

   (B) LEASED items (not owned by Seller): _____

   (C) EXCLUDED fixtures and items: _____

Figure 7:9 – Sample Real Estate Sales Contract Extract – Page 2

Specific details pertaining to the fixtures and personal property that will be included in the sale of the real estate will be shown on the sales agreement.

The removal or addition of fixtures and personal property will affect the value of the property and may alter the approval terms of the loan.

Many loan guidelines will require the removal of any value assessed to personal property transferring as part of the transaction. This value removal will lower the basis for the loan amount provided to the borrower.

Example: If the sales agreement sets the sales price of a property at $150,000 and the loan approval dictates an eighty percent loan to value, the loan amount for the transaction would be $120,000.

The borrower would need to provide the $30,000 shortfall between the sales price and the loan amount as part down payment funds.

If the same sales agreement dictates that the buyer keeps $10,000 worth of furnishings, decorations, and other personal property as part of the negotiations, the value of these items is not a part of the value of the property and underwriting will deduct this value from the overall sales price.

That would mean that the loan amount would now be based on $140,000 ($150,000 sales price - $10,000 furniture and goods = $140,000 property purchase price).

Using the same 80% loan to value, the new loan amount would be $112,000.

The borrower would now need to prove that they have $38,000 to use as down payment funds.

---

5. **DATES / TIME IS OF THE ESSENCE**

   (A) The settlement date and all other dates and times referred to for the performance of the obligations of this Agreement are of the essence and are binding.

   (B) For purposes of this Agreement, the number of days will be counted from the date of execution, excluding the day this Agreement was executed and including the last day of the time period. The Execution Date of this Agreement is the date when Buyer and Seller have indicated full acceptance of this Agreement by signing and/or initialing it. All changes to this Agreement should be initialed and dated.

   (C) The settlement date is not extended by any other provision of this Agreement and may only be extended by mutual written Agreement of the parties.

   (D) Certain time periods are pre-printed in this Agreement as a convenience to the Buyer and Seller. All pre-printed time periods are negotiable and may be changed by striking out the pre-printed text and inserting a different time period acceptable to all parties.

Figure 7:10 – Sample Real Estate Sales Contract Extract – Page 2

When the sales agreement negotiations are finalized, specific dates for action will be incorporated into the contract.

These dates set the timeline expectations for the transaction.

Some dates such as the term for a pest inspection are listed based upon industry standard expectations and may be open to negotiation such.

Other dates are negotiated dates between the buyer and the seller and as such are considered fixed dates that must be met.

If a specifically negotiated date cannot be met for any reason, an alteration to the contract, signed by all parties, must be created. This type of date includes items such as the mortgage application and approval dates and the expected close date.

It is very important that you use these dates to set the timeline for the transaction and ensure that all of your required activity is finalized by the expected close date. Additional details pertaining to the expected time flow of a transaction and potential delays to the closing date and methods that you may use to overcome these potential delays are included later in the course.

---

6. **MORTGAGE CONTINGENCY**
   __ WAIVED This sales is NOT contingent on mortgage financing, although Buyer may still obtain mortgage financing.
   __ ELECTED

Figure 7:11 – Sample Real Estate Sales Contract Extract – Page 2

The borrower may elect to incorporate a mortgage contingency clause into the sales agreement. This clauses states that the offer to purchase is contingent on your offices ability to structure a loan that enables the borrower to purchase the property.

The mortgage contingency clause is one of the most common reasons that an offer to purchase will be cancelled.

It is critical that you ensure that you complete all of the functions related to the obtainment of the mortgage in a timely manner and in compliance with the terms set forth in the sales agreement.

A) The sale is contingent on Buyer obtaining mortgage financing as follows:

First Mortgage on the Property	Second Mortgage on the Property
Loan Amount $_____	Loan Amount $_____
Minimum Term _____ years	Minimum Term _____ years
Type of Mortgage _____	Type of Mortgage _____
Mortgage Lender _____	Mortgage Lender _____
Interest Rate _____ % however, Buyer agrees to accept the interest rate as may be committed by the mortgage lender, not to exceed a maximum interest rate of _____ %. Discount points, loan origination, loan placement, and other fees charged by the lender as a percentage of the mortgage loan (excluding any mortgage insurance premiums or VA funding fee) not to exceed _____ % (1% if not specified)	Interest Rate _____ % however, Buyer agrees to accept the interest rate as may be committed by the mortgage lender, not to exceed a maximum interest rate of _____ %. Discount points, loan origination, loan placement, and other fees charged by the lender as a percentage of the mortgage loan (excluding any mortgage insurance premiums or VA funding fee) not to exceed _____ % (1% if not specified)

Figure 7:12 – Sample Real Estate Sales Contract Extract – Page 2

Specific parameters under which the buyer may decline mortgage funding or must accept mortgage funding will often be included in the sales agreement.

The minimum and maximum terms of the mortgage that the borrower believes will be acceptable will be outlined. You should review this clause and compare it to the financing that the borrower may actually obtain.

If there is a discrepancy between the approval that the borrower receives and the terms outlined in the sales agreement, the sales contract may need to be modified. This modification of the borrower's expectations ensures that the mortgage clause matches the true loan terms and limits the probability that the transaction will be cancelled later in the process. A late cancellation can be expensive to all of the parties involved and will be frustrating to you because you will have invested a great deal of time and effort into the completion of the loan package.

The interest rate(s) and fee(s) provisions in paragraph 6(A) are satisfied if the mortgage lender(s) gives Buyer the right to guarantee the interest rate(s) and fee(s) at or before the maximum levels stated. Buyer gives Seller the right at Seller's sole option and as permitted by law and the mortgage lender(s) to contribute financially, without promise of reimbursement to the buyer and or the mortgage lender(s) to make the above mortgage terms available to the Buyer.

(B) Within _____ days (10 if not specified) from the Execution Date of this Agreement, Buyer will make a completed, written mortgage application for the mortgage terms stated above to the mortgage lender(s) defined in paragraph 6(A), if any, otherwise to a responsible mortgage lender(s) of Buyer's choice. Broker for Buyer, if any, otherwise Broker for Seller, is authorized to communicate with the mortgage lender(s) to assist in the mortgage loan process.

(C) Should Buyer furnish false or incomplete information to Seller, Broker(s), or the mortgage lender(s) concerning Buyer's legal or financial status, or fail to cooperate in good faith in processing the mortgage loan application, which results in the mortgage lender(s) refusing to approve a mortgage loan commitment, Buyer will be in default of this Agreement.

(D) 1. Mortgage commitment date: _____ if Seller does not receive a copy of Buyer's mortgage commitment by this date, Buyer and Seller agree to extend the mortgage commitment date until the Seller terminated this Agreement buy written notice to the Buyer

2. Upon receiving a mortgage commitment, Buyer will promptly deliver a copy of the commitment to the Seller.

3. Seller may terminate this Agreement, in writing, after the mortgage commitment date, if the mortgage commitment
   a. is not valid until the date of settlement , OR
   b. is conditional upon the sale and settlement of any other property, OR
   c. does not satisfy all the mortgage terms as stated in paragraph 6(A), OR
   d. Contains any other conditions not specified in this Agreement that is not satisfied and or removed in writing by the mortgage lender(s)

4. If this Agreement is terminated pursuant to paragraph 6(D)(1) or (3), or the mortgage loan(s) is not obtained for settlement, all deposit monies will be returned to Buyer according to the terms of paragraph 30 and this Agreement will be VOID. Buyer will be responsible for any costs incurred by Buyer for any inspections or certifications obtained according to the terms of this Agreement and any costs incurred by Buyer for (1) Title search, title insurance and or mechanics' lien insurance, or any fee for cancellation. (2) Flood insurance and or fire insurance with extended coverage, mine subsidence insurance or any fee for cancellation (3) Appraisal fee and charges paid in advance to mortgage lender(s)

Figure 7:13 – Sample Real Estate Sales Contract Extract – Page 2

Timelines for application and approval of mortgage funding will be included in the contract. These dates will assist you in setting the time flow and activity sheets for the application remittal, documentation needs, and other preparations you must undertake to meet the expected close date.

Additional details that may be applicable to your transaction such as costs, fees, and other matters may be incorporated. Any detail included within the sales agreement under the mortgage contingency clause should be transferred to your loan package.

STANDARD AGREEMENT FOR THE SALE OF REAL ESTATE
(Continued)

(E) If the mortgage lender(s), or an insurer providing property and casualty insurance s required by the mortgage lender(s), requires repairs to the Property, Buyer will, upon receiving the requirements, deliver a copy of the requirements to the Seller. Within ___ DAYS of receiving the copy of the requirements, Seller will notify Buyer whether Seller will make the required repairs at Seller's expense.

1. If Seller makes the required repairs to the satisfaction of the mortgage lender(s) or insurer, Buyer accepts the Property and agrees to the RELEASE in paragraph 27 of this Agreement.

2. If Seller will not make the required repairs, or if Seller fails to respond within the time given, Buyer will, within ___ days, notify Seller of Buyer's choice to:
   a. Make the required repairs, at Buyer's expense, with permission and access to the Property given by Seller; permission and access may not be unreasonably withheld by Seller, OR
   b. Terminate this Agreement by written notice to Seller, with all deposit monies returned to Buyer according ot the terms of paragraph 30 of this Agreement.

(F) **Seller Assist**
   __ NOT APPLICABLE
   __ APPLICABLE, Seller will pay:
   $_____, or _____% of Purchase Price, maximum, toward Buyer's costs as acceptable to the mortgage lender(s)

Figure 7:14 – Sample Real Estate Sales Contract– Page 3

FHA/VA, IF APPLIABLE

(G) It is expressly agreed that notwithstanding any other provisions of this contract, Buyer will not be obligated to complete the purchase of the Property described herein or to incur any penalty by forfeiture of earnest money deposits or otherwise unless Buyer has been given, in accordance with HUD/FHA or VA requirements, a written statement by the Federal Housing Commissioner, Veterans Administration, or a Direct Endorsement Lender setting forth the appraised value of the Property of not less than $_____ (the dollar amount to be inserted is the sales price as stated in this Agreement). Buyer will have the privilege and option of proceeding with consummation of the contract without regard to the amount of the appraised valuation. The appraised valuation is arrived at to determine the maximum mortgage the Department of Housing and Urban Development will insure. HUD does not warrant the value nor the condition of the Property as acceptable.

Warning: Section 1010 of Title 18, U.S.C., Department of Housing and Urban Development and Federal Housing Administration Transactions, provides, "Whoever for the purpose of... influencing in any way the action of such Department, makes, passes, utters or publishes any statement, knowing the same to be false... shall be fined under this title or imprisoned not more than two years or both."

(H) **U.S. Department of Housing and Urban Development (HUD) NOTICE TO PURCHASERS: Buyer's Acknowledgement**
___   Buyer has received the HUD Notice "For Your Protection: Get a Home Inspection." Buyer understands the importance of getting an independent home inspection and has thought about this before signing this Agreement. Buyer understands that FHA will not perform a home inspection nor guarantee the price or condition of the Property.

(I) **Certification** We the undersigned, Seller(s) and Buyer(s) party to this transaction each certify that the terms of this contract for purchase are true to the best of our knowledge and believe, and that any other agreement entered into by any of these parties in connection with this transaction is attached to this Agreement.

7. **WAIVER OF CONTINGENCIES**
If this Agreement is contingent on Buyer's right to inspect and/or repair the Property, or to verify insurability, environmental conditions, boundaries, certifications, zoning classification or use, or any other information regarding the Property, Buyer's failure to exercise any of Buyer's options within the times set forth in this Agreement is a WAIVER of that contingency and Buyer accepts the Property and agrees to the RELEASE in paragraph 27 of this Agreement.

8. **PROPERTY INSURANCE AVAILABILITY**
___   WAIVED. This Agreement is NOT contingent upon Buyer obtaining property and casualty insurance for the Property, although Buyer may still obtain property and casualty insurance.
___   ELECTED. Contingency Period: ___ DAYS (15 if not specified) from the Execution Date of this Agreemetn.
Within the Contingency Period, Buyer will make application for property and casualty insurance for the Property to a responsible insurer. **Broker for Buyer, if any, otherwise Broker for Seller, may communicate with the insurer to assist in the insurance process.** If Buyer cannot obtain property and casualty insurance for the Property on terms and conditions reasonably acceptable to Buyer, Buyer will, within the Contingency Period:
(A) Accept the Property and agree to the RELEASE in paragraph 27 of this Agreement, OR
(B) Terminate this Agreement by written notice to Seller, with all deposit monies returned to Buyer according to the terms of paragraph 30 of this Agreement, OR
(C) Enter into a mutually acceptable written agreement with Seller.
If Buyer and Seller do not reach a written agreement during the Contingency Period, and Buyer does not terminate this Agreement by written notice to Seller within that time, Buyer will accept the Property and agree to the RELEASE in paragraph 27 of this Agreement.

9. **INSPECTIONS**
(A) Seller will provide access to insurers' representatives and, as may be required by this Agreement, to surveyors, municipal officials, and inspectors. If Buyer is obtaining mortgage financing, Seller will provide access to the Property to appraisers and others reasonably required by the mortgage lender(s). Buyer may attend any inspections.

Figure 7:15 – Sample Real Estate Sales Contract– Page 3

(E) If the mortgage lender(s), or an insurer providing property and casualty insurance s required by the mortgage lender(s), requires repairs to the Property, Buyer will, upon receiving the requirements, deliver a copy of the requirements to the Seller. Within ___ DAYS of receiving the copy of the requirements, Seller will notify Buyer whether Seller will make the required repairs at Seller's expense.

1. If Seller makes the required repairs to the satisfaction of the mortgage lender(s) or insurer, Buyer accepts the Property and agrees to the RELEASE in paragraph 27 of this Agreement.
2. If Seller will not make the required repairs, or if Seller fails to respond within the time given, Buyer will, within ___ days, notify Seller of Buyer's choice to:
   a. Make the required repairs, at Buyer's expense, with permission and access to the Property given by Seller; permission and access may not be unreasonably withheld by Seller, OR
   b. Terminate this Agreement by written notice to Seller, with all deposit monies returned to Buyer according ot the terms of paragraph 30 of this Agreement.

Figure 7:16 – Sample Real Estate Sales Contract Extract – Page 3

The loan commitment provided by underwriting will detail any repairs that must be made to the property in order for the loan to be completed.

These repairs are typically based on the inclusions and descriptions contained within the appraisal report and will include any matter that must be remedied in order to stabilize the value and condition of the property.

If such stipulations exist, you must ensure that the borrower negotiates an addendum to the sales contract that dictates who will make said repairs and bear the cost of the repairs.

(F) **Seller Assist**
   __ NOT APPLICABLE
   __ APPLICABLE, Seller will pay:
   $_____, or _____% of Purchase Price, maximum, toward Buyer's costs as acceptable to the mortgage lender(s)

Figure 7:17 – Sample Real Estate Sales Contract Extract – Page 3

The practice of requesting assistance toward the payment of closing costs from the seller in a transaction is becoming more common.

Many standard real estate sales agreements have incorporated a specific clause pertaining to this negotiation.

Seller concessions are the specific amount of funds a seller will allocate toward paying buyers closing costs out of the sellers closing proceeds.

The amount of seller assistance must comply with the maximum amount set forth in the underwriting guidelines for the loan program. Many programs have maximum amounts of seller assistance that they will allow.

If seller assistance is incorporated into the sales agreement, these figures should be included within the financial details section of the 1003. Any financial modification that you make to the 1003 will carry with it a requirement that you remit the application package to the underwriter so that they may review and approve the changes.

Many borrowers require assistance in obtaining all of the required funds for closing and seller assistance is one tool that will enable the borrower to source the necessary funds. It is important that you understand that seller assistance funds come from the transaction. What this means is that the funds appear as a credit from the seller, but the money used will actually come from the loan funds and down payment money that the borrower brings to the table.

You should verify all of the seller assistance details, allowed costs offsets, and the inclusion of such assistance on the HUD 1 prior to beginning the settlement meeting. All of the entries relating to closing cost assistance must comply with the requirements of the loan guidelines. If any wording or allocation agreement relating to the closing cost assistance does not meet the requirements of the loan guidelines, the sales agreement will need to be modified to bring the negotiations into line with the mortgage approval terms.

At times, errors in the calculations or application of the seller assistance funds can occur during the preparation of the closing documents. It is important that all allowable seller assistance be credited to the borrower at the closing and that the assistance is credited in the correct location on the HUD 1 Settlement Statement.

Example: The loan guidelines dictate that the seller assistance may be applied to non-recurring closing costs. The allocation of seller assistance on the HUD 1 must be in entries related to non-recurring closing costs.

If the closing agent preparing the settlement statement enters some of the seller assistance money in the area detailing payment for homeowners insurance, a problem may arise that delays the closing.

- Homeowner's insurance premiums are recurring closing costs.

- The entry of the seller assistance funds in this area may cause underwriting to invalidate the transaction until the funds are applied according to the guidelines.

The ability to review all of the closing documents before the commencement of closing will enable you to isolate and correct issues before the parties arrive to close the transaction. Gaining a reputation for processing loan packages that lead to a smooth closing is one element that will assist you in growing your business and ensuring satisfied customers and future referrals from each loan that you close.

STANDARD AGREEMENT FOR THE SALE OF REAL ESTATE
(Continued)

10. INSPECTION CONTINGENCY OPTIONS

The inspection contingencies elected by Buyer in paragraphs 11-15 are controlled by the Options set forth below. The time periods in these Options will apply to all inspection contingencies in paragraphs 11-15 unless otherwise stated in this Agreement.

Option 1. Within the Contingency Period, as stated in paragraphs 11-15, Buyer will:

1. Accept the Property with the information stated in the report(s) and agree to the RELEASE in paragraph 27 of this Agreement, OR
2. If Buyer is not satisfied with the information stated in the report(s), terminate this Agreement by written notice to the Seller, with all deposit monies returned to the Buyer according to the terms of paragraph 30 of this Agreement, OR
3. Enter into a mutually acceptable written agreement with the Seller providing for any repairs or improvements to the Property and or any credit to Buyer at settlement, as acceptable to the mortgage lender(s), if any.

   If Buyer and Seller do not reach a written agreement during the specified Contingency Period, an Buyer does not terminate this Agreement by written notice to Seller within that time, Buyer will accept the Property and agree to the RELEASE in paragraph 27 of this Agreement.

Option 2. Within the Contingency Period, as stated in paragraphs 11-15, Buyer will:

1. Accept the Property with the information stated in the report(s) and agree to the RELEASE in paragraph 27 of this Agreement, OR
2. If Buyer is not satisfied with the information stated in the report(s), present the report(s) to Seller with a Written Corrective Proposal ("Proposal") listing corrections and/or credits desired by Buyer. The Proposal may, but is not required to, include the name of a properly licensed or qualified professional to perform the corrections requested in the Proposal, provisions for payment, including retests, and a projected date for completion of the corrections. Buyer agrees that Seller will not be held liable for corrections that do not comply with mortgage lender or governmental requirements if performed in a workmanlike manner according to the terms of Buyer's Proposal, or by a contractor selected by Buyer.
   a. Within ___ days (7 if not specified) of receiving Buyer's Proposal, Seller will inform Buyer in writing of Seller's choice to:
      1. Satisfy the terms of Buyer's Proposal, OR
      2. Credit Buyer at settlement for the cost to satisfy the terms of Buyer's Proposal, as acceptable to mortgage lender(s), if any, OR
      3. Not satisfy the terms of Buyer's Proposal or to credit Buyer at settlement for the costs to satisfy the terms of Buyer's Proposal.
   b. If Seller agrees to satisfy the terms of Buyer's Proposal or to credit Buyer at settlement as specified above, Buyer accepts Property and agrees to the RELEASE in paragraph 27 of this Agreement.
   c. If seller chooses not to satisfy the terms of Buyer's Proposal and not to credit Buyer at settlement as specified above, of if Seller fails to choose any option within the time give, Buyer will within ____ days (5 if not specified);
      1. Accept the Property with the information stated in the report(s) and agree to the RELEASE in paragraph 27 of this Agreement, OR
      2. Terminate this Agreement by written notice to Seller, with all deposit monies returned to Buyer according to the terms of paragraph 30 of this Agreement, OR
      3. Enter into a mutually acceptable written agreement with Seller providing for any repairs or improvements to the Property and/or any credit to Buyer at settlement, as acceptable to the mortgage lender(s) if any.

11. **PROPERTY INSPECTION CONTINGENCY** (See Property and Environmental Inspection Notices)

Buyer understands that property inspections, certifications and/or investigations can be performed by professional contractors, home inspectors, engineers, architects and other properly licensed or otherwise qualified professionals, and may include, but are not limited to: structural components; roof; exterior windows and exterior doors; exterior siding, fascia, gutters and downspouts; swimming pools, hot tubs and spas; appliances; electrical, plumbing, heating and cooling systems; water penetration; environmental hazards (e.g., mold, fungi, indoor air quality, asbestos, underground storage tanks, etc.); electromagnetic fields; wetlands inspection; flood plain verification; property boundary/square footage verification; and any other items Buyer may select. Buyer is advised to investigate easements, deed and use restrictions (including any historic preservation restrictions or ordinances) that apply to the Property and to review local zoning ordinances. Other provisions of this Agreement may provide for inspections, certifications and/or investigations that are not waived or altered by Buyer's election here.

___ WAIVED Buyer has the option to conduct property inspections, certifications, and/or investigations. Buyer WAIVES THIS OPTION and agrees to the RELEASE in paragraph 27 of this agreement.

___ ELECTED Contingency Period: ___ days (15 if not specified) from the Execution Date of this Agreement.

(A) Within the Contingency Period, Buyer, at Buyer's expense, may have inspections, certifications and/or investigations completed by properly licensed or otherwise qualified professionals. If Buyer elects to have a home inspection of the Property, as defined in the Pennsylvania Home Inspection Law (see Information Regarding the Home Inspection Law), the home inspection must be performed by a full member of a national home inspection association, in accordance with the ethical standards and code of conduct or practice of that association, or by a properly licensed or registered professional engineer, or a properly licensed or registered architect. This contingency does not apply to the following conditions or items: _____

(B) If Buyer is not satisfied with the condition of the Property as stated in the written inspection report(s), Buyer will proceed under one of the following Options as listed in paragraph 10 within the Contingency Period:

___ Option 1

___ Option 2 For the purposes of Paragraph 11 only, Buyer agrees to accept the Property with the results of any report(s) and agrees to the RELEASE in paragraph 27 of this Agreement if the total cost to correct the conditions stated in the report(s) is less than $_____ ($0 if not specified) (the "Deductible Amount"). Otherwise, all provisions of paragraph 10, Option 2, shall apply, except that Seller will be deemed to have satisfied the terms of Buyer's Proposal if Seller agrees to perform corrections or offer credits such that the cumulative cost of any uncorrected or uncredited condition(s) is equal to the Deductible Amount.

Figure 7:19 – Sample Real Estate Sales Contract– Page 4

STANDARD AGREEMENT FOR THE SALE OF REAL ESTATE
(Continued)

2. WOOD INFESTATION INSPECTION CONTINGENCY

__ WAIVED. Buyer has the option to have the Property inspected for wood infestation by an inspector certified as a wood-destroying pests pesticide applicator. BUYER WAIVES THIS OPTOIN and agrees to the RELEASE in paragraph 27 of this Agreement.

__ ELECTED. Contingency Period ___ days (15 if not specified) from the Execution Date of this Agreement.

(A) Within the Contingency Period, Buyer, at Buyer's expense, may obtain a written "Wood Destroying Insect Infestation Inspection Report" from an inspector certified as a wood-destroying pests pesticide applicator and will deliver it an all supporting documents and drawings provided by the inspector to Seller. The report is to be made satisfactory to and in compliance with applicable laws, mortgage lender requirements, and/or Federal Insuring and Guaranteeing Agency requirements, if any. The inspection is to be limited to all readily visible and accessible areas of all structures on the Property except fences and the following structures, which will not be inspected:

_____

(B) If the inspection reveals active infestation(s), Buyer, at Buyer's expense, may within the Contingency Period, obtain a proposal from a wood-destroying pests pesticide applicator to treat the Property.

(C) If the inspection reveals damage from active or previous infestation(s), Buyer, at Buyer's expense, may within the Contingency Period, obtain a written report from a professional contractor, home inspector, or structural engineer that is limited to structural damage to the Property caused by wood-destroying organisms and a Proposal to repair and/or treat the Property.

(D) If Buyer is not satisfied with the condition of the Property as stated in the written inspection report(s), Buyer will proceed under one of the following Options as listed in paragraph 10 within the Contingency Period:

__ Option 1

__ Option 2

3. STATUS OF RADON

(A) Seller has no knowledge concerning the presence or absence of radon unless checked below:

__ 1. Seller has knowledge that the Property was tested on the dates, by the methods (e.g., charcoal canister, alpha track, etc.), and with the results of the test indicated below:

DATE   TYPE OF TEST   RESULTS (picocuries/liter or working levels)

_____

__ 2. Seller has knowledge that the Property underwent radon reduction measures on the date(s) and by the method(s) indicated below:

DATE   RADON REDUCTION METHOD

_____

COPIES OF ALL AVAILABLE TEST REPORTS will be delivered to Buyer with this Agreement. SELLER DOES NOT WARRANT EITHER THE METHODS OR RESULTS OF THE TESTS.

(B) RADON INSPECTION CONTINGENCY

__ WAIVED. Buyer has the option to have the Property inspected for radon by a certified inspector. BUYER WAIVES THIS OPTION and agrees to the RELEASE in paragraph 27 of this Agreement.

__ ELECTED. Contingency Period: ____ Days (15 if not specified) from the Execution Date of this Agreement.

Within the Contingency Period, Buyer, at Buyer's expense, may obtain a radon test a radon test of the Property from a certified inspector. If Seller performs any radon remediation, Seller will provide Buyer a certification that the remediation was performed by a properly licensed and certified radon mitigation company.

1. If the written test report reveals the presence of radon below 0.02 working levels or 4 picoCuries/liter(4 pCi/L), Buyer accepts the Property and agrees to the RELEASE in paragraph 27 of this Agreement.

2. If the written test report reveals the presence of radon at or exceeding 0.02 working levels or 4 picoCuries/liter (4 pCi/L), Buyer will proceed under one of the following options as listed in paragraph 10 within the Contingency Period.

__ Option 1

__ Option 2

4. STAUTS OF WATER

(A) Seller represents that the Property is served by:

__ Public Water

__ On-site Water

__ Community Water

__ None

_____

(B) WATER SERVICE INSPECTION CONTINGENCY

__ WAIVED. Buyer has the option to have an inspection of the quality and or quantity of the water system for the Property. BUYER WAIVES THIS OPTION and agrees to the RELEASE in paragraph 27 of this Agreement.

__ ELECTED. Contingency Period ___ days (15 if not specified) from the Execution Date of this Agreement.

1. Within the Contingency Period, Buyer, at Buyer's expense, may obtain an inspection of the quality and/or quantity of the water system from a properly licensed or otherwise qualified water/well testing company.

2. If required by the inspection company, Seller, at Seller's expense, will locate and provide access to the on-site (or individual) water system. Seller also agrees to restore the Property, at Seller's expense, prior to settlement.

3. If Buyer is not satisfied with the condition of the water system as stated in the written inspection report(s), Buyer will proceed under one of the following options as listed in paragraph 10 within the Contingency Period:

__ Option 1

__ Option 2

Figure 7:19 – Sample Real Estate Sales Contract– Page 5

Certain specific inspections of the property may be written into the agreement. It is important for you to know some basic facts pertaining to these inspections. You will need to locate the

- Information detailing who will pay for the inspection

- The agreement regarding when the payment for the inspections will be made

The payment for any required inspections may be made outside of closing or these payments may become part of the closing costs paid at the settlement meeting.

All billings pertaining to the transaction that are not paid prior to close must be addressed at the closing table so that the transaction may close without additional obligations coming to the surface for either the buyer or the seller at some point in the future.

When inspections are completed, specific issues may become known that must be addressed or corrected prior to the closing of the loan.

For Example: If a termite inspection is completed and termites are found on the subject property, one party will likely be responsible for having the problems relating to the termites corrected.

This could cause closing delays while the problem is corrected.

Any matter that must be corrected may also result in additional costs and the payment of these costs must be negotiated.

The handling of deficiencies should be written into the contracts and all inspections should be ordered early in the loan process. Addressing these items early helps to ensure that there is adequate time to remedy any issues that are discovered.

STANDARD AGREEMENT FOR THE SALE OF REAL ESTATE
(Continued)

(C) In the event any notices (including violations) and/or assessments are received after Seller has signed this Agreement and before settlement, Seller will provide a copy of the notices and/or assessments to Buyer and will notify Buyer in writing within ___ days after receiving the notices and/or assessments that seller will:
  1. Fully comply with the notices and/or assessments at Seller's expense before settlement. If Seller fully complies with the notices and/or assessments, Buyer accepts the Property and agrees to the RELEASE in paragraph 27 of this Agreement OR
  2. Not comply with the notices and/or assessments. If Seller chooses not to comply with the notices and/or assessments, or fails within the time given to notify Buyer whether Seller will comply, Buyer will notify Seller in writing within ___ days that Buyer will:
     a. Comply with the notices and/or assessments at Buyer's expense, accept the Property, and agree to the RELEASE in paragraph 27 of this Agreement OR
     b. Terminate this Agreement by written notice to Seller, with all deposit monies returned to Buyer according to the terms of paragraph 30 of this Agreement.
        If Buyer fails to respond within the time stated in paragraph 18 (C) (2) or fails to terminate this Agreement by written notice to the Seller within that time, Buyer will accept the Property and agree to the RELEASE in paragraph 27 of this Agreement.
(D) If required by law, within ___ DAYS From the Execution Date of this Agreement, but in no case later than 15 days prior to settlement, Seller will order at Seller's expense a certification from the appropriate municipal department(s) disclosing notice of any uncorrected violations of zoning, housing, building, safety, or fire ordinances and/or a certificate permitting occupancy of the Property. If Buyer receives notice of any required repairs/improvements, Buyer will promptly deliver a copy of the notice to the Seller.
  1. Within ___ DAYS of receiving notice form the municipality that repairs/improvements are required, Seller will notify Buyer in writing that the Seller will:
     a. Make the required repairs/improvements to the satisfaction of the municipality. If Seller makes the require repairs/improvements, Buyer accepts the Property and agrees to the RELEASE in paragraph 27 of this Agreement OR
     b. Not make the required repairs/improvements. If Seller chooses not to make the required repairs/improvements, Buyer will notify Seller in writing within ___ DAYS that Buyer will:
        (1) Make the repairs/improvements at Buyer's expense, with permission and access to the Property given by Seller, which will not be unreasonably withheld, OR

Figure 7:20 – Sample Real Estate Sales Contract– Page 6

(2) Terminate this Agreement by written notice to Seller, with all deposit monies returned to Buyer according to the terms of paragraph 30 of this Agreement.

If Buyer fails to respond within the time stated in paragraph 18 (D) (1) (b) or fails to terminate this Agreement by written notice to Seller within that time, Buyer will accept the Property and agree to the RELEASE in paragraph 27 of this Agreement, and Buyer accepts the responsibility to perform the repairs/improvements according to the terms of the notice provided by the municipality.

2. If Seller denies Buyer permission to make the required repairs/improvements, or does not provide Buyer access before settlement to make the required repairs/improvements, Buyer may, within ___ DAYS, terminate this Agreement by written notice to Seller, with all deposit monies returned to Buyer according to paragraph 30 of this Agreement

3. If repairs/improvements are required and Seller fails to provide a copy of the notice to Buyer as required in paragraph 18 (D), Seller will perform all repairs/improvements as required by the notice at Seller's expense. Paragraph 18(D)(3) will survive settlement.

19. TITLE, SURVEYS & COSTS

(A) The Property will be conveyed with good and marketable title as is insurable by a reputable title company at the regular rates, free and clear of all liens, encumbrances, and easements, EXCEPTING HOWEVER the following: existing deed restrictions; historic preservation restrictions or ordinances; building restrictions; ordinances; easements of roads; easements visible upon the ground; easements of record; and privileges or rights of public service companies, if any.

(B) Buyer will pay for the following: (1) Title search, title insurance and/or mechanics' lien insurance, or any fee for cancellation; (2) Flood insurance, fire insurance with extended coverage, mine subsidence insurance, or any fee for cancellation; (3) Appraisal fees and charges paid in advance to mortgage lender(s); (4) Buyer's customary settlement costs and accruals.

(C) Any survey or surveys required by the title insurance company or abstracting attorney for preparing an adequate legal description of the Property (or the correction thereof) will be obtained and paid for by Seller. Any survey or surveys desired by Buyer or required by the mortgage lender will be obtained and paid for by Buyer.

(D) If Seller is unable to give a good and marketable title and such as is insurable by a reputable title insurance company at the regular rates, as specified in paragraph 19 (A), Buyer will:

1. Accept the Property with such title as Seller can give, with no change to the purchase price, and agree to the RELEASE in paragraph 27 of this Agreement, OR

2. Terminate this Agreement by written notice to Seller, with all deposit monies to Buyer according to the terms of paragraph 30 of this Agreement. Upon termination, Seller will reimburse Buyer for any costs incurred by Buyer for any inspections or certifications obtained according to the terms of this Agreement, and for those items specified in paragraph 19 (B) items (1), (2), (3) and in paragraph 19 (C).

(E) The property is not a "recreational cabin" as defined in the Pennsylvania Construction Code Act unless otherwise stated here (see information regarding Recreational Cabins): _____

20. CONDOMINIUM/PLANNED COMMUNITY (HOMEOWNER ASSOCIATION) RESALE NOTICE
__ NOT APPLICABLE
__ APPLICABLE

Figure 7:20 – Sample Real Estate Sales Contract– Page 6 Continued

---

19. TITLE, SURVEYS & COSTS

(A) The Property will be conveyed with good and marketable title as is insurable by a reputable title company at the regular rates, free and clear of all liens, encumbrances, and easements, EXCEPTING HOWEVER the following: existing deed restrictions; historic preservation restrictions or ordinances; building restrictions; ordinances; easements of roads; easements visible upon the ground; easements of record; and privileges or rights of public service companies, if any.

(B) Buyer will pay for the following: (1) Title search, title insurance and/or mechanics' lien insurance, or any fee for cancellation; (2) Flood insurance, fire insurance with extended coverage, mine subsidence insurance, or any fee for cancellation; (3) Appraisal fees and charges paid in advance to mortgage lender(s); (4) Buyer's customary settlement costs and accruals.

(C) Any survey or surveys required by the title insurance company or abstracting attorney for preparing an adequate legal description of the Property (or the correction thereof) will be obtained and paid for by Seller. Any survey or surveys desired by Buyer or required by the mortgage lender will be obtained and paid for by Buyer.

(D) If Seller is unable to give a good and marketable title and such as is insurable by a reputable title insurance company at the regular rates, as specified in paragraph 19 (A), Buyer will:

1. Accept the Property with such title as Seller can give, with no change to the purchase price, and agree to the RELEASE in paragraph 27 of this Agreement, OR

2. Terminate this Agreement by written notice to Seller, with all deposit monies to Buyer according to the terms of paragraph 30 of this Agreement. Upon termination, Seller will reimburse Buyer for any costs incurred by Buyer for any inspections or certifications obtained according to the terms of this Agreement, and for those items specified in paragraph 19 (B) items (1), (2), (3) and in paragraph 19 (C).

Figure 7:21 – Sample Real Estate Sales Contract Extract – Page 6

Kenney

Specific terms relating to

- The marketability of the title
- The ability to insure the title
- Restrictions specific to the property
- Easements, rights and privileges pertaining to the property
- The costs pertaining to the searching and insuring the title
- Survey completion and costs

may be incorporated into the sales agreement. If any negotiated item within the sales agreement cannot be met, the options available to the parties should be outlined.

These terms should be verified, specifically those relating to the party who will bear the costs associated with each of these contingency clauses. If any question exists pertaining to which party will pay for the costs associated with any clause, you should contact the buyer, seller or real estate agent to obtain a formalized agreement between the parties prior to completing the financial calculations of the transaction.

The payment of these items could affect the loan terms, approval, and cash required from the borrower to complete the process.

---

23. POSSESSION
    (A) Possession is to be delivered by deed, keys and:
        1. Physical possession to vacant Property free of debris, with all structures broom-clean at day and time of settlement, AND/OR
        2. Assignment of any existing lease(s), together with any security deposits and interest, at day and time of settlement, if Property is leased at the execution of this Agreement, unless otherwise stated in this Agreement.
    (B) Buyer will acknowledge existing lease(s) by initialing the lease(s) at the execution of this Agreement, unless otherwise specified herein.
    (C) Seller will not enter into any new leases, extensions of existing leases or additional leases for the Property without the written consent of Buyer.

Figure 7:22 – Sample Real Estate Sales Contract Extract – Page 6

Details regarding possession of the property as well as any lease assignments relating to the property should be incorporated into the sales agreement.

- Many standard agreements contain a clause that provides default instructions for a transaction.

- Any alteration to this clause would appear in an addendum to the contract.

You should confirm the specific negotiations pertaining to possession. If possession is to occur at some point in the future or is based upon an unusual negotiation, you should confirm that these occupancy options meet with the approval guidelines of the loan.

Loan approval is often based on the occupancy plans that the borrower has for the property with an owner-occupied property being approved for a higher loan to value than a non-owner occupied property. Any change to the planned or

94

agreed upon occupancy of the property could create a delay during the underwriting processes or even result in a change to the loan to value approval status of the borrower.

---

30. TERMINATION & RETURN OF DEPOSITS

(A) Where Buyer terminates this Agreement pursuant to any right granted by this Agreement, all deposit monies paid on account of purchase will be returned to the buyer and this agreement will be VOID. The broker holding the deposit monies may only release the deposit monies according to the terms of a fully executed written agreement between Buyer and Seller ands as permitted by the rules and regulations of the State Real Estate Commission.

(B) If there is a dispute over entitlement to deposit monies, a broker is not legally permitted to determine if a breach occurred or which party is entitled to deposit monies. A broker holding monies is required by the Rules and Regulations of the State Real Estate Commission to retain the monies in escrow until the dispute is resolved. In the event of litigation over deposit monies, a broker will distribute monies according to the terms of a final order of court or a written agreement of the parties. Buyer and Seller agree that, if any broker or affiliated licensee is joined in litigation regarding deposit monies, the attorney's fees and costs of the broker(s) and licensee(s) will be paid by the party joining them.

Figure 7:23 – Extract Sample Real Estate Sales Contract– Page 6

Details regarding the earnest money deposit, the application of the deposit toward costs, and the specifics of how or when the buyer may regain or loose rights to the earnest money deposit should be outlined within the contract.

Standard contracts typically contain a specific clause dealing with the earnest money deposit, but these standard clauses can be altered through additions to the contract or by addendums to the sales agreement. Non-standard contracts should specify the pertinent handling of earnest money funds.

The handling of the earnest money deposit and method of applying this deposit will be important to the loan structure process, the sourcing of down payment money, and the calculation of the cash that the borrower will need to bring to the closing table.

Other conditions or contingencies may be written into the sales agreement. Any item that is of concern or interest to either party may become part of the agreement for transfer. You should review the entire contract, addendums and other paperwork remitted to your office to gain a better understanding of the unique details in each transaction. As you can see, the specifics of the transaction will alter the methodology, details, and handling of the loan package. By gaining a complete understanding of each potential alteration to the sales agreement, you gain the ability to make the loan and closing processes smoother for all parties.

---

34. SPECIAL CLAUSES

(A) The following are part of this Agreement if checked:

__ Sale & Settlement of Other Property   __ Settlement of Other Property Contingency Addendum
__ Tenant-Occupied Property   __
__   __

Figure 7:24 – Sample Real Estate Sales Contract– Page 6

Chapter

5

GOOD FAITH ESTIMATE

It is essential that you understand the components of a Good Faith Estimate and gain the knowledge necessary to generate the estimate. The inclusions on the good faith estimate serve many functions during the loan process from assisting in the creation of the HUD 1 Settlement Statement to setting borrower expectations with regard to the costs that they will incur during the obtainment of their mortgage loan. Setting the expectations of costs at the proper level is one of the most important acts you can perform. This single act is essential to ensuring smooth closings and good relationships – with your borrowers, with the real estate offices, with the closing agents and with your closing team!

Many of the costs involved in closing a loan including appraisal fees, pest inspections, and title costs are standard in the industry or in the region where you conduct your business.

Your funding source will require you to charge other costs that are specific to the funding source and may vary among different lenders. You will want to refer to your underwriting guidelines to determine what fees a particular lender requires.

Other costs in the good faith estimate are part of your offices payment structure. These costs should remain similar for all borrowers. It is inappropriate to charge one borrower a $500.00 application fee and another borrower a $50.00 application fee.

In general, the structure and inclusions of the good faith estimate will depend on the type of loan you are processing, the funding source of the loan, and the transaction details negotiated within the sales agreement and dictated by the lending approval.

Lender:	Sales Price:
Address:	Base Loan Amount:
	Total Loan Amount:
Applicant(s):	Interest Rate:
	Type of Loan:
Property Address:	Preparation Date:
	Loan Number

The information provided below reflects estimates of the charges which you are likely to incur at the settlement of your loan. The fees listed are estimates – actual charges may be more or less. Your transaction may not involve a fee for every item listed.

THE NUMBERS LISTED BESIDE THE ESTIMATES GENERALLY CORRESPOND TO THE NUMBERED LINES CONTAINED THE HUD-1 OR HUD-1A SETTLEMENT STATEMENT WHICH YOU WILL BE RECEIVEING AT THE SETTLEMENT. THE HUD-1 OR HUD-1A SETTLEMENT STATEMENT WILL SHOW YOU THE ACTUAL COST FOR ITEMS PAID AT SETTLEMENT.

800	ITEMS PAYABLE IN CONNECTION WITH LOAN;		1100	TITLE CHARGES	
801	Origination Fee @ % + $	$_____	1101	Closing or Escrow Fee	$_____
802	Discount Fee @ %+$	$_____	1102	Abstract or Title Search	$_____
803	Appraisal Fee	$_____	1103	Title Examination	$_____
804	Credit Report	$_____	1105	Document Preparation Fee	$_____
805	Lender's Inspection Fee	$_____	1106	Notary Fee	$_____
806	Mortgage Insurance Application Fee	$_____	1107	Attorney's Fee	$_____
807	Assumption Fee	$_____	1108	Title Insurance	$_____
808	Mortgage Broker Fee	$_____			$_____
810	Tax Related Service Fee	$_____			$_____
811	Application Fee	$_____			$_____
812	Commitment Fee	$_____			$_____
813	Lender's Rate Lock-In Fee	$_____			$_____
814	Processing Fee	$_____			$_____
815	Underwriting Fee	$_____			$_____
816	Wire Transfer Fee	$_____			$_____

900	ITEMS TO BE PAI DIN ADVANCE ;		1200	GOVERNMENT RECORDING AND TRANSFER CHARGES	
901	Interest for 1 days @ $13.78 day	$_____	1201	Recording Fee	$_____
902	Mortgage Insurance Premium	$_____	1202	City/County Tax/Stamps	$_____
903	Hazard Insurance Premium	$_____	1203	State Tax/Stamps	$_____
904	County Property Taxes	$_____	1205	Intangible Tax	$_____
905	Flood Insurance	$_____			$_____

1000	RESERVES DEPOSITED WITH LENDER		1300	ADDITIONAL SETTLEMENT CHARGES	
1001	Hazard Ins 3 Mo @ $ 35 Per Mo	$_____	1201	Survey	$_____
1002	Mortgage Ins. Mo@$ Per Mo	$_____	1202	Pest Inspection	$_____
1004	Tax & Assmt. 7 Mo@$110 Per Mo	$_____	1203		$_____
1006	Flood Insurance	$_____	1205		$_____
		$_____		TOTAL ESTIMATED SETTLMENT CHARGES	$_____
S/B designates these costs to be paid by Seller / Broker			A designates those costs effecting APR		

TOTAL ESTIMATED MONTHLY PAYMENT			TOTAL ESTIMATED FUNDS TO CLOSE	
Principal & Interest	$_____			
Real Estate Taxes	$_____	Down Payment	$_____
Hazard Insurance	$_____	Estimated Closing Costs (not financed)	$_____
Flood Insurance	$_____	Estimated Prepaid Items/Reserves	$_____
Mortgage Insurance	$_____	Total Paid Items (subtract)	$_____
Other	$_____	Other	$_____
TOTAL MONTHLY PAYMENT	$_____	CASH FROM BORROWER	$_____

Figure 8:1 – Form Sample Good Faith Estimate Page 1 – HUD Release

The first section of the good faith estimate will define items that are payable in connection with the obtainment of the loan. The inclusions of each good faith estimate will vary slightly because the items charged to the borrower will be dependent on the structure of the loan being provided.

Always remember that alternative fees or 'junk fees' should remain similar for all borrowers regardless of their specific loan product or situation.

800	ITEMS PAYABLE IN CONNECTION WITH LOAN;	
801	Origination Fee @ % + $	$_____
802	Discount Fee @ %+$	$_____
803	Appraisal Fee	$_____
804	Credit Report	$_____
805	Lender's Inspection Fee	$_____
806	Mortgage Insurance Application Fee	$_____
807	Assumption Fee	$_____
808	Mortgage Broker Fee	$_____
810	Tax Related Service Fee	$_____
811	Application Fee	$_____
812	Commitment Fee	$_____
813	Lender's Rate Lock-In Fee	$_____
814	Processing Fee	$_____
815	Underwriting Fee	$_____
816	Wire Transfer Fee	$_____

Figure 8:2 – Form Sample Extract Good Faith Estimate Page 1 – HUD Release

800.   ITEMS PAYABLE IN CONNECTION WITH THE LOAN

801.   Origination Fee

The Origination Fee is usually known as a loan origination fee but is sometimes called a "point" or "points".

The origination fee covers the lenders administrative costs in processing the loan.

Often this fee is expressed as a percentage of the loan.

Generally, the buyer pays these fees. If the buyer and the seller negotiate a different method of payment, it will be defined within the sales agreement.

These points are charged on behalf of you or your branch. When working for a bank or a broker you have a negotiated commission schedule for all fees and points charged on the loan. You will also have a maximum limit to the points that you are allowed to charge.

You may charge points in two ways.

The first method of charging points is to wrap the points into the interest rate that you offer to the borrower. This will be discussed further in "pricing the loan".

The second method of charging points is as an up-front fee during the closing. Any up-front points will be reflected on the good faith estimate. If you do not include these fees within the good faith estimate, you will not be able to collect up-front fees on the loan.

A point is 1% of the loan amount.

802	Discount Fee	A discount fee is also called a loan discount point. A loan discount is a one-time charge imposed by the lender or broker to lower the rate at which the lender or broker would otherwise offer the loan.

This fee may vary.

In effect, the borrower is paying up front to reduce the overall monthly debt related to the loan. You may use the application of a discount fee to reduce the interest rate on a loan if the monthly payment exceeds the D. T. I. Ratio and the necessary funds are available to pay the discount fee.

This is also an excellent tool for your borrowers if the sellers have agreed to pay a set closing cost amount and the funds have not been utilized elsewhere.

These fees are paid to the lender.

803	Appraisal Fee	The Appraisal Fee covers the cost of the Appraisal.

The amount the appraisal fee is set by the appraisal company.

- The appraisal fee is often paid in advance.

    You will note this payment as paid in the details of transaction summary.

- The appraisal fee may be charged at the settlement.

These funds are paid to the Appraisal Company.

804	Credit Report	Any costs associated with the completion of the Credit Report will be disclosed on the good faith estimate.

Many lenders or brokers require the credit report charges be paid on all closed loans.

This amount is paid as a reimbursement to the lender.

The cost of the credit report is set regionally or by branch location. You should check with your branch manager for the amount.

At times, a lender may require the credit report fee be paid at the application meeting. In these cases, you will note the payment in the details of transaction summary as a fee paid in advance.

805	Lender's Inspection	If the lender requires an inspection of the property for Underwriting purposes or another reason, the costs are the responsibility of the borrower.
806	Mortgage Insurance Application Fee	If Mortgage Insurance is necessary for the loan; any associated Application Fee should be included in the good faith estimate. This fee covers the processing of an application for mortgage insurance.
807	Assumption Fee	If a loan is being assumed from the seller of the property, the lender assigning the

loan to the new borrower may charge an Assumption Fee.

This fee is charged when a buyer "assumes" or takes over the duty to pay the seller's existing mortgage loan

| 808 | Mortgage Broker Fee | Some states or specific funding lenders require that all fees charged by the Broker be differentiated on the good faith estimate. Mortgage Broker Fees are categorized with in this section of the good faith estimate. |

This separate disclosure helps to differentiate for the borrower the costs they are paying to the lending entity and the costs that they are paying for the Brokerage services.

| 810. | Tax Service Fee | Some lenders will use a service to verify the tax payment status of the property. Other lenders will rely on the settlement and closing company to perform this verification activity. |

If a separate tax service entity is used to obtain the tax payment amounts and payment status, they will charge a fee for completing this action. The amount of the fee will vary by Service Company.

| 811 | Application Fee | Some lenders or mortgage brokerage offices charge an up-front application fee. |

This amount may include the credit report charges, appraisal fee, or additional costs as determined by the branch location.

- Often these charges are credited toward the closing in the event the loan is completed.

- These payments are typically kept to offset any costs incurred by the branch in the event the loan does not close.

The decision to charge an application fee is determined by a particular branch location or lender. You will want to verify whether your office charges an application fee, the amount of the fee, and how the fee will be allocated at loan closing.

You will want to be sure to note this payment in the details of transaction section of the 1003.

| 812 Commitment Fee | | If your offices or the funding lender requires that the borrower pay a Commitment Fee, you must enter the amount into the good faith estimate. This is often termed a "junk fee". |

This is a fee charged by the lender in addition to points.

These fees are sometimes split per the negotiated commission schedule with the loan processor or loan officer.

| 813 Lender's Lock Rate Fee | | Some lenders will charge a specific fee for the task of locking the interest rate. This fee could be a service charge or may be a fee associated with the obtainment of a specific rate. |

This fee is different from the discount points paid to buy down the interest rate.

814 Processing Fee	If your offices or the funding lender requires that the borrower pay a Processing Fee, you must enter the amount into the good faith estimate. This is often termed a "junk fee".	

This is a fee charged by the lender in addition to points.

These fees are sometimes split per the negotiated commission schedule with the loan processor.

815 Underwriting Fee

If your office or the funding lender requires that the borrower pay an Underwriting Fee, you must enter the amount into the good faith estimate. This is often termed a "junk fee".

This is a fee charged by the lender in addition to points.

These fees are sometimes split per the negotiated commission schedule with the loan underwriter, loan officer, or loan processor but are more frequently credited entirely to the lender.

816 Wire Transfer Fee

Some lenders may charge a Wire Transfer Fee to cover the costs of wiring the required funds to close the loan.

This fee is a "buyer non-allowable fee" under some program guidelines. If a wire transfer fee is being charged on behalf of the branch or lender, you should incorporate the cost of this fee into the good faith estimate.

900	ITEMS TO BE PAI DIN ADVANCE	
901	Interest for 1 days @ $13.78 day	$_____
902	Mortgage Insurance Premium	$_____
903	Hazard Insurance Premium	$_____
904	County Property Taxes	$_____
905	Flood Insurance	$_____
		$_____

Figure 8:3 – Form Sample Extract Good Faith Estimate Page 1 – HUD Release

900 ITEMS REQUIRED BY THE LENDER TO BE PAID IN ADVANCE

Some fees related to the closing are recurring fees. These fees relate to costs associated with the carrying of the loan. The lender may require that the borrower pre-pay a specific quantity of these recurring fees as a condition of the loan closing. Some of these items would be accrued interest, mortgage insurance premiums, and homeowner's hazard insurance.

901 Interest

Lenders often require borrowers to pay the interest that accrues from the date of settlement or closing to the date that they will make the first monthly payment

This interest is prorated daily and based on the new loans interest rate.

902 Mortgage Insurance Premium

If mortgage insurance is a requirement of the loan being obtained, an up-front Premium may be charged. This premium may also be financed into the loan amount.

If the borrower pays the insured loan off within the first seven years, they may be entitled to a prorated refund of the fee.

You will include any up front premium in the good faith estimate and on the 1003.

903 Hazard Insurance Premium

Hazard insurance protects the borrower and the lender against loss due to fire, windstorm, and other hazards.

Lenders often require that the borrower to bring a paid-up first year's hazard insurance policy to the settlement or to pay for the first year's premium at settlement.

The premium amount should be included on the good faith estimate as a cost to close the loan. If the borrower pays this premium before closing, you will enter the amount of the payment into the pre-paid items on the 1003.

904 City Property Taxes

The city where the property is located may charge property taxes on real estate. The costs will be prorated between the buyer and the seller based on the closing date of the property and the negotiations included on the sales agreement. You will enter the borrower's estimated share of these costs into the good faith estimate.

905 Flood Insurance

If the lender requires flood insurance as a condition of the loan, it is usually listed within the segment of the good faith estimate relating to items to be paid in advance. Many lenders will require that the borrower bring a fully paid policy illustrating flood coverage for the first year of homeownership as a condition of loan closing.

1004 County Property Tax

The County will assess property taxes on real estate.

The amount of property taxes collected will vary depending on the date of closing, billing cycle of the taxes, and negotiations between the borrower and the seller.

The lender may require that the borrower escrow property taxes. Escrowing taxes means that the borrower pays a portion of the expected tax billing to the lender each month. The lender or servicer then holds these payments until the tax billing becomes due. The lender or servicer then uses the funds paid by the borrower to pay the tax bills related to the property.

1100	TITLE CHARGES	
1101	Closing or Escrow Fee	$_____
1102	Abstract or Title Search	$_____
1103	Title Examination	$_____
1105	Document Preparation Fee	$_____
1106	Notary Fee	$_____
1107	Attorney's Fee	$_____
1108	Title Insurance	$_____

Figure 8:4 – Form Sample Extract Good Faith Estimate Page 1 – HUD Release

1000 TITLE CHARGES

Any costs or charges associated with securing a clear title to the property and closing of the loan will be incorporated into the good faith estimate. Although these are not lender fees, lenders must provide a quote of the estimated costs of these items and services. These quotes may vary significantly. Title charges may cover a variety of services performed by title companies and others.

| 1101 | Closing/Escrow Fee | A Closing or Escrow Fee is paid to the settlement agent or escrow holder. Responsibility for the payment of this fee should be negotiated between the seller and the buyer and will appear on the sales agreement provided to you by either the real estate agent or the borrower. |

| 1102 | Abstract/Title Search | Any fees required for the completion of the Abstract or Title Search on the property will be charged by the Title Company to the borrower. |

The payment of these fees may be negotiated as part of the sales agreement between the borrower and the seller.

You can contact the closing company handling the settlement to obtain a figure for this field.

| 1105 | Document Preparation Fee | Any cost charged by the title company for the service of preparing all of the closing documents not provided by the funding company will be entered into the good faith estimate under Document Preparation Fee. |

Lender or Funding Company charges for document preparation costs will be included within a different section of the good faith estimate.

| 1106 | Notary Fee | The charge incurred for the notary who verifies the signatures of all parties on the documents during the closing should be included within the good faith estimate. |

You can contact the closing company handling the settlement to obtain a figure for this field.

| 1107 | Attorney's Fee | In the event that the services of an attorney are required during any portion of the loan application, processing, or closing activity, the costs charged by the attorney for these services should be entered into the good faith estimate. |

The attorney will provide you with an estimate of his or her charges for the requested services.

1200 GOVERNMENT RECORDING AND TRANSFER CHARGES	
1201	Recording Fee	$_____
1202	City/County Tax/Stamps	$_____
1203	State Tax/Stamps	$_____
1205	Intangible Tax	$_____

Figure 8:5 – Form Sample Extract Good Faith Estimate Page 1 – HUD Release

1200   GOVERNMENT RECORDING AND TRANSFER

Fees charged at the courthouse where the mortgage documents are filed will be allocated in association with the loan. The borrower typically pays these costs, but you should refer to the sales agreement to ensure that no other negotiations relating to the payment of these fees has been made. These fees are payable to the government.

| 1201 | Recording fee | A recording fee is the amount charged for the recording of each item that must be filed within the public records system. These items are filed for the protection of both the borrower and the lender. |

Recording costs vary depending on the region where the recording will occur. You will want to verify the costs with your Title Company, courthouse, or branch manager.

1202   City/County Tax Stamps

City and County Taxes and Stamps are the taxes assessed when real property is transferred within a city and county.

Different areas have different tax costs. You will want to verify this figure with your Title Company, courthouse, or branch manager.

1203   State Tax Stamps

State Tax Stamps are the state required taxes involved with the transfer of the property.

Different states have different tax costs and you will want to verify this figure with your Title Company, courthouse, or branch manager.

1300   ADDITIONAL SETTLEMENT CHARGES:

Any additional charges incurred during the loan processes that have not been addressed previously will be explained and entered within the final area of the good faith estimate

1301   Survey

Many lenders accept a survey affidavit from the Title Company as verification of the property location and boundary lines.

If a survey must be performed for the property to clear underwriting, these charges are negotiated as paid by the buyer or the seller of the property and the figure is paid to the Survey Company at settlement.

1302   Pest Inspections

Pest Inspections are required by some loan programs and are requested in some cases by the buyer

The payment for these fees is negotiated on the Real Estate Sales Agreement.

These payments are paid to the inspection provider based on a billing presented at the closing table.

1303   Flood Certification

A Flood Certification or verification that the property is not in a flood plain may be requested by underwriting.

If the flood certification is completed through a service retained by underwriting, the costs of the certification are paid to the lender at the time of closing and the lender pays the certification service.

If another certification service is used to verify the flood status of the property, the name of the service will be entered into the good faith estimate and the charges imposed by the service included.

Payment to the service provider may be made during the loan process or as part of the settlement process. You should enter the applicable details into the good faith estimate.

1304   Courier Fees

Courier Fees may be charged by either the funding company or closing company for the transfer of documents via courier.

Lender: Address: Applicant(s): Property Address:		Sales Price: Base Loan Amount: Total Loan Amount: Interest Rate: Type of Loan: Preparation Date: Loan Number		

The information provided below reflects estimates of the charges which you are likely to incur at the settlement of your loan. The fees listed are estimates – actual charges may be more or less. Your transaction may not involve a fee for every item listed.THE NUMBERS LISTED BESIDE THE ESTIMATES GENERALLY CORRESPOND TO THE NUMBERED LINES CONTAINED THE HUD-1 OR HUD-1A SETTLEMENT STATEMENT WHICH YOU WILL BE RECEIVEING AT THE SETTLEMENT. THE HUD-1 OR HUD-1A SETTLEMENT STATEMENT WILL SHOW YOU THE ACTUAL COST FOR ITEMS PAID AT SETTLEMENT.

800	**ITEMS PAYABLE IN CONNECTION WITH LOAN;**		**1100**	**TITLE CHARGES**	
801	Origination Fee @ % + $	$2550.00	1101	Closing or Escrow Fee	$ 295.00
802	Discount Fee @ %+$	$	1102	Abstract or Title Search	$
803	Appraisal Fee	$ 275.00	1103	Title Examination	$
804	Credit Report	$ 50.00	1105	Document Preparation Fee	$
805	Lender's Inspection Fee	$	1106	Notary Fee	$ 35.00
806	Mortgage Insurance Application Fee	$	1107	Attorney's Fee	$
807	Assumption Fee	$	1108	Title Insurance	$ 618.75
808	Mortgage Broker Fee	$			$
810	Tax Related Service Fee	$ 98.00			$
811	Application Fee	$			$
812	Commitment Fee	$			$
813	Lender's Rate Lock-In Fee	$ 200.00			$
814	Processing Fee	$ 250.00			$
815	Underwriting Fee	$ 400.00			$
816	Wire Transfer Fee	$			$

900	**ITEMS TO BE PAI DIN ADVANCE ;**		**1200**	**GOVERNMENT RECORDING AND TRANSFER CHARGES**	
901	Interest for 1 days @ $13.78 day	$ 13.78	1201	Recording Fee	$ 33.50
902	Mortgage Insurance Premium	$	1202	City/County Tax/Stamps	$ 80.00
903	Hazard Insurance Premium	$ 420.00	1203	State Tax/Stamps	$ 80.00
904	County Property Taxes	$1320.00	1205	Intangible Tax	$
905	Flood Insurance	$			$

1000	**RESERVES DEPOSITED WITH LENDER**		**1300**	**ADDITIONAL SETTLEMENT CHARGES**	
1001	Hazard Ins 3 Mo @ $ 35 Per Mo	$ 105.00	1201	Survey	$
1002	Mortgage Ins. Mo@$ Per Mo	$	1202	Pest Inspection	$
1004	Tax & Assmt. 7 Mo@$110 Per Mo	$ 770.00	1203		$
1006	Flood Insurance	$		TOTAL ESTIMATED SETTLMENT CHARGES $	
S/B designates these costs to be paid by Seller / Broker			A designates those costs effecting APR		

TOTAL ESTIMATED MONTHLY PAYMENT			**TOTAL ESTIMATED FUNDS TO CLOSE**	
	Principal & Interest	$ 616.00		
	Real Estate Taxes	$ 110.00	Down Payment	$
	Hazard Insurance	$ 35.00	Estimated Closing Costs (not financed)	$7743.03
	Flood Insurance	$	Estimated Prepaid Items/Reserves	$
	Mortgage Insurance	$	Total Paid Items (subtract)	$
	TOTAL MONTHLY PAYMENT	$ 761.00	CASH FROM BORROWER	$

Figure 8:6 – Form Sample Good Faith Estimate Page 2 – HUD Release

Kenney

APPROVED SERVICE PROVIDER LIST

Some mortgage lenders will use specific service providers when completing the processing and closing of a loan application. If the mortgage lender uses a specific service provider and the borrower will be responsible for the billing that is incurred because of this use, the lender must provide a disclosure to the borrower detailing the referral and relationship. This disclosure enables the borrower to make an informed decision applicable to the costs that they will incur.

Addendum to the standard "Good Faith Estimate" of Settlement Costs

_____ requires the use of certain providers in the processing and settlement of your loan. These providers are chosen from an approved list and we require that you pay for all portions of the services provided from these providers. The costs of these services are based on the charges of these providers or industry standards. Please refer to your attached Good Faith Estimate form for an estimate of each proposed charge. The following providers have been repeatedly used for the designated services within the last 12 months.

1. CREDIT REPORTING AGENCIES:

2. APPRAISAL SERVICES:

3. PRIVATE MORTGAGE INSURANCE PROVIDERS:

4. OTHER:

I/we acknowledge that we received a copy of this notice:

_____   _____
Borrower Signature   Date

_____   _____
Co-Borrower Signature   Date

Figure 8:7 – Form Sample Approved Service Provider – HUD Release

CHAPTER

9

APPRAISALS

A comprehensive understanding of appraisals is another area in which you must obtain knowledge. Much of your training focuses on the borrower situation and approval guidelines.

An important factor that everyone involved in the transaction must consider is that the property is as important as the borrower in the loan process.

The underwriter will base the borrower approval upon the factors that influence the likelihood that the borrower will pay the mortgage debt as agreed. These likelihood calculations are based upon historical data dictating the actions of past borrowers and are simply predictions of the performance of your borrower, not guarantees of their performance.

In the event that the borrower defaults on their mortgage loan, the property will then become the medium that the lender holding the loan will employ to regain their capital investment.

It is critical that the property condition and value has the ability to meet the needs of the lender if a default should occur. One method that the lender will use to determine the capability of the property to provide this security is through the appraisal.

The borrower is responsible for repaying the loan. The property acts as collateral, in the event the borrower does not fulfill this obligation.

The Underwriting team will scrutinize property appraisals and other property related information. In an effort to facilitate smoother loan processes and stronger loan packages, you should understand the appraisal process, the components of an appraisal, and areas within the appraisal that present red flags to Underwriters.

A Red flag is any information that indicates an issue exists that will lower the security of a loan package.

Appraisers are important elements in a variety of components of the lending process. The valuation and accuracy of an appraisal must be dependable. Appraisals will be used for

- Sales Price Negotiation

- Loan-to-Value Assessment

- Collateral Security

- Homeowner's Insurance Policies

- Title Insurance Policies

- Borrower Equity

- Determining necessary repairs to the property

- Private Mortgage Insurance Premiums

- Equity assessment

This is not to be considered an all-inclusive list. The listing is a basic assessment of the appraisal uses. Appraisals may affect other facets of the mortgage and home-buying process.

Many lenders have approved appraisers that they prefer to have complete the appraisal on any property being considered for a loan. The approval of an appraiser is based on the historical ability of that appraiser to provide appraisals that reflect the fair value of the property and do not contain exceptions to the preferred appraisal guidelines of the lender.

The most common appraisal form that you will counter is the *Uniform Residential Appraisal Report* or URAR.

UNIFORM RESIDENTIAL APPRAISAL REPORT

The purpose of this summary appraisal report is to provide with an accurate, and adequately supported opinion of market value of the subject property

Property Address		City	State	Zip Code
Borrower	Owner of Public Record		County	

Legal Description

Assessor's Parcel #		Tax Year	R.E. Taxes $
Neighborhood Name		Map Reference	Census Tract

Occupant __ Owner __ Tenant __ Vacant　　　Special Assessments $　　　　　　　__ PUD　HOA $　　　　__ per year __ per month

Property Rights Appraised ___ Fee Simple ___ Leasehold ___ Other (describe)

Assignment Type ___ Purchase Transaction ___ Refinance Transaction ___ Other (describe)

Lender Client		Address	

Is the subject property currently offered for sale or has it been offered for sale in the twelve months prior to the effective date of this appraisal __ yes __ no

Report data source(s) used offering prices(s), and date(s)

I __ did __ did not analyze the contract for sale for the subject purchase transaction. Explain the results of the analysis of the contract for sale or why analysis was not performed.

Contract Price $　　　　　Date of Contract　　　　Is the property seller the owner of public record __ Yes __ No Data Source(s)

Is there any financial assistance (loan charges, sale concessions, gift or down payment assistance, etc.) to be paid by any party on behalf of the borrower? __ Yes __ No If yes, report the total dollar amount and describe the items to be paid.

Note: Race and racial composition of the neighborhood are not appraisal factors

Neighborhood Characteristics			One-Unit Housing	Present Land Use %
	One-Unit Housing Trends			
Location ___ Urban ___ Suburban ___ Rural	Property Values ___ Increasing ___ Stable ___ Declining		PRICE AGE	One-Unit %
Built-Up ___ Over 75% ___ 25-75% ___ Under 25%	Demand Supply ___ Shortage ___ In Balance ___ Over Supply		$ (000) (yrs)	2-4 Unit %
Growth ___ Rapid ___ Stable ___ Slow	Marketing Time ___ Under 2 mth ___ 3-6 mths ___ Over 6 mths		Low	Multi-Family %
Neighborhood Boundaries			High	Commercial %
			Pred.	Other %

Neighborhood Description

Market Conditions (including support for the above conclusions)

Dimension	Area	Shape	View

Specific Zoning Classification　　　Zoning Description

Zoning Compliance ___ Legal ___ Legal Nonconforming (Grandfathered use) ___ No Zoning ___ Illegal (describe)

Is the highest and best use of the subject property as improved (or as proposed per plans and specifications) the present use? ___ Yes ___ No If No, describe

Utilities	Public Other (describe)		Public Other (describe)	Off-site Improvements – Type	Public	Private
Electricity		Water		Street		
Gas		Sanitary Sewer		Alley		

FEMA Special Hazard Area ___ Yes ___ No FEMAL Flood Zone　　　Fema Map #　　　FEMA Map Date

Are the utilities and off-site improvements typical for the market area ___ Yes ___ No If No, describe

Are there any adverse site conditions or extreme factors (easements, encroachments, environmental conditions and uses, etc.)? ___ Yes ___ No If Yes, describe

General Description	Foundation	Exterior Description materials/condition	Interior materials/condition
Units ___ One ___ One w Accessory Unit	Concrete Slab ___ Crawl Space	Foundation Walls	Floors
# of Stories	Full Basement ___ Partial Basement	Exterior Walls	Walls
Type ___ Det ___ Att ___ S-Dec / End Unit	Basement Area ___ sq ft	Roof Surface	Trim/Finish
___ Existing ___ Proposed ___ Under Cons	Basement Finish ___ %	Gutters & Downspouts	Bath Floor
Design (Style)	Outside Entry/ Exist ___ Sump Pump	Window Type	Bath Wainscot
Year Built	Evidence of ___ Infestation	Storm Sash / Insulated	Car Storage ___ None
Effective Age (Yrs)	___ Dampness ___ Settlement	Screens	Driveway # of Cars
Attic ___ None	Heating ___ FWA ___ HWBB ___ Radiant	Amenities ___ Woodstove(s)	Driveway Surface
___ Drop Stair ___ Stairs	___ Other ___ Fuel	___ Fireplaces # ___ Fence	___ Garage # of Cars
___ Floor ___ Scuttle	Cooling ___ Central Air Conditioning	___ Patio/Deck ___ Porch	___ Carport # of Cars
___ Finished ___ Heated	___ Individual ___ Other	___ Pool ___ Other	___ Att ___ Det ___ Built-in

Appliances ___ Refrigerator ___ Range/Oven ___ Dishwasher ___ Disposal ___ Microwave ___ Washer/Dryer ___ Other (describe)

Finished area above grade contains:　　　Rooms　　　Bedrooms　　　Bath(s)　　　Square Feet of Gross Living Area Above Grade

Additional Features (special energy efficient items, etc.)

Describe the conditions of the property (including needed repairs, deterioration, renovations, remodeling, etc.)

Are there any physical deficiencies or adverse conditions that affect the livability, soundness, or structural integrity of the property? ___ Yes ___ No If Yes, describe

Figure 9:1 – Form Uniform Residential Appraisal Report – Page 1 – HUD Release

Subject

Property Address		City	State	Zip Code
Borrower	Owner of Public Record		County	
Legal Description				
Assessor's Parcel #		Tax Year	R.E. Taxes $	
Neighborhood Name		Map Reference	Census Tract	
Occupant __ Owner __ Tenant __ Vacant	Special Assessments $		__ PUD HOA $	__ per year __ per month
Property Rights Appraised __ Fee Simple __ Leasehold __ Other (describe)				
Assignment Type __ Purchase Transaction __ Refinance Transaction __ Other (describe)				

Figure 9:2 – Form Extract Uniform Residential Appraisal Report – Page 1 – HUD Release

The upper portion of the URAR contains identifying data, general details of the property being assessed, and information relating to the individuals involved in the transaction.

You should compare the details of this section to the application details from your files. If any discrepancy between the appraisal report and your file details exists, you should ensure that the error or variation is corrected before submitting the appraisal to the underwriting team. You should compare the

- Property Address

- Borrower Name

- Legal Description

entries to the 1003. These entries should match the application data exactly.

- Owner of Public Record

- Assessor's Parcel Number
  Tax Year
  Real Estate Tax Amount

- Neighborhood Name
  Map Reference
  Census Tract

should match the sales agreement entries. If a discrepancy exists, you must have the incorrect document corrected. Some of these details will be used to create the loan closing documents and having correct details ensures that all of the paperwork is correct and helps to stabilize the lender's security in the property.

The details relating to the occupancy refer to the present occupancy status of the property.

- Occupancy of the Property
  Owner
  Tenant
  Vacant

The area relating to special assessments will be important to the loan.

- Special Assessments
  PUD

HOA
Terms

You should ensure that any special assessments noted by the appraiser that are recurring costs are entered into the 1003. These assessments will become a factor in the borrower's DTI ratio. If the appraiser notes special assessments that you have not included on the 1003, these could become a red flag issue and underwriting will require that the application be modified and the DTI Ratio be recalculated. At times, special assessments could result in a loan approval being changed to a denial or the terms of the loan approval being modified so that the borrower's DTI Ratio falls within the guidelines.

The appraiser will define the rights being appraised. This section of the URAR refers to the rights that are available for transfer by the current owner of the property.
Property Rights Appraised

Fee Simple
Leasehold
Other

The rights being transferred through the transaction may alter the security of the loan. It is important that you verify that these rights match the information remitted on the loan application.

The appraiser will note the type of transaction being conducted.

Assignment Type

Purchase Transaction
Refinance Transaction
Other

You should review each entry within this section and confirm that these entries match the information submitted on the loan application and sales agreement.

If you note an error in a document, you must determine which document contains the error. If it is simple typing error or name entry method, the error can be easily corrected by the individual responsible for creating the document. If it is a more serious error, such as one relating to special assessments, you should re-assess the loan application and ensure that the borrowers are still able to qualify for the present loan program. Once you have recalculated the loan specifics and corrected the application package details, you must submit the loan package to the underwriter so that they may issue a new approval that includes the corrected items.

CONTRACT

I __ did __ did not analyze the contract for sale for the subject purchase transaction. Explain the results of the analysis of the contract for sale or why analysis was not performed.

Contract Price $	Date of Contract	Is the property seller the owner of public record __ Yes __ No Data Source(s)
Is there any financial assistance (loan charges, sale concessions, gift or down payment assistance, etc.) to be paid by any party on behalf of the borrower? __ Yes __ No If yes, report the total dollar amount and describe the items to be paid.		

Figure 9:3 – Form Extract Uniform Residential Appraisal Report – Page 1 – HUD Release

Data pertaining to any sales contract or other contract that is a part of the transaction will be included within this section.

You will wish to supply a copy of the contract to the appraiser at the time of the appraisal request.

Upon receipt of the completed appraisal, you should review the inclusions within this section to confirm that they match the details of the transaction you used to structure the application.

The appraiser will note whether the details of the contract were or were not reviewed during the completion of the appraisal.

- Contract Price

- Date of Contract

- Confirmation of Seller

- Financial Assistance
  Seller Concessions
  Gift Funds
  Down payment Assistance

You should review the financial details that the appraiser enters into the appraisal report including details relating to seller concessions, down payment assistance, and gift funds. The appraiser will take these details from the sales agreement. You should ensure that these inclusions match those that you incorporated into your 1003.

Neighborhood

Note: Race and racial composition of the neighborhood are not appraisal factors									
Neighborhood Characteristics				One-Unit Housing Trends				One-Unit Housing	Present Land Use %
Location	Urban	Suburban	Rural	Property Values	Increasing	Stable	Declining	PRICE AGE	One-Unit %
Built-Up	Over 75%	25-75%	Under 25%	Demand Supply	Shortage	In Balance	Over Supply	$ (000) (yrs)	2-4 Unit %
Growth	Rapid	Stable	Slow	Marketing Time	Under 2 mth	3-6 mths	Over 6 mths	Low	Multi-Family %
Neighborhood Boundaries								High	Commercial %
								Pred.	Other %
Neighborhood Description									

Figure 9:4 – Form Extract Uniform Residential Appraisal Report – Page 1 – HUD Release

Neighborhood Information

Details concerning the neighborhood of the property will be considered during the appraisal process.

Each line of the neighborhood assessment should be completed by the appraiser. There should be no blank lines or unchecked boxes. If an area is incomplete, you should contact the appraiser and request that they make the appropriate notations on the report before you submit the package to underwriting for review.

Neighborhood Red Flags

Assessments within the neighborhood section present vital information that may effect the loan terms and approval.

Any variance from a positive answer or an uncommon answer will be scrutinized by the underwriter as these entries may affect the ability of the property to serve as security in the event of a borrower default. If any item entered into the neighborhood assessment is negative in nature, you should discuss these variances with the Appraiser to determine if the information is correct.

Example: A property whose neighborhood is considered Rural may require additional comparable properties to substantiate the valuation of the property.

These additional comparables help to offset the distance factor inherent to most underwriting guidelines relating to appraisers.

Most underwriting guidelines require that the appraiser use sales from comparable properties that are within a certain, pre-set proximity to the subject property. Rural areas often exceed these limitations due to the oversize land owned by each property owner.

Red Flag Action

If a need exists for additional comparables on the appraisal, it is a more effective and a faster process to request the appraiser provide these immediately rather than waiting for the Underwriter to generate a stipulation for the additional comparable property.

Market Characteristics and Conditions

Market Conditions (including support for the above conclusions)

Figure 9:5 – Form Extract Uniform Residential Appraisal Report – Page 1 – HUD Release

The appraiser will provide an assessment of market comparison and market conditions. You should review the appraiser's comments. Any comment that could be considered a negative factor may affect the loan approval. If the appraiser states that the market for property similar to the subject property is below average, the security inherent in the property may be lessened. This could result in a change in the loan approval or even a denial of the loan to the borrower for this specific property. The borrower may need to choose another home to purchase or renegotiate the purchase agreement the seller in order to meet the new conditions imposed by underwriting for that particular property.

SITE

Dimension	Area	Shape	View	
Specific Zoning Classification	Zoning Description			
Zoning Compliance __ Legal __ Legal Nonconforming (Grandfathered use) __ No Zoning __ Illegal (describe)				
Is the highest and best use of the subject property as improved (or as proposed per plans and specifications) the present use? __ Yes __ No If No, describe				
Utilities Public Other (describe)	Public Other (describe)	Off-site Improvements – Type Public Private		
Electricity	Water	Street		
Gas	Sanitary Sewer	Alley		
FEMA Special Hazard Area __ Yes __ No FEMAL Flood Zone	Fema Map #	FEMA Map Date		
Are the utilities and off-site improvements typical for the market area __ Yes __ No If No, describe				
Are there any adverse site conditions or extreme factors (easements, encroachments, environmental conditions and uses, etc.)? __ Yes __ No If Yes, describe				

Figure 9:6 – Form Extract Uniform Residential Appraisal Report – Page 1 – HUD Release

The site segment of the appraisal describes the parcel on which the subject property is built and any issue regarding site usage that are apparent.

Any issues with the use of the land including easements, encroachment, boundary line issues, or other factors affecting the land should be reviewed and addressed. Issues affecting the use of the land may need to be corrected before the closing of the loan. Underwriting guidelines will dictate what generates a red flag stipulation regarding site and site usage.

The buyer and the seller may need to negotiate an addendum to the sales agreement relating to the correction of any site usage issues and who will pay for the correction of these issues.

The loan closing may be delayed while a site usage issue is corrected.

Improvements

General Description	Foundation	Exterior Description materials/condition	Interior materials/condition
Units ___ One ___ One w Accessory Unit	Concrete Slab ___ Crawl Space	Foundation Walls	Floors
# of Stories	Full Basement ___ Partial Basement	Exterior Walls	Walls
Type ___ Det ___ Att ___ S-Dec / End Unit	Basement Area ___ sq ft	Roof Surface	Trim/Finish
___ Existing ___ Proposed ___ Under Cons	Basement Finish ___ %	Gutters & Downspouts	Bath Floor
Design (Style)	Outside Entry/ Exist ___ Sump Pump	Window Type	Bath Wainscot
Year Built	Evidence of ___ Infestation	Storm Sash / Insulated	Car Storage ___ None
Effective Age (Yrs)	___ Dampness ___ Settlement	Screens	Driveway ___ # of Cars
Attic ___ None	Heating ___ FWA ___ HWBB ___ Radiant	Amenities ___ Woodstove(s)	Driveway Surface
___ Drop Stair ___ Stairs	___ Other ___ Fuel	Fireplaces # ___ Fence	Garage ___ # of Cars
___ Floor ___ Scuttle	Cooling ___ Central Air Conditioning	Patio/Deck ___ Porch	Carport ___ # of Cars
___ Finished ___ Heated	___ Individual ___ Other	Pool ___ Other	Att ___ Det ___ Built-in
Appliances ___ Refrigerator ___ Range/Oven	___ Dishwasher ___ Disposal ___ Microwave	Washer/Dryer ___ Other (describe)	
Finished area above grade contains:	Rooms ___ Bedrooms ___	Bath(s) ___ Square Feet of Gross Living Area Above Grade	
Additional Features (special energy efficient items, etc.)			
Describe the conditions of the property (including needed repairs, deterioration, renovations, remodeling, etc.)			
Are there any physical deficiencies or adverse conditions that affect the livability, soundness, or structural integrity of the property? ___ Yes ___ No If Yes, describe			

Figure 9:7 – Form Extract Uniform Residential Appraisal Report – Page 1 – HUD Release

Many of the red flags that occur with an appraisal review will occur in the area of the appraisal that relates to the improvements. The term improvement refers to the actual building of the property. All portions of the subject property should obtain at least a rating of average.

If any area relating to the property receives a rating of less than average, the seller and the buyer will need to determine the steps that will be taken to improve the rating or condition of the property.

The appraiser will check the boxes that relate to the property.

# of Units   These will include the number of units contained within the subject property. You should ensure that the number of units reflected on the appraisal is the same as the number of units indicated on the 1003.

# of Stories   The number of stories included in the property will affect the desirability of the property. The comparables used for the valuation portion of the appraisal should be of a similar number of stories.

Status   The appraiser will note the status of the property including whether the improvements are existing, under construction or planned improvements. The status of the property should match the loan type that you are requesting.

    Example: Proposed Improvements   =   Construction Loan

Design   The design of the property will affect the desirability of the property. The comparables used for the valuation portion of the appraisal should be of a similar design and appeal.

Year Built and Effective Age   The year that the property was built and the effective age of the property will affect the value. The year built is the actual age. Improvements, renovations, and updating are factored into the effective age. A home may be a number of decades old and have a much younger effective age if the property has been renovated to bring it into line with newer construction.

Attic   The inclusion or exclusion of an attic may affect both the desirability and the value of a property. Square foot value is typically assessed to those areas that are heated and cooled. These areas are considered to be living square feet. If the attic is used as living square feet, it will be factored as part of the dollar per square foot valuation process. If the attic is used for storage and does not qualify as living square footage, it will still be a factor during underwriting, but more often as a determination that the property of similar design and appeal as the comparables used during the valuation processes.

Foundation   The type of foundation, including the type of basement that they property contains will effect both the desirability and the value of the property. Similar to an attic, a finished basement with a heat source may be considered as living square footage and factored as part of the dollar per square foot valuation. A basement used as storage will be apply as a determination that the subject property is of a similar design and appeal as the comparables used during the valuation process.

Issues   The appraiser will note any issues that are apparent in the basement area of the property. Any issues, including dampness, infestation, or settlement of the property may need to be addressed before the loan can proceed to closing. These issues may put the value and condition of the property at risk if left unaddressed. The job of the underwriter relating to the property is to gain the strongest collateral position possible. If an issue is left unaddressed, the property may continue to deteriorate and result in a loss of value over time.

Heating / Cooling   The type of heating and cooling contained within the subject property may affect the value and appeal of the property. The comparables used for valuation should contain a similar type of heating and cooling sources as the subject property.

Exterior/ Interior   The interior and exterior of the property should be in good condition. The underwriter will confirm that there is not a large discrepancy between the materials of the subject property and the materials of the comparable properties, but will be most interested in the appraiser notes relating to condition. The condition rating set by the appraiser should be at least average. Any condition rating below average may need to be addressed before the loan can proceed to closing.

Amenities   will add value to the property. The appraiser will note any special features or amenities relevant to the subject property. The underwriter will look at the information entered under the comparable property to see if they have any of the same amenities. If the subject property has either a great many or far fewer amenities and features than the comparables, the underwriter may request an explanation from the appraiser or may determine that an alteration in value from that shown on the appraisal is in order.

Appliances   The inclusion of appliances in the transfer of real estate is not a factor unless the value of the appliances equals a substantial amount of the overall value of a property or if the comparables do include a much greater number or quality of appliances in the transfer.

Square Feet   The appraiser will enter the total square feet of the property and the number of rooms encompassed by this square footage. He will also note the number of these rooms that are bedrooms and bathroom space.

The appraiser will make adjustments during the valuation processes for the differences in square footage between the subject property and the comparable property. The appraiser will also make adjustments based on the use of the square footage.

Comment   The URAR form provides the appraiser with an area to provide opinion about the property. This option section has places available to comment on

- Additional features of the property

- Condition of the property including items that
  - presently require repairs
  - are in a state of deterioration

- are undergoing renovations
- have other apparent issues that the appraiser feels may affect the value of the property

- Deficiencies that affect the livability, soundness or structural integrity of the property

- Neighborhood in comparison to the subject property

The appraiser will enter any comments that they feel are important to the ability of the subject property to maintain its present value. If any item is defined within the comments area that creates a potential for a loss in value, the underwriter will typically require that the issue be cured, or corrected, before the transaction can proceed to closing.

You will want to review each entry within the Improvements Comment section and ensure you understand the problems that may arise. You will also wish to inform any applicable parties to the transaction about the comments.

We recommend contacting your appraiser if you note a discrepancy, error, or issue on the appraisal report. This recommendation does not indicate that you should influence the appraiser's decision and comments in any manner.

The purpose of the contact is to confirm the information in the URAR is correct according to the appraiser's record.

The only alterations you should request to a completed appraisal are alterations arising because of an error or omission.

You should never attempt to influence or alter the opinion of the appraiser.

UNIFORM RESIDENTIAL APPRAISAL REPORT

. There are	comparable properties currently offered for sale in the subject neighborhood ranging in price from $			to $		
There are	comparable sales in the subject neighborhood within the past twelve months ranging in sales price from $			to $		

FEATURE	SUBJECT	COMPARABLE SALE #1		COMPARABLE SALE #2		COMPARABLE SALE #3	
Address							
Proximity to Subject							
Sale Price	$	$		$		$	
Sale Price/Gross Liv Area	$ sq ft	$ sq ft		$ sq ft		$ sq ft	
Data Source(s)							
Verification Source(s)							
VALUE ADJUSTMENTS	DESCRIPTION	DESCRIPTION	Adjustment	DESCRIPTION	Adjustment	DESCRIPTION	Adjustment
Sales or Financing Concessions							
Date of Sale / Time							
Location							
Leasehold/Fee Simple							
Site							
View							
Design (Style)							
Quality of Construction							
Actual Age							
Condition							
Above Grade Room Count	Total Bdrms Baths	Total Bedrms Baths		Total Brms Baths		Total Brms Baths	
Gross Living Area	sq ft	sq ft		sq ft		sq ft	
Basement & Finished Rooms Below Grade							
Functional Utility							
Heating / Cooling							
Energy Efficient							
Garage / Carport							
Porch/Patio/Deck							
Net Adjustment		+ -	$	+ -	$	+ -	$
Adjusted Sales Price of Comps		Net Adj % Gross Adj %	$	Net Adj % Gross Adj %	$	Net Adj % Gross Adj %	$

I __ did __ did not research the sale or transfer history of the subject property and comparable sales. If not, explain

My research __ did __ did not reveal any prior sales or transfers of the subject property for the three years prior to the effective date of this appraisal.
Data source(s)

My research __ did __ did not reveal any prior sales or transfers of the comparables sales for the year prior to the date of sale of the comparable sale.
Data source(s)

Report the results of the research and analysis of the prior sale or transfer history of the subject property and comparable sales (report additional on pg 3)

ITEM	SUBJECT	COMPARABLE SALE #1	COMPARABLE SALE #2	COMPARABLE SALE #3
Date of Prior Sale/Transfer				
Price of Prior Sale/Transfer				
Data Source(s)				
Effective Date of Data Source(s)				

Analysis of prior sale or transfer history of the subject property and comparable sales

Summary of Sales Comparison Approach

Indicated Value by Sales Comparison Approach $

Indicated Value by: Sales Comparison Approach $ Cost Approach (if developed) $ Income Approach (if developed)$

Figure 9:8 – Form Uniform Residential Appraisal Report – Page 2 – HUD Release

FEATURE	SUBJECT	COMPARABLE SALE #1		COMPARABLE SALE #2		COMPARABLE SALE #3
Address						
Proximity to Subject						
Sale Price	$	$		$		$
Sale Price/Gross Liv Area	$ sq ft	$ sq ft		$ sq ft		$ sq ft
Data Source(s)						
Verification Source(s)						
VALUE ADJUSTMENTS	DESCRIPTION	DESCRIPTION	Adjustment	DESCRIPTION	Adjustment	DESCRIPTION
Sales or Financing Concessions						
Date of Sale / Time						
Location						
Leasehold/Fee Simple						
Site						
View						
Design (Style)						
Quality of Construction						
Actual Age						
Condition						
Above Grade Room Count	Total / Bdrms / Baths	Total / Bedrms / Baths		Total / Brms / Baths		Total / Brms / Baths
Gross Living Area	sq ft	sq ft		sq ft		sq ft
Basement & Finished Rooms Below Grade						
Functional Utility						
Heating / Cooling						
Energy Efficient						
Garage / Carport						
Porch/Patio/Deck						
Net Adjustment		+ -	$	+ -	$	+ -
Adjusted Sales Price of Comps		Net Adj % Gross Adj %	$	Net Adj % Gross Adj %	$	Net Adj % Gross Adj %

Figure 9:9 – Form Extract Uniform Residential Appraisal Report – Page 2 – HUD Release

Page two of the URAR will contain the valuation and cost analysis the appraiser completes when assessing the value of the property. The cost analysis may take two forms either the Cost Approach or the Sales Comparison Approach.

You will see the sales comparison approach used more frequently within your files than the cost approach.

The sales comparison data assesses the characteristics and condition of the subject property as compared to other, similar properties sold within a given time period and in the same area as the subject property. Underwriting guidelines will have standards that must be met with regard to the comparable property that may be used. The property should be

- Similar in design and appeal as the subject property
- Similar in size and condition as the subject property
- Similar in features and amenities as the subject property
- Similar in site design, use, and view as the subject property
- Within a defined distance of the subject property

    Example: Within the same neighborhood

- Sold within a pre-set time limit of the date of the appraiser

118

If a comparable property included on the appraisal does not meet one of these qualifications, the appraiser will need to explain the reason that the comparable was selected as a data source.

Example: Rural property often exceeds the distance requirement as the mass of land encompassed by rural property often makes it difficult to locate many pieces of sold property within the same neighborhood and within the sales time limit.

At times, underwriting may require additional actions if the comparables used by the appraiser do not meet the standards set within the guidelines of the loan program. Common stipulations that relate to an unacceptable data source inclusion would be to request two additional comparables be incorporated into the appraisal or that an appraisal field review be conducted to verify the value and other information included within the original appraisal.

The subject property will be compared to each of the comparables selected by the appraiser.

Proximity　The distance between the properties being compared effects the value.

The appraiser should locate similar properties sold within a reasonable time that are close in location to the subject property.

Property values vary greatly from one neighborhood to the next. It is important that property comparisons use properties that are located in similarly valued areas.

A comparable property that exceeds reasonable proximity guidelines as set by underwriting for your loan program will require an explanation by the appraiser.

Additional comparables may be needed to validate the value indicated within the appraisal. Some loan programs will dictate that comparables that do not meet the neighborhood requirement will require a reduction in the LTV approval for the loan or a decrease in the value indicated by the appraisal.

Sales Price　The sales price of the comparables is the starting basis that will be used to determine the value of your subject property.

The factors listed below sales price will increase or decrease the value of the subject property in comparison with other closed sales in the area.

Any area of the subject property that is lacking as compared to the comparison properties will result in a decrease to the sales price baseline of the comparable.

Any area of the subject property that is a positive as compared to the comparison properties will result in an increase to the sales price baseline of the comparable.

Sales Price / Gross Living　A dollar figure will be determined for the cost per square foot of the comparable property.

This figure is determined by dividing the total sales price by the total square foot of each property.

Data Sources　The appraiser will note the source from which they obtained each entry included in the appraisal.

The comparable property sales price will be adjusted based on comparison factors between the subject property and the comparable property. Each of these adjustment items will result in a change in the price valuation.

Concessions　Any concession relating to the transfer of the comparison property will be included as part of the appraisal. These concessions may alter the transaction through an increase in overall value.

The appraiser will also review the sales agreement relating the subject property to determine if it contains any negotiations relating to seller or finance concessions.

Date of Sale   A date that is too far removed (past) will need to be addressed.

This is a red flag issue.

The loan guidelines for the loan program being obtained will dictate how far in the past a sale may have occurred and still be considered viable for comparison purposes. All comparison property sales should occur within a reasonable time to ensure the correct market conditions are being addressed in regards to value.

At times, the appraiser may exceed the time limitations set by underwriting. This exception could occur for a variety of reasons including a slow market in which very few homes have transferred or a neighborhood that contains an exceptionally high number of long-term residences and few property transfers.

The appraiser should include an explanation regarding any property sale used for comparison purposes that exceeds the sale date requirements. The underwriter may require other actions to offset the exception in sale date including additional comparables, an appraisal field review, an LTV changes, a property value alteration, or other action.

Location   An assessment of average or above is desired with regard to property location.

Any assessment below average will need to be addressed.

This may be a red flag.

Any variance between the property assessment level and the assessment of the comparison property may result in an alteration to value.

Estate Type   The type of estate of the subject property should match the type of estate listed on the 1003. Any differences between the documents will need to be addressed. Most loan programs require that the fee simple estate be transferred because of the sale. Any limitations or changes to the estate type may affect the value and desirability of the property.

The estate transferred on each of the comparable properties should be the same as the type of estate being transferred in the subject property.

A variance between the estate types of the properties may result in an alteration to the value.

Site Size   The sites should be similar in size. A large difference between the land included with the transfer of the subject property and a comparable property will need to be addressed.

A variance between the site sizes of the properties will result in an alteration to the value. Most program guidelines have specific parameters regarding the percentage of the overall property value allocated to the land and the percentage allocated to improvements, setting very specific limits on the amount of the overall value that may be allocated to the land transferred in the sale.

This issue typically arises in the transfer of rural property.

If the land value of the subject property is excessive, the underwriter may reduce the value by the amount allocated to the land that is in excess of the loan program guidelines.

If there is a large discrepancy between the site size of a comparable and the subject property, the appraiser will need to include an explanation as to why this comparable was chosen as a data source. The underwriter may dictate additional actions required on the appraisal or changes to the loan program because of the variation in site size.

View

The sites should be of similar rating concerning view assessment.

A difference in the assessment of the view level between the properties may result in an alteration in the value of the subject property.

An assessment that indicates a below average rating of the view of the subject property will need to be explained by the appraiser and may result in stipulations or value changes by the underwriter.

Design / Style

The properties should be of similar design and appeal levels. A difference in the design and style of the properties will require an explanation by the appraiser. The appraiser will need to define the reason that they chose a comparable property of a different design or style than the subject.

If the subject property obtains a below average design and appeal assessment this may be a red flag to the underwriter. Any item that receives a below average rating may require actions on the part of the buyer or seller to correct the issue, additional stipulations, or an alteration to the value assessed to the property.

Quality of Construction

The properties should be of similar quality. Any difference in the quality levels of the property will need to be explained by the appraiser.

A difference in the quality of construction may result in an alteration in the value allowed by underwriting.

An assessment that the subject property is of below average construction quality may result in underwriting refusing financing on this property, a stipulation that specific repairs be completed to correct the item that is considered to be below average, a change in the value assessment allowed on the property or another action.

Age of Property

The properties used for comparison purposes should be similar to the age of the subject property. The age of a property affects its value and the appraiser will need to define the reason that the comparables used as data sources are of a different age basis than the subject property.

Room Count /Square Ft

The room counts and square footage of the properties should be similar.

A difference in the room count between the subject property and the comparable property will result in a change to the value assessment assigned by the appraiser.

Underwriting may require additional actions or explanations relating to the differences in property room count.

The dollar value per square foot calculations will be completed by the appraiser. These act as a baseline for the other value calculations. A large discrepancy in square footage between the subject property and the comparison property will alter the value assessed by the appraiser.

Basement The size and use of the basement of the subject property and comparable properties should be similar. If the basement of the subject property is finished, the basement area of the comparable properties should also be finished.

A variance between the properties will result in an alteration in value.

Functional Utility The functional utility of all of the properties should be similar. A difference in the functional utility of the subject property from the comparables will require an explanation by the appraiser.

A difference in the quality of construction may result in an alteration in the value allowed by underwriting.

An assessment that the subject property is of below average construction quality may result in underwriting refusing financing on this property, a stipulation that specific repairs be completed to correct the item that is considered to be below average, a change in the value assessment allowed on the property or another action.

The subject property should obtain an assessment of at least average.

An assessment below average will need to be addressed.

This is a red flag.

Heating / Cooling The heating and cooling systems of the properties will need to be similar.

A difference between the types or inclusion of heating or cooling systems may result in an alteration in value. The type of heating and cooling systems may not be a red flag depending on the region and the commonality of the various heating and cooling systems in use. The addition or exclusion of a cooling system or the age of the heating and cooling system may be a factor.

Energy Efficient The properties should be of similar levels of energy efficiency.

A large discrepancy in the energy efficiency levels of the properties may result in an alteration in value. The subject property must obtain a rating of at least average. A rating of below average will need to be addressed.

This may be a red flag.

Some programs may require alterations to the property to obtain an assessment of at least average in relationship to energy efficiency.

Some loan program guidelines consider a high level of energy efficiency to be a compensating factor.

Garage / Carport The inclusion of a garage or carport should be similar between all properties. The appraiser will assess a value to the garage or carport. The comparison section of the appraisal should reflect the alteration in value that results from the inclusion or lack of a garage or carport in one of the properties.

If either the subject property or one of the comparables has or lacks a garage or carport and the other property does not, you should confirm that the value adjustments have been entered into the appropriate field by the appraiser. If there is no value adjustment relating to the inclusion or lack of a garage or carport, you should question the appraiser regarding the lack of an adjustment.

The appraisal may need to be modified to include this value change.

Porch /
Patio / Deck The inclusion of a porch, patio, or deck should be similar between all properties. The appraiser will assess a value to the porch, patio, or deck. The comparison section of the appraisal should reflect the alteration in value that results from the inclusion or lack of a porch, patio, or deck in one of the properties.

If either the subject property or one of the comparables has or lacks a porch, patio, or garage and the other property does not, you should confirm that the value adjustments have been entered into the appropriate field by the appraiser.

If there is no value adjustment relating to the inclusion or lack of a porch, patio, or carport, you should question the appraiser regarding the lack of an adjustment.

The appraisal may need to be modified to include this value change.

An alteration to this inclusion will result in an alteration in the value.

I ___ did ___ did not research the sale or transfer history of the subject property and comparable sales. If not, explain				
My research ___ did ___ did not reveal any prior sales or transfers of the subject property for the three years prior to the effective date of this appraisal.				
Data source(s)				
My research ___ did ___ did not reveal any prior sales or transfers of the comparables sales for the year prior to the date of sale of the comparable sale.				
Data source(s)				
Report the results of the research and analysis of the prior sale or transfer history of the subject property and comparable sales (report additional on pg 3)				
ITEM	SUBJECT	COMPARABLE SALE #1	COMPARABLE SALE #2	COMPARABLE SALE #3
Date of Prior Sale/Transfer				
Price of Prior Sale/Transfer				
Data Source(s)				
Effective Date of Data Source(s)				
Analysis of prior sale or transfer history of the subject property and comparable sales				
Summary of Sales Comparison Approach				
Indicated Value by Sales Comparison Approach $				

Figure 9:10 – Form Extract Uniform Residential Appraisal Report – Page 2 – HUD Release

Adjustments and Sales Price

The appraiser will enter details relating to the subject property and each comparable selected as a data source for the determination of value. The upper portion will contain details relating to the sale or transfer of each property, including the date of the sale or transfer. The date entered into the date field must be within the time term established by the underwriter. If the sale date of a comparable property exceeds the limitations set by underwriting.

A date that is too far removed (past) will need to be addressed.

This is a red flag issue.

The loan guidelines for the loan program being obtained will dictate how far in the past a sale may have occurred and still be considered viable for comparison purposes. All comparison property sales should occur within a reasonable time to ensure the correct market conditions are being addressed in regards to value.

At times, the appraiser may exceed the time limitations set by underwriting. This exception could occur for a variety of reasons including a slow market in which very few homes have transferred or a neighborhood that contains an exceptionally high number of long-term residences and few property transfers.

The appraiser should include an explanation regarding any property sale used for comparison purposes that exceeds the sale date requirements. The underwriter may require other actions to offset the exception in sale date including additional comparables, an appraisal field review, an LTV changes, a property value alteration, or other action.

Net
Adjustments   The net adjustments section of the appraisal is the area that the appraiser will use to enter the value calculation factors that will help to determine the final value assessed to the subject property.

Each item that the appraiser assesses for comparison between the properties will be assigned a value.

Any item that was lacking in the subject property but present in the comparison property will result in a reduction from the sales price of the comparable.

Any item that was lacking in the comparable but present in the subject will result in an increase to the sales price of the comparable.

Adjusted
Sales Price   These value adjustments will be added to or subtracted from the sales price of the   comparable.

Example: Sales Price   199,900
                Garage   + 1,500
                Adjusted Sales Price   201,400

The total dollar figure resulting from these adjustments is the figure the appraiser believes the subject property would have sold for if given the same buyer, the same time, and the same conditions.

This is the comparison approach to property valuation.

Signature   The signature of the appraiser indicates he has completed the appraiser and certifies that the market value of the property has been duly determined per appraiser guidelines.

Analysis and Indicated Value

The appraiser will place the value figure he has obtained through comparison, adjustments, and market research on the appraisal page.

This is the final appraised value of the property.

PAGE 3 - Additional Comments

The third page of the appraisal has space for comments of the appraiser.

Any issue noted in the first pages of the appraisal should be addressed in this area.

You should review all of the comments to ensure that you have located each potential red flag contained within the appraisal.

You should ensure the appraiser has addressed each issue that you have noted during your review of the appraisal inclusions.

Indicated Value by: Sales Comparison Approach $	Cost Approach (if developed) $	Income Approach (if developed)$

Figure 9:11 – Form Extract Uniform Residential Appraisal Report – Page 2 – HUD Release

COST APPROACH TO VALUE

The cost approach is used to determine value based upon the replacement cost of the subject property. The cost approach is not usually used for a mortgage loan.

INCOME APPROACH TO VALUE

The income approach to value will often be used for rental or other income producing property. The income approach uses many of the same data indicators as the core appraisal but adds the factor of income to the final value of the property.

PUD PROJECT INFORMATION

If the transaction is being based upon a Planned Unit Development, the PUD section of the appraisal will play a role in the final value determination of the property. You should review this section for any additional red flags that may become apparent if your transaction involves a PUD.

FIELD REVIEWS

Any discrepancy, red flag, or issue on the appraisal may result in a requirement for a field review appraisal. The purpose of a field review is to confirm the opinion of the original appraiser as to condition, value, location and other factors concerning the subject property.

- Underwriting guidelines will stipulate what conditions create the need for a field review.

- Underwriting guidelines will define who is responsible for the cost for a field review.

- The underwriting department will typically request the field review appraisal directly form the appraiser and you will usually not be given the opportunity to review the inclusions of the field review before the underwriter has received a copy.

An example of a field-review appraisal form generated from HUD is included from your review.

You should note the items that the field review appraisal would inspect.

Always remain aware that appraisals are not to be altered in any manner.

You will usually be aware of the need for a field review and the results of the field review, but will not be an integral part of the field review processes.

We recommend contacting your appraiser if you note a discrepancy, error, or issue on the appraisal report. This recommendation does not indicate that you should influence the appraiser's decision and comments in any manner.

The purpose of the contact is to confirm the information in the URAR is correct according to the appraiser's record.

The only alterations you should request to a completed appraisal are alterations arising because of an error or omission.

You should never attempt to influence or alter the opinion of the appraiser.

RIGHT TO RECEIVE A COPY OF THE APPRAISAL

When an appraisal has been conducted as a part of the transaction, the borrower has a right to obtain a copy of the appraisal.

- The appraisal will often be delivered directly to the lender during the course of the loan process.

- You should provide instructions to the buyer on how to obtain a copy of the appraisal if they desire one at or before the settlement meeting.

- These instructions must be signed and witnessed during the closing process.

NOTICE REGARDING YOUR
UNIFORM RESIDENTIAL APPRAISAL REPORT

You are advised that you have the right, under the Equal Credit Opportunity Act, to obtain a copy of your *Uniform Residential Appraisal Report*.

If you wish a copy, please write us at the address shown below. We must hear from you no later than 90 days after we notify you about the action taken on your credit application or you withdraw your application.
Please send your written request to:

In your letter, give the following information:

    Loan or application number (if known)
    Date of application
    Name(s) of loan applicant(s)
    Property address
    Current mailing address

A copy of your Uniform Residential Appraisal Report shall be mailed to you within 30 days after receipt of your request.

Please acknowledge receipt of this Notice by signing and dating below.

Figure 9:12 – Form Notice Regarding Your Uniform Residential Appraisal Report – HUD Release

Chapter

10

THE GUIDELINE MATRIX

A guideline matrix is a chart that dictates the approval requirements, underwriting basis, and specific approval terms of each loan product that you might use for a borrower. You should view the matrix as a snapshot of the full underwriting guidelines that will be applied to the loan packages that you submit for approval.

The ability to review the matrix and determine where an application package will fall within the matrix will enable you to determine what loan programs might suit the needs of your borrower. The matrix will include data that enables you to assess the documentation that will be requested with the loan package, and begin the process of structuring the loan immediately upon the review of all of the application documentation.

- Each lender your work with will have a variety of loan products available.

- Each product will come with its own set of rules or guidelines that must be met in order to secure that loan for your borrowers.

It is impossible to convey to you the importance of learning the guidelines for each loan program that you have available. The more familiar with the loan guidelines you become, the more capable you will be at placing your borrowers in the appropriate program.

It is our goal to teach you the basics of Mortgage Origination and Loan Submission and to make you a Specialist at these tasks.

It must be your continued goal to review the loan programs available for your use. You must become familiar with the specifics of each program that you may use for your borrower. Your employer should have manuals detailing specific guidelines for each program available. If these are not available at your branch office, you will want to request a guideline manual from the Underwriting Department or have your manager do so.

Learning loan guidelines is imperative to your continued success within the mortgage industry.

Each loan program will have a product matrix available. These matrixes are a snapshot of the minimum requirements that are necessary to place a loan in a particular approval tier or level.

Approval guidelines should not be confused with proper documentation. Most approval guidelines are based on your borrower credit and debt ratios. Earlier we asked you to complete two practice forms. These forms were:

Credit Scoring

Debt-to-Income Ratio

You should locate these two forms and use them for this section of the course. If you have not yet completed the practice lessons, you will need to do so now. The practice materials we will review in placing and pricing the loan require these forms. The completed forms will contain valuable information you will need when determining loan placement and adherence to minimum level criteria.

SAMPLE PRODUCT MATRIX

Credit Grade	Credit Score	Mortgage History	Consumer History	Bankruptcy/ Foreclosure	Maximum Debt Ratio	Maximum LTV	Maximum CLTV
A	660+	0x30	1x30	3/3	41%	97%	97%
A-	620-669	1x30	2x30	3/3	45%	95%	97%
B	590-619	2x30	1x60	2/2	47%	90%	95%
B-	560-589	1x60	2x60	2/2	50%	85%	95%
C	540-559	2x60	1x90	1/1	50%	80%	90%
C-	520-539	1x90	2x90	1/1	55%	75%	90%
D	490-519	2x90	3x90	>1year	55%	70%	85%
Contact U/W	>490	>2x90	>3x90	>1 year	55%	Contact U/W	Contact UW

Figure 10:1 Sample Product Matrix

Matrix Limitations/Key

The sample matrix applies to a non-conforming loan product. The sample matrix includes the minimum guideline requirements for each level. The minimum guidelines indicated by this particular matrix are included below. You should review these minimum requirements and limitations and compare the entries to the example matrix. This practice will assist you in gaining an understanding of how you will locate the limitations and requirements for each matrix that you will use.

- Maximum mortgage and consumer late payments are rated using the worst rating in history.

- All late payments lower than the worst rating mortgage and consumer history late payments may usually be discounted.

Example: a 1x60 negates the use of all 30-day late payments.

- Mortgage and Consumer late payments are calculated over the preceding 12-month or 24-month period only.

- Credit scores requirements may be waived if adequate compensating factors exist in the credit profile.

- Foreclosure and Bankruptcy dates indicate the date of completion or discharge only.

- Maximum debt ratio limitations may be exceeded if adequate compensating factors exist in the credit profile

- Collection accounts under $2500 may be left unpaid for approval levels of B- or lower. Approval status of B or above must pay all open collections.

- Charge off accounts and all judgment accounts must be paid in full before closing for all approvals above C-. Approvals below C- must be reviewed by underwriting.

- Medical collections may be left unpaid for all approvals of B or below.

- Medical collections must be paid in full for approvals of A or A-.

- All approval levels require a minimum of three open lines of consumer credit.

- Mortgage/Rental history must be verified through a third party source.

This matrix is for example purposes only. Each loan program will have specific guidelines and approval levels. You should refer to your guideline manual for the approval guidelines of a particular loan program.

GRADING

Each loan program will have a product matrix available. These matrixes are a snapshot of the minimum requirements that are necessary to place a loan in a particular approval tier or level for a specific loan program.

Example:	Borrower	1st Matrix Level Approval Rate
Credit Score	589	B- (on tier possible bump)
Mortgage History	0x30	A
Consumer History	1x60	B
Bankruptcy	None	A
Foreclosure	None	A
Debt Ratio	43%	A-

Using this borrower example criterion and the data included within the sample product matrix, the borrower would qualify for an approval rating of B or a B-. B is the better approval rating and will provide the borrower with a more desirable LTV, CLTV, and interest rate pricing. Therefore, you desire a B for your borrower.

In order to qualify as a B rating compensating factors must used to improve the base approval of the borrower. The credit score in the example places the borrower within the B- tier, but all of the other factors are within the

A or B approval level. A common compensating factor baseline request is that the credit score falls within a few points of the next highest approval tier.

The cover sheet you submit with the loan application for this borrower would indicate all compensating factors regarding your borrower and state the request for an underwriting exception with regard to the credit score.

In this scenario, we will assume the underwriter approved the credit-grade exception request based on the compensating factors within the borrower's profile.

The B credit-grade approval level carries the following details:

- LTV   90%

- CLTV   95%

- All collection accounts must be paid in full before closing.

- All charge off and judgment accounts must be paid in full before closing.

- Medical collections may remain unpaid.

We have placed the borrower within a B credit-grade approval level. As a B credit grade approval, the borrower is qualified for an LTV of 90%, a CLTV of 95%.

If the basic criteria of the approval tiers suits the needs of the borrower, your next step is to price the loan to determine the interest rate level and to confirm that the debt ratio of the borrower meets the program guidelines.

The DTI ratio may change after you complete the pricing process due to the actual rate the borrower can receive. The debt ratio may continue to change as interest rate offerings fluctuate. Once the borrower locks in the rate using the rate lock / float option form, you can finalize the DTI ratio calculations.

Some underwriting criteria allow for exceptions to the debt ratio levels if there are adequate compensating factors in the borrower's profile to substantiate the exception.

Our example borrower has obtained an exception to the credit score requirement so compensating factors would need to carry a high impact with the underwriter to obtain a second exception.

If the new housing expense exceeds ratio limitations and you cannot obtain an exception, there would be alternative options available to you:

- Reduce the maximum sales price and loan amount your borrower may obtain.

- Reduce the points wrapped into the interest rate and accept a lower commission or obtain payment for your services on the front-end.

- Pay off consumer debt in an attempt to reduce debt load.

*   Caution The action of paying off debt may reduce the credit score.

- Obtain seller assistance toward closing costs or additional borrower funds so that there is money available to buy down the interest rate to a level that generates a payment that fits within the debt ratio guidelines.

- Search for a different program whose approval tier gives a higher DTI ratio limit. This program change may enable the borrower to approve at the levels needed to close the loan under the present circumstances.

It is important to note that each approval grade provides a maximum LTV and CLTV. When you review the section relating to pricing the loan, you will note that a lower LTV compared to the maximum possible under a credit grade, the lower the interest rate will become. Even if your borrowers only require an LTV of 80%, you will still wish to locate the highest-grade approval possible for the borrower's profile because the grade approval will affect all elements of the loan process, not just the maximum LTV and CLTV.

This is a sample of a credit grading process. Each loan program will have different guidelines and factors that may affect the process. Each borrower will have a variety of factors that effect the approval options. You should review the guideline matrix for each program that you may use for a borrower to determine other variables that may affect the grading and approval practices of your office.

CONVENTIONAL LOAN UNDERWRITING GUIDELINES

		MANUAL UNDERWRITING	AUTOMATED UNDERWRITING
ELIGIBILITY	Programs	30-Year Fixed, 40-Year Fixed, 35-Year Interest Only	
	Loan Purpose	Purchase Transactions Only	
	Occupancy Status	Owner-Occupied Primary Residence Only	
	LTV / CLTV Limits	Maximum LTV 100%, Maximum CLTV 107% (90% Maximum LTV/CLTV on Manufactured Housing on 30 and 40-year only. Manufactured housing is NOT permitted on interest only	
	Minimum Contribution	None Required	
CREDIT	Minimum Credit Score	620 (regardless of automated underwriting findings)	
	Alternative Credit	Permitted. Minimum of four sources with a twelve month satisfactory payment record. One of the sources must be a twelve month VOR	
	BK / NOD / Foreclosure	Minimum 3 years since discharge/sale date and evidence of reestablished credit required	
	Collections	If individual account balance is less than $250 or the total of all such accounts is $1000 or less not required to pay at closing.	Determined by automated approval
	Student Loan	Must not be in default. Deferred allowed as long as payment calculated in debt ratios	
RATIOS & INCOME	Back End Ratio	45% (35-Year Interest Only qualified as 35-Year fully amortized)	55% regardless of underwriting findings
	Temporary Buy downs	Temporary buy downs allowed on 30-Year & 40-Year Fixed Rate loans only. No buy downs permitted on Interest Only. LTV > 95% qualify at note rate. LTV < or = 95% qualify at buy down + 1	Determined by automated approval
	Non-Occupancy Co-Signor	Permitted on 30-Year & 40-Year Fixed rate loans only with LTV, or = 90%. Occupant borrower(s) total debt ratio max 55%, combined max 45%	
	Boarder Income	None Permitted	
	PT / OT / 2nd Job / Bonus Income	Permitted with a minimum 12 month history	Determined by automated approval
PROPERTY	Eligible Property Types	Single Family (no in laws suites/ granny flats) 5 acres maximum. Condominiums must meet FNMA Condominium Project Acceptance Policy or be FHA Approved PUD. Manufactured Housing – limited to 90% LTV/CLTV with 10% down payment from borrower's own funds on 30 and 40-year	
	Appraisals	One of the following appraisal forms is required: Uniform Residential Appraisal Report (URAR) Fannie Mae/Freddie Mac for 1004 (Single Family / PUD) Form 1004C (Manufactured Home Appraisal Report) Form 1073 (Individual Condominium Appraisal Report)	
FUNDS TO CLOSE	Minimum Down Payment	No minimum down payment required except for manufactured home loans which require 10% borrowers own funds	
	Cash Reserves	1 month	Determined by automated approval
	Gift Funds	Permitted. No Maximum. May be used to supplement cash reserves	
	Seller Contribution	Contributions by any interested party towards recurring and/or non-recurring closing costs are limited to: 3% of the purchase price if LTV is > 90% 6% of the purchase price if LTV is < or = 90% Any contribution exceeding these limits requires a downward adjustment to the sales price to reflect the amount that exceeds the limits	

MORTGAGE INSURANCE — Monthly Mortgage Insurance Rates							
Required on all loans with an LTV >80%							
30-Year Fixed / 40-Year Fixed / 35-Year IOP (non-conforming loan)				35-Year IOP (conforming loan)			
LTV	Coverage	Pricing		LTV	Coverage	Pricing	
95.01-100	35%	85		97.01 – 100	20%	59	
90.01 – 95	35%	75		95.01 – 97	18%	50	
85.01 – 90	35%	55		90.01 – 95	16%	46	
80.01 – 95	35%	41		85.01 – 90	12%	34	
				80.01 - 95	6%	23	

Figure 10:2 Sample Product Matrix

CHAPTER 11

PRICING THE LOAN

Loan program pricing is the process of determining the interest rate that the lender will apply to the borrower's new loan. Rate factors, including approval tiers, maximum limitations, and wrapped points will influence the interest rate that you can offer to the borrower.

After you have chosen a loan program for your borrower, you will need to price the loan based on the current rate sheet for that particular program.

You will want to be certain you are using the most up to date rate sheet to avoid errors in pricing.

- Before beginning the pricing process, you should review the rate sheet to determine if there are any restrictions to the pricing.

  Restrictions will include any internal requirement and applicable laws regarding loan pricing for the loan program you have chosen for the borrower.

  Example: Loans under $50,000 may not contain a pre-payment penalty.

  You will want to ensure that you comply with all of the applicable restrictions on the rate sheet.

- The second item to review will be the qualifying guidelines on the rate sheet.

  These guidelines should match the product matrix you used to determine the approval level of your borrower.

It is important that you confirm the matrix guidelines match the approval guidelines that you applied when placing the borrower within a credit tier. Loan programs are changed frequently and you must ensure that you are using the most up-to-date details when pricing the loan.

You should note that some rate sheets might not contain guideline qualification information.

- You should familiarize yourself with the format of the rate sheet. Every lender has a variation on the rate sheet format that they like to use.

The rate sheets will contain the same basic information. The layout used will be different.

- Locate the column on the rate sheet that contains the preferred loan terms for your borrower.

Example: 30 year fixed

Example: 3/1 ARM

- Once you have located the correct column, you will locate the row that is applicable to the borrower approval rating.

A, A-, B or another credit approval designation depending on the lender to whom you are submitting the loan package

- Within the credit level designation, you will find various LTV's. You should locate the LTV that your borrower requires.

- You will scroll over within the LTV row to the column that indicates the pricing that you must obtain to make the loan figures work.

Example: if you must price at par and will obtain payment up front, you will use the rate designated under the PAR column.

Example   If you must wrap 1 point into the rate, you will use <1.00>

- Locate the corresponding interest rate.

You will offer this rate for your borrower.

You should enter this rate into all applicable documents and recalculate the loan payments.

It is important that you confirm the payment is entered correctly on the loan application documents. A small change in the monthly payment can alter the entire loan approval.

RATE SHEET

Grade	LTV	3/1 ARM			Margin	30 Year Fixed			15 Year Fixed		
		Par	<1.00>	<2.00>		Par	<1.00>	<2.00>	Par	<1.00>	<2.00>
A	97%	8.000	8.500	9.000	4.125	8.500	9.000	9.500	8.000	8.500	9.000
660+	95%	7.875	8.375	8.875	3.875	8.125	8.625	9.125	7.875	8.375	8.875
Mtg 0X30	90%	7.625	8.125	8.625	3.375	8.000	8.500	9.000	7.625	8.125	8.625
Con 1X30	85%	7.250	7.875	8.375	3.250	7.875	8.125	8.625	7.375	7.875	8.375
3/3	80%	7.000	7.500	8.000	3.125	7.750	8.250	8.750	7.000	7.500	8.000
41%	75%	6.750	7.250	7.775	3.000	7.625	8.125	8.625	6.750	7.250	7.775
A-	95%	8.500	9.000	9.500	3.875	9.750	10.250	10.750	8.500	9.000	9.500
620-669	90%	8.125	8.625	9.125	3.375	9.500	10.000	10.500	8.125	8.625	9.125
Mtg 1X30	85%	8.000	8.500	9.000	3.250	9.125	9.625	10.125	8.000	8.500	9.000
Con 2X30	80%	7.875	8.125	8.625	3.125	8.875	9.375	9.875	7.875	8.125	8.625
3/3	75%	7.750	8.250	8.750	3.000	8.375	8.875	9.375	7.750	8.250	8.750
45%	70%	7.625	8.125	8.625	2.875				7.625	8.125	8.625
B	90%	9.750	10.250	10.750	4.125	10.250	10.750	11.250	9.750	10.250	10.750
590-619	85%	9.500	10.000	10.500	3.875	9.625	10.125	10.625	9.500	10.000	10.500
Mtg 2X30	80%	9.125	9.625	10.125	3.375	9.375	9.875	10.375	9.125	9.625	10.125
Con 1X60	75%	8.875	9.375	9.875	3.250	9.250	9.750	10.250	8.875	9.375	9.875
2/2	70%	8.375	8.875	9.375	3.125	8.875	9.250	9.750	8.375	8.875	9.375
47%											
B-	85%	10.250	10.750	11.250	5.250	10.875	11.375	11.875	10.250	10.750	11.250
560-589	80%	9.625	10.125	10.625	5.125	10.250	10.750	11.250	9.625	10.125	10.625
Mtg 1X60	75%	9.375	9.875	10.375	5.000	9.625	10.125	10.625	9.375	9.875	10.375
Con 2X60	70%	9.250	9.750	10.250	4.875	9.375	9.875	10.375	9.250	9.750	10.250
2/2											
50%											
C	80%	10.875	11.375	11.875	6.250	11.625	12.125	13.125	10.875	11.375	11.875
540-559	75%	10.250	10.750	11.250	6.000	10.875	11.375	12.375	10.250	10.750	11.250
Mtg 2X60	70%	9.625	10.125	10.625	5.875	10.250	10.750	11.750	9.625	10.125	10.625
Con 1X90	65%	9.375	9.875	10.375	5.625	9.750	10.125	11.250	9.375	9.875	10.375
1/1											
50%											
C-	75%	11.625	12.125	13.125	7.500	12.375	12.875	13.250	11.625	12.125	13.125
520-539	70%	10.875	11.375	12.375	6.875	11.750	12.250	12.750	10.875	11.375	12.375
Mtg 1X90	65%	10.250	10.750	11.750	6.250	11.125	11.625	12.125	10.250	10.750	11.750
Con 2X90											
1/1											
55%											
D	70%	12.375	12.875	13.250	7.875	12.875	13.250	13.875	12.375	12.875	13.250
490-519	65%	11.750	12.250	12.750	7.325	12.250	12.750	13.125	11.750	12.250	12.750
Mtg 2X90											
Con 2X90											
>1 Year											
55%											

Pricing assumes 3-year prepayment penalty.
Add .250 to rate for 1-year prepayment penalty.
Add .500 to rate for 0-year prepayment penalty.
No prepayment penalty may be charged on loans >50K.
Loans under 30K require a .500 rate adjustment.

Figure 11-1 Sample Rate Sheet

Pre-pricing Quick List

- Qualifying level of your borrower

- LTV required by your borrower

- CLTV required by your borrower

- ARM or Fixed priced loan program

- Prepayment penalty option

- How you are being paid. Will you receive up front fees or must you wrap points

To determine your borrower's approval level, you will want to refer to the credit scoring forms you completed earlier.

You will also need to verify the DTI Ratios to be certain they fall within the guidelines of the level you wish to place your borrowers.

Note that each level has different LTV options.

- In general, the lower the LTV as compared to the maximum allowed the lower the interest rate.

The higher the credit-grade status of your borrowers the better interest rate they can expect.

- Keep in mind that using the maximum available options for the borrower's Credit Grade typically will increase the interest rate.

You must know the options that the borrower has chosen for the loan. If the borrower has not chosen term and penalty options, you might price all of the variables and provide your borrower with a range of program offerings at the approval meeting. ARM vs. Fixed Rate programs and the use of Prepayment Penalties are explained on the following pages.

Determine commission payment options before pricing the loan.

<table>
<tr><td colspan="3" align="center">PRICING THE LOAN
Quick Guide</td></tr>
<tr><td>Credit Grade</td><td>You will need to refer to your credit worksheet to determine the credit grade for which your borrower's will qualify.

Upon reviewing your Product Matrix and Guidelines, you should have developed you own system for charting the credit grade of your borrower's package under the various programs you are considering.</td><td>Each program will have a different set of terminology for their credit grades.

Many will put the basic minim requirements for each grade level on the rate sheet so that you can double-check the approval tier as you price the loan.</td></tr>
<tr><td>Credit Score</td><td>You will want to verify that the credit score you have determined as applicable for the program meets the minimum requirements for the grade level that you are pricing.</td><td>Keep in mind that different lender's will dictate the score that will apply to the loan program.

Some lenders require the use of the middle credit score ranked by numbers and some will require the use of the most regionally accurate score for the borrower's location.</td></tr>
<tr><td>Mortgage History</td><td>The rate sheet or guideline matrix will define the number and the time allowed for that grade with regard to mortgage late payments.</td><td>If the mortgage history is not on the credit report, you will need to provide documentation proving the mortgage or rental history status over the applicable period the chosen loan program.</td></tr>
<tr><td>BK/FC</td><td>All credit grades require that a bankruptcy or foreclosure be 'seasoned" for a period. This refers to the date of discharge.</td><td>If the date is not apparent on the credit report, you will need to provide documentation proving the discharge date.</td></tr>
<tr><td>Consumer Credit</td><td>As with mortgage history most Credit Grades will require that, the consumer history meets certain minimums requirements with regard to the number and term of any late payments evident on the history.</td><td>Some Credit Grade sheets will remove consumer history as a criterion. These lenders rely on credit scores to reflect the consumer history.</td></tr>
<tr><td>Debt Ratio</td><td>Many rate sheets provide you with the maximum debt ratio allowed under that grade.

If your borrower's ratio exceeds the requirements of the loan program, they will be dropped to the next lowest credit grade whose minimum requirements they do meet.</td><td>Bear in mind that the Debt Ratios must include the new housing payment and any subordinate financing payments the borrower plans to incur because of the purchase.

Also, bear in mind that the Underwriting Team will typically pull another credit report just before closing. Any additional debt your borrower's incur between these credit reports will be factored into the debt ratio.

Counsel your borrowers not to make credit purchases even if the credit is available to them until the new mortgage loan is closed.</td></tr>
<tr><td>LTV (Loan To Value)</td><td>This section lists the maximum loan to value options available for each credit grade</td><td>You will note that there are listings below the maximum LTV available to the borrower.

In most cases, the lower the actual LTV as compared to the maximum LTV allowed the lower the interest rate offered.</td></tr>
<tr><td>ARM/FIXED</td><td>The next columns show the program term options.

The term that your borrower chooses for the amortization of the loan will affect the interest rate offered to them by the lender.</td><td>You should discuss the term options with the borrower and assist them in choosing the amortization term and method that best suits their needs and plans.

You should not simply choose a term to</td></tr>
</table>

			achieve the best interest rate. The amortization term and method must be chosen to meet the needs of the borrower.
	PAR	Directly below the term option you will see the pricing details available the loan program. PAR, <1.00>, <2.00> and <3.00> To price at par means that there are no points included in the interest rate and you must obtain your commission points as an up-front payment at the closing. You will include these up front points in the good faith estimate and on the HUD Settlement Statement.	To price at <1.00> means that you are receiving 1% of the loan amount as back end commission. <2.00> means 2% commission points and <3.00> means 3% of the loan amount as back end commission. This is known as wrapping points or being paid on the back-end.
	Margin	Beside the Par section, you will see the word Margin. This only appears on the ARM options. The margin refers to the rate of adjustment that may occur after the fixed portion of the loan program expires.	It is essential that you explain the rate adjustment term and margin to the borrower before placing them in an adjustable rate program. ARM's can be useful tools if the borrower's plans match the adjustment term but should be used with caution. The borrower must be able to meet the terms of the newly adjusted loan. If you place a borrower in an ARM program and the DTI Ratio cannot support the adjusted monthly payment or the borrower cannot refinance or sell the home, the borrower's payment stability may be at risk.
Pricing		You will now incorporate all of the applicable pricing options to arrive at an interest rate quote. • find the correct credit grade • determine the desired loan to value • follow the column over to the correct loan term option and pricing (back end points)	The rate shown is the interest rate you will quote to your borrowers.
Examples		Borrower A is rated a credit grade A and requires a 95% LTV. You need to incorporate 2 points into the rate. The borrower is able to take a 3/1 ARM with a 3-year prepayment penalty	Rate Quote: 8.875
		If Borrower A is willing to pay all points up front, you can drop his interest rate accordingly.	Rate Quote: 7.875
		If Borrower A were able to secure gift funds from a family member in the amount of 10% of the sales price, your LTV would drop to 85% LTV. All other items remain the same as in example one.	Rate Quote: 8.375

A rate sheet will often have a variables box somewhere on the page. The variable box allows you to alter the rate by choosing additional options.

Example: if you chose a 1-year prepayment penalty with the loan examples above, you would add .250 to the rate quote.

If you choose no prepayment penalty, with the examples above, you might be required to increase the rate quote by .500.

Variables are very important to the pricing process because it is up to you to sell the borrower on the interest rate. It would also be up to you to explain why the rate changed if you missed a variable that was going to cause a rate increase.

We have included some sample credit reports in the Chapter Career Building Tools. We recommend you use the samples and forms included to practice preliminary product approvals and rate quotes.

ARM or Fixed Rate Options

You will typically have both ARM and Fixed Rate offerings available for your borrower. The decision to use an ARM or fixed rate program is one that you and the borrower must carefully consider.

Both program types carry potential benefits as well as potential drawbacks. You should review the borrower's present situation, plans, and the market conditions in order to educate your borrower and assist them in making the best possible decision.

Adjustable Rate Program

An adjustable rate mortgage is a mortgage program that carries a variable interest rate that can change over the life of the loan. The rate applied to the principal borrowed under an adjustable rate mortgage may go up or down depending on the status of the index to which it is linked.

Adjustable-rate mortgage programs are created with a pre-set margin. The margin or adjustment base is set on a major mortgage index such as the Libor. An adjustable rate mortgage program has the ability to affect the borrower's monthly payments through the application of the new interest rate that occurs at each adjustment period. This adjusting rate could place some borrowers at risk if economic conditions dictate that the rate goes up and the borrower's debt to income ratio is unable to bear the new monthly mortgage payment applied because of the increased interest rate.

An adjustable rate mortgage program can be customized around your borrower's homeownership plans, credit rehabilitation program, or the market prediction of rate activity.

- The credit rehabilitation program is the program you develop as a service to your borrower in an effort to secure future purchase and refinance loans from that borrower. This program offers them methods of rebuilding and repairing their credit in time to refinance before the rate adjustment occurs. You will want to familiarize yourself with conventional minimum guidelines before offering rehabilitation advice.

- When market fluctuations are expected to occur and the borrower plans to refinance the mortgage at the time of these occurrences, an ARM will allow a lower interest during the payment term. The ARM should be set to expire at or about the time of market condition changes.

- If the borrower intends to move or sell the home within a specified number of years, an adjustable rate program may help to decrease the costs of homeownership during the years that the borrower remains in the mortgage.

  Example: A borrower who works for a national corporation or serves in the military may be aware of future transfer plans. An adjustable rate loan program may be a good choice if the transfer plans are solid and the program can be customized around this expected move date.

In many cases, the adjustable rate programs will offer a rate discount to the borrower well below the basic fixed rate program offerings.

Many adjustable rate programs offer a 2, 3, even 5-year fixed rate term before the first adjustment.

Because of the rate adjustment period, you may also have the opportunity to write a prepayment penalty into the loan package.

A pre-payment penalty option provides the benefit of lowering the interest rate even further.

You should carefully consider the risk of incorporating a pre-payment penalty or adjustable rate into any borrower's loan program.

- An adjustable rate carries the risk that the payment may adjust by a large margin if the borrower is unable to refinance or sell the home before the adjustment period.

- A pre-payment penalty inhibits the refinance or sale activity of the borrower until the pre-payment penalty expires. If the borrower chooses to refinance the loan or sell the home before the date of the expiration, a fee or penalty will be imposed.

If your borrower desires an ARM and Pre-Payment penalty loan, you must assist the borrower in customizing the prepayment period to expire in time for the refinance but before the rate adjustment.

If a borrower's primary dwelling is going to be secured by an Adjustable Rate or Variable Rate loan, The Truth-in-Lending Act requires that additional disclosures be provided to the borrower.

When working with a borrower that is obtaining an adjustable rate mortgage, you must provide the borrower with educational notices and disclosures that assist them in understanding the loan program that they are obtaining.

- The Consumer Handbook on Adjustable Rate Mortgages

- A disclosure for each variable rate program offered to the borrower.

The disclosures must contain all the necessary information required by Regulation Z.

The Truth-in-Lending Act also requires loan servicers to provide disclosures to consumers each month an adjustment to the interest rate occurs.

ADJUSTABLE RATE MORTGAGE DISCLOSURE STATEMENT

IMPORTANT MORTGAGE LOAN INFORMATION
PLEASE READ CAREFULLY

PROGRAM NAME: _____

You have expressed an interest in applying for an Adjustable Rate Mortgage loan (ARM). This disclosure contains information regarding the differences between this ARM and other mortgage loans. This disclosure describes the features of the specific ARM that you are considering. Upon request, we will provide you with information about any other Adjustable Rate Mortgage programs we have available.

ADJUSTABLE RATE MORTGAGE LOAN: This loan is an Adjustable Rate Mortgage loan. The interest rate may change based upon movements of a specific interest rate index. Changes in the interest rate will be reflected by increases or decreases in the amount of your payments. The date or dates on which changes can occur will be specified in the ARM loan documents. This ARM is based on the terms and conditions of the program in which you have expressed an interest. We have based this disclosure on recent interest rates, index and margin values, and fees.

THIS DISCLOSURE: This disclosure is not a contract or loan commitment. The matters discussed in this disclosure are subject to change by us at any time without notice. DETERMINING THE INTEREST RATE: Your interest rate will be determined by means of an index that is subject to change.

Your interest rate is based on the Index value plus a margin. A change in the index generally will result in a change in the interest rate. If the Index rate change since the previous adjustment is less than _____, the interest rate will not change. The amount that your interest rate change may also be affected by periodic interest rate change limitations and the lifetime interest rate limits set forth in your loan program.

    Interest Rate Adjustments Your interest rate under this ARM can change every _____ years.

    Your interest rate cannot increase or decrease more than ____ percentage points at each adjustment.

    Your interest rate cannot increase or decrease more than ____percentage points over the term of your loan.

    Rate adjustments under this ARM will be reflected in higher or lower payments.

DETERMINING THE PAYMENTS: Your initial monthly payment of principal and interest will be determined based on the interest rate, loan term, and loan balance when your loan is closed.

Your payment will be set to amortize the loan over a period of ___ payments.

Frequency of Payment Changes: Based on increases or decreases in the Index, payment amounts under this ARM loan can change every ____ years. Your monthly payment amount could change more frequently if there is a change in other loan factors not relating to the ARM. These factors may include taxes, assessments, insurance premiums, or other charges required when creating an escrow or impound account.

Limitations on Payment Changes: Your payment can change every ___ years based on changes in the interest rate, loan term, or loan balance.

Adjustment Notices: You will be notified if interest rate changes occur. If an interest rate change effects your monthly payment, you will be notified at least 25 calendar days before the changed payment is due. The notice will indicate the adjusted payment amount, interest rate, Index value, and the outstanding loan balance at that time.

** INSERT AN EXAMPLE AND INDEX TABLES AS THEY APPLY TO THE ARM UNDER DISCUSSION.

I/we acknowledge that we have received a copy of this disclosure:

Borrower Signature   Date   Co-Borrower Signature   Date

_____   _____   _____   _____

Figure 11-3 Sample Adjustable Rate Mortgage Disclosure Statement – HUD Release

What is a pre-payment penalty?

- A prepayment penalty is a monetary penalty that is assessed for the early payoff of a loan that contains a prepay clause. Most lenders offer 0, 2, 3, and 5-year prepayment penalties.

- These penalties offer the lender the security that the borrower will retain the loan for a certain period of time. This helps to secure a minimum financial return for the investor based on the expected interest payments over the pre-set term. If the borrower were to make an early payoff on the loan, the penalty is designed to offset the loss of interest suffered by the lender.

- Lenders will offer a reduction of initial interest rate in exchange for the prepayment clause because of the added longevity of loans on the books.

- Pre-payment penalties may not be a workable option for some borrowers. If you are working with a borrower who desires a pre-payment penalty or requires a lower interest rate than the base offering, you should ensure that the borrower's situation and plans could meet the requirements of the pre-payment penalty term.

Penalty Verbiage

If within the first (option #) of years full prepayment is made, the prepayment charge is an amount equal to the payment of six (6) months advance interest, at the interest rate provided under the note, on the amount prepaid which is in excess of twenty (20) percent of the original principal amount.

Some states have laws governing the use of prepayment penalties. You will want to familiarize yourself with your state law pertaining to the use of prepayment penalties.

RATE LOCK OR FLOAT OPTION

The borrower must complete a rate lock or float option form. This form specifies the borrower's determination as to whether they wish to lock in the offered interest rate now or wait on the chance that the interest rate will change for the better during the loan processing stage.

The upper section of the form should provide identifying details relating to the borrower, the property, and the loan.

The form will have two areas that relate to the choices the borrower is making. The borrower should complete and sign the area that relates to their choice with regard to the offered interest rate.

If the borrower wishes to lock in the currently offered interest rate, they will complete the RATE LOCK section of the form. The rate lock section will show the offered rate, any points associated with the obtainment of this rate, and the number of days that the rate lock offer is applicable.

The borrower will sign and date the form to illustrate their acceptance of the offered rate and terms.

If the borrower wishes to wait to lock the rate in the hopes that the market will improve thus improving the interest rate that they can obtain, the borrower will complete the DO NOT LOCK section of the form by signing and dating the applicable area.

The borrower should receive a copy of the completed rate lock form.

RATE LOCK

Loan Amount $_____

Property Address _____

City, State, Zip   _____

This is to certify that I DO want to exercise my interest rate lock option at this time.

A.   My guaranteed interest rate will be _____%.

B.   The total points paid at settlement will not exceed _____. This total does not include settlement costs such as title insurance, homeowners insurance, transfer taxes, etc.

C.   This agreement will end _____ days from today. This date is called the ending date.

ACKNOWLEDGEMENT

_____   _____

Signed   Date

_____   _____

Signed   Date

This is to certify that I DO NOT want to exercise my interest rate lock option at this time.

A.   I understand that my lender cannot predict interest rate changes.

B.   If I want to obtain an interest rate commitment in the future, I may do so at any time up to ___ days before the closing of my mortgage loan.

C.   I understand that I must sign an interest rate lock-in agreement to obtain a guaranteed interest rate lock.

D.   I understand that it is my responsibility to advise the lender of my desire to obtain interest rate commitment.

ACKNOWLEDGEMENT

_____   _____

Signed   Date

_____   _____

Signed   Date

Figure 11-4 Sample Form – Rate Lock / Float Option

CHAPTER 12

BASIC LOAN PROCESS

You will establish your own personal system for fulfilling all the myriad of tasks involved with a loan process from initial contact to closing the loan. The loan officer with whom you work will have other specific methods they choose to use in the loan process. A large portion of the loan processor day will be spent moving the loan process toward a speedy closing. The more organized you become at incorporating all of the necessary tasks into your workflow the more vital to the office you will become.

To aid you in creating your own loan system, we have created a process overview that encompasses the required tasks in a timely manner.

Complete the Pre-Qualification Questionnaire

You will need to have the Pre-Qualification forms available at all times, preferably bound in a reference Binder.

Pull Credit

Pull the Credit report for both the borrower and the co borrower.

Review Credit Report

The loan officer will typically complete the review of the credit report. As you gain in knowledge and skills, the task of reviewing the credit report may become one of your duties. Reviewing the credit report is typically an advanced processing task. If you feel comfortable with the basics of loan processing, you may wish to consider obtaining training in processor advancement skills so that you can become even more proficient at your chosen profession and more valuable to the loan office.

For now, the loan officer will provide you with a copy of the completed credit review form. This form will enable you to note additional documentation requirements that the borrower may need to provide because of an entry on the credit report.

Qualify loan

The loan officer usually completes this task. You should provide all the applicable forms and documents to the loan officer so that they may begin planning the loan strategy. If you feel comfortable with the basics of loan processing, you may wish to consider obtaining training in processor advancement skills so that you can become even more proficient at your chosen profession and more valuable to the loan office.

For now, you will provide the loan officer with all of the applicable forms necessary to begin qualifying the loan package, these include the

Pre-Qualification Questionnaire

Credit Report

D. T. I. Ratio Form

Credit History Form

Screen for possible programs

The loan officer will compare the borrower profile with the requirements of the different loan programs to choose a loan offering for the borrower. The loan officer will have the applicable lender matrix and guideline manuals available for their use.

If you feel comfortable with the basics of loan processing, you may wish to consider obtaining training in processor advancement skills so that you can become even more proficient at your chosen profession and more valuable to the loan office.

Rate/Price Loan

Once the loan officer has chosen a loan program suitable for the borrower's goals and whose guidelines fit the profile of the borrower, the loan officer will determine a Rate and Price basis for the loan. If you feel comfortable with the basics of loan processing, you may wish to consider obtaining training in processor advancement skills so that you can become even more proficient at your chosen profession and more valuable to the loan office.

For now, you must ensure that the loan officer has all of the necessary documents, manuals, and forms required to complete the pricing tasks. To price the loan, the loan officer will need all of the documents from the loan file and the Product Matrix for the chosen loan product and the most up to date rate sheet for the loan program being considered. You should ensure that these items are available to the loan officer so that they can accomplish the necessary pricing tasks.

The loan officer will usually complete the pricing processes. The loan officer will have the applicable forms and documents available.

Product Matrix

Rate Sheet

Worksheets

Set Appointment/
Request Documentation

Once the loan officer has completed their tasks on the loan file, they will typically return the package to you so that you can contact the borrower to set an appointment for the completion of the application and obtainment of file documents.

You will request documentation based on the guidelines of the loan program chosen for the borrower and on the borrower's specific situation.

You will nearly always request that the borrower bring

- 2 years W-2s,

- Year To Date pay stubs

   The borrower should bring pay stubs that cover the full 30 day period prior to the meeting.

- If the borrower rents from an individual rather than an entity, you should request 12 months proof of timely rental payments in the form of rent checks.

- Credit Documents

- Contested Items

- Divorce Decree etc

- Any additional items you feel may be requested by underwriting based on information on Pre-qualification Questionnaire and Credit report

Appointment

Once the preliminary file assessment, loan planning, and documentation list is complete, you will contact the borrower and set an Appointment for the application meeting.

The loan officer will typically be the one who conducts the application meeting, but it will be a part of your function to ensure that the borrower understands what documentation they must bring to the meeting.

You should ensure that the loan file contains all of the necessary data, disclosure forms, and application materials that the loan officer will need during the meeting.

Once the application meeting is complete, you will receive the file back for review and submittal. You should review all of the documents contained in the loan file before submitting the package to underwriting.

If any discrepancies exist on the file, you will need to bring it to the loan officer's attention so that they can correct the file inclusions before the submittal.

Stack Loan Package

You will stack the submittal items according to the preferences of the particular lender chosen of the loan package. You will use the underwriting checklist or Submittal summary Form to ensure that the documents are stacked correctly and that all of the necessary items are included.

If the borrower is completing the application by mail or telephone, you will mail the required signature documents and disclosures to the borrower.

You may be required to create a loan cover letter for the borrower. You should carefully review the loan file to ensure that you have an understanding of the plans the loan officer has made with and for the borrower. If you have any questions regarding the file, you should confer with the loan officer before completing the loan cover letter. Remember, the initial submittal is the time to set the stage with underwriting. The cover letter should contain a brief summary of the planned loan, borrower qualifications and compensating factors, and missing documentation.

Submit Loan Package

You will submit the loan package according to the preferences of the lender. Some underwriting teams will accept fax transmittals while others require that you mail a hard copy of the package to their offices. You should ensure that you send all submittals in a timely manner.

Receive Loan Approval

After reviewing the loan file, underwriting will issue a decision. This decision can be denied, approved, or suspended.

- Denied means that aspects of the loan file do not meet the criteria for the loan program.

  The reason for the denial will be included with the denial notice.

  You should discuss the denial with the loan officer to determine if an action or additional documentation will correct the necessary aspects of the loan file.

  ➢ If the issue was a simple error or correctable file matter, the loan officer will handle the remittal.

  ➢ If the issue is not a result of a simple error or correctable matter, you must issue a notice of denial to the borrower. You will save the file and all of the file contents in the location your office has designated for old loan file storage.

- If underwriting issues a suspension, they will provide you with details that define the reasons the file is suspended.

  A suspended file is missing some critical element that is necessary for underwriting to make a determination about the loan request.

  You should review the reason for the suspension with the loan officer, take the steps necessary to correct the file deficiency and then resubmit the package for review by underwriting.

- Each time you submit an initial loan package to the underwriting department, you are seeking an approval with stipulations.

  This stipulation list will become your primary focus over the coming days with regard to this loan file. You will gather the documentation items necessary to meet the stipulation list inclusions.

Upon receiving the notice of file approval with stipulations, you will inform the loan officer of the approval and stipulation requirements.

The loan officer will review the approval and confirm that the terms meet the parameters of the loan the borrower is expecting.

You will then proceed with the documentation and file processing requirements.

Documentation Requests

The first resource for obtaining missing documentation or file information is often the borrower. You should call the borrower with a list of the required stipulations. During the conversation, you will want to confirm the commitment terms of the file with the borrower to ensure that they have a full understanding of the loan and to solidify their commitment to your loan program.

You should also mail a list of the necessary stipulations, commitment letter, and welcome letter to the borrower.

If a real estate agent is involved in the transaction, you should send a copy of the commitment letter to the Real Estate Agent. If the borrower is not yet working with an agent, you should discuss the outbound referral with the loan officer. A part of the loan officer's job is to build referral and affinity relationships. Referring a borrower to a real estate agent is an excellent tool in building and solidifying the relationship your loan officer is building with that agent.

Documentation Orders (Borrower)

After providing notice of the approval and stipulations to all of the parties; you will document the required details that relate to the borrower profile. For example, you will order a V. O. R. or V. O. M. to verify the status of the mortgage.

You should order any third party documentation requested on the stipulation list relating to the borrower to ensure that these items are available in the file to facilitate a speedy closing. You will order the property related stipulations after the borrower has chosen a home to purchase.

Each loan program will have different documentation requirements.

Receive Sales Agreement

When the borrower has located the home they wish to purchase and negotiated an agreement with the seller for that purchase, you will receive a copy of the sales agreement

You should provide the loan officer with the sales agreement. They will restructure deal as needed to conform to the terms in the sales agreement.

Examples of items that may need restructured within the loan documents after your office receives the final sales agreement are

>Seller Concession

>Sales Price

>Source of Funds

Issue Additional Disclosures

The borrower may need to receive certain disclosures again after the final restructuring of the transaction. You will need to review the signed notices and disclosures and obtain the borrowers signature on any missing items.

Revise GFE/TIL

The loan officer will revise the Good Faith Estimate and Truth in Lending to conform to the final financial details dictated by the sales agreement. Upon completion of the restructured loan package, you will need to disclose the Good Faith Estimate and the Truth in Lending to the borrowers a second time. These revised documents will contain actual numbers rather than 'to be decided' information. This re-disclosure enables the borrower to see the best estimate of closing costs based on an actual property agreement.

Obtain missing documentation

At this time it is imperative that you secure any outstanding stipulations from the borrower or from third party sources.

Documentation Orders (Property)

You will Order the Title Search, Appraisal, and Inspections where applicable.

The type of inspections necessary will be dependent on the loan program and the negotiations within the sales agreement.

>Title Request Form

>Inspections (where applicable)

>Appraisal Request Form

>Other inspections or documents

You should ensure that you order all of the necessary paperwork, inspections, title work, and other documentation in a timely manner. Pay close attention to the section of the sales agreement that dictates the settlement date for the transaction.

Finalize Conditions

Once you have obtained all of the conditions listed on the stipulation list, you will submit the package to underwriting for a final review and approval.

You should stack this submission in the order that they appear on the stipulation list. In most cases, it is not a good idea to send each stipulation as it comes into the office. Most underwriting teams prefer that you submit all of the necessary stipulations in one packaged submittal. This enables them to have all of the necessary information to issue a loan approval. The exception is the appraisal.

You should submit the appraisal as soon as you receive it in your office. The underwriter may issue additional stipulation requirements because of the inclusions of the appraisal.

You should also review each stipulation that you receive to ensure that it does not contain any detail or issue that will create a delay in obtaining the approval. For example, if you receive the borrower's tax returns from the previous year and note a large discrepancy in income, you will wish to discuss this issue with the loan officer. The loan officer will wish to discuss the matter with the borrower and obtain the documentation necessary to address the discrepancy.

Perform Pre-Close

Once underwriting has issued the final loan commitment and the closing is scheduled, you should contact the borrower to perform a pre-close discussion.

If possible, arrange a meeting for the loan officer to meet with the borrower.

The loan officer will review the final terms of the loan with the borrower during the meeting. If the borrower has not chosen to lock the interest rate prior to this time, the loan officer will prepare a lock request for you to submit.

It is a good idea to be certain the borrower understands every term on their finalized loan commitment. This helps to avoid turmoil at closing because of miscommunication or memory issues.

Closing

Most loan officer will attend their closings. Following closing it is a good idea to send a post-close package and referral request. As part of our marketing program, we have a whole system of post-close fliers and referral requests to use.

We recommend you send each borrower and the agents involved in the transaction certain items. These could include Thank You cards, Customer Surveys, Realtor Surveys, and Gift Certificates towards closing cost discounts that they may pass along to a future referral.

FILE DOCUMENTATION

Your primary functions are to process borrower applications, obtain substantiating documentation proving all of the information on the loan application, and process the loan to a closing. To accomplish these tasks, you must gain a comprehensive understanding of the classification methodology applied to the various borrower situations by the mortgage industry.

Most borrowers are classified into two groups based upon the loan products for which they can qualify. These are

- A Paper, which is also called prime or conforming paper

- And B/C Paper sometimes called sub-prime or non-conforming paper.

The fundamental difference between a conforming and a non-conforming loan is that the standards set by Fannie Mae and Freddie Mac dictates the guidelines of a conforming. Fanny Mae and Freddie Mac are the two of the largest entities that purchase mortgage loans from lenders to package into securities and sell to investors within the secondary mortgage market. Because these two entities are the largest purchasers of mortgage portfolios, the guidelines that they establish are, the industry standard with regard to borrower credit, income, down payment, debt ratio, and maximum loan amounts.

Any lending institution that intends to sell their packaged loans to an investor within the secondary mortgage market must consider these guidelines when providing mortgage funds to an applicant. If the application package does not meet the standards set forth by Fanny Mae and Freddie Mac, the likelihood of the lending institution being able to transfer the loan to an investor is diminished.

Within the category of conforming or conventional loans there is a sub-category termed Government Loans. Government loans sometimes enable a borrower whose situation or specifics falls outside of the standard conforming parameters to obtain a mortgage loan. The government will underwrite loans that fall within the category of Government loans. These loans will typically carry an insurance against default known as private mortgage insurance. This insurance enables borrowers whose credit, employment history, down payment amount, or other factors do not meet standard lending guidelines to obtain financing. These types of loans also carry very strict guidelines and parameters but the requirements are slightly lower in nature than those in the base conforming market.

The most common government loans are the F. H. A. and V.A. loans. Within these broad loan types are sub-types that offer different program specifics, approval parameters, and guidelines that will enable still more borrowers to qualify for mortgage financing.

The packages created by bundling groups of government underwritten loan products are often sold through Ginnie Mae. Ginnie Mae purchases mortgage loans from lenders to package into securities and sell to investors within the secondary mortgage market. Ginnie Mae loans are the most popular type of mortgage-backed securities because the U.S. government provides a guarantee of payment on the loan. These loans also usually provide higher returns than investment opportunities outside of the mortgage offerings.

Non-conforming loans are loans with a different set of criteria than the guidelines set forth by Fannie Mae and Freddie Mac. This criterion still considers all of the aspects of a borrowers file such as credit history, employment history, down payment, and debt to income ratios but sets the minimum levels for each item at a lower level than the conforming parameters. The types of borrowers who seek non-conforming loans include individuals whose situation is different from what is considered the norm. An example of a commonly encountered, non-conforming profile would be the self-employed borrower. Guidelines also exist that enable individuals with poor credit histories to obtain mortgage financing but these guidelines will require higher costs and fees, down payment amount, and other matters than the conforming loan products.

The fact that the non-conforming loan is structured under a set of guidelines that will fall below those sought by investors interested in the Fannie Mae, Freddy Mac and Ginnie Mae loan portfolios does not mean that these loans are not commonly transferred on the secondary mortgage market. The non-conforming loan will carry a higher interest rate and more costs than the conforming loan. This higher rate helps to offset the increased investment risk associated with the lower guideline standards of the non-conforming loan. Investing pools seeking to purchase the non-conforming loan portfolios will be those who can bear a higher level of risk in exchange for potentially higher returns.

Each of these general programs will have various approval levels and loan products. Each of these specific programs will have slightly different borrower qualifications and documentation requirements. We have been illustrating the basis for the loan programs and the general documentation necessary throughout the coursework. You should become familiar with the specifics of each loan program your office uses to obtain funding for borrowers and gain an understanding of the documentation requirements of each program. In general, you will need to gain the documentation necessary to prove the creditworthiness of the borrower and the value of the property that secures the loan. To do this, you will obtain documentation from many sources, compile all of the documentation into an understandable order, and remit all of the documentation to the underwriter assigned to the loan file.

After the initial meeting with the borrower, you will have a variety of documents to submit to the Underwriter. These are items such as the loan application, credit report, and all available substantiating documents provided by the borrower. The underwriter will review of the information and make sure that it conforms to the guidelines that the specific loan program requested has set forth. The underwriter will review the borrowers.

- Income and Debt Ratios

- Employment History

- Credit History

- Savings / Source of Money for Down Payment

- The sales contract and the property appraisal if these are available at the time of the submittal.

Once the underwriter has reviewed the entire file, they will issue a written decision. This decision can take one of three forms.

Approved   means that everything in the file meets the guidelines for the loan program.

Conditional   or suspended meaning that Additional documentation is necessary to issue final determination on the file.

Denied   meaning that aspects of the file do not conform to the guidelines

If the loan is approved, the underwriter will provide you with a written loan approval that defines any additional item or documents that the borrower may need to provide before the approval can be cleared for closing. These items are called "Conditions" or stipulations. A loan may be approved but still require updated "conditions" or items.

There are two types on conditions:

Prior to Loan Conditions   are items that the underwriter must review and approve before the issuance of loan closing documents.

     Prior to loan conditions must be given to the underwriter before the closing date can be scheduled.

Prior to Closing Conditions   are items that must be the underwriter or loan closer must receive and review before they will release the funds necessary to close the loan.

     Prior to closing conditions can be provided to the underwriter at any time up to the time of the closing meeting.

The loan processing of the file is the most time consuming aspect of the loan process.

The true definition of loan processing is the preparation of the loan file for presentation to the underwriting department.

If the borrower did not provide all of the original documents necessary to process the file at the initial application meeting, the processing stage is the time you will request these items again.

The processing stage is comprised of gathering all of the documents necessary to substantiate the creditworthiness of the borrower, value, and condition of the property, and ability of the seller to transfer the title to the property free and clear of any blemishes.

Some of the file documents required by underwriting must be verified by what is considered an uninterested third party. These verifications require that you contact a resource besides the borrower, seller, or real estate agent to obtain proof that the information contained in the borrower application and loan file is correct. You will use the borrower consent form and the forms created for the specific entity to which you are requesting information to obtain a statement verifying the specific detail.

Each aspect of the loan file must be fully documented in compliance with the underwriting guidelines applicable to the specific loan program. Ensuring that the correct and complete documentation is included in the loan file is your job.

You must properly document every loan package you submit to the Underwriting Department. Without the ability to review all proper documentation necessary, the Underwriting team cannot make a valid decision on your loan package. If the documentation is incomplete or missing, the underwriting department will request additional items or stipulations.

STACKING THE FILE

The loan process is much smoother if you provide all necessary documentation at the time of submission rather than submitting documentation based on a stipulation lists. We have been reviewing applicable documentation requirements throughout the coursework.

Each time you submit a stipulation the Underwriter in charge of that particular loan must re-review the entire package. This is a time consuming and lengthy method of gaining approvals. Many times, additional items will be required to clarify the stipulations you have just submitted. Most important – sending packages in pieces is a very irritating practice that will not endear you to the underwriting team! By submitting packages piece meal, you create additional work for the underwriting team.

If you do not gather as many stipulations as possible at the initial application, you will gain a reputation of "stipping a loan to death". This reputation will cause referral partners and borrowers to doubt your professionalism and capabilities. It is also more time consuming to return to referral partners and borrowers for documentation necessary to close the loan.

Each time you submit a loan package there will be a transmittal summary or underwriting submission form your team prefers to have as a cover sheet. This sheet will usually contain a checklist of items the underwriting team requires to adequately review a loan package and make a decision for pre-approval. You will need to stack the items you are submitting in the order they appear on the submission form.

If there is no submission form, a best practice is to stack the items according to the usefulness and importance.

STACKING ORDER CHECKLIST

____   Loan Coversheet

____   Loan Submission Form

____   Stacking Order Checklist

____   Full 1008 or underwriting transmittal summary

____   Full, signed 1003 application

____   Purpose of Refinance Letter if applicable to the transaction

____   Credit Report

____   Credit Supplements if any are applicable to the loan file

____   Letter of explanation regarding any questionable or derogatory item on the credit report

____   A verification of mortgage or rent form or 12 months cancelled rent checks

____   All Bankruptcy Discharge Documentation if it is applicable to the transaction

____   A Divorce Decree if it is applicable to the transaction

____   A verification of deposit if checking or savings funds will be used toward the funds to close

____   A breakdown of the source of funds for closing

____   Gift letters signed by donors if they are applicable to the transaction

____   Verification of employment forms

____   Most Recent 30 Days Pay stubs

____   W-2's or full tax returns from preceding two years

____   Documentation of other income if it is applicable to the transaction

____   Sales Agreement including all pages and addendums

____   Rental or Lease Agreements if they are applicable to the transaction

____   Appraisal Report with original photographs

____   Preliminary Title Report

____   Title Commitment

____   Copy of any exiting note if the transaction is a refinance transaction

____   Escrow or funding instructions

____   Original Good Faith Estimate and Truth in Lending disclosures

____   ECOA, Fair Lending, and other Applicable Disclosures

____   Broker Agreements

____   And any other documentation specific to the loan file.

Figure 13:1 Sample Form - Stacking Order Checklist

UNDERWRITING SUBMISSION FORM

FAX _____

Date: _____ Broker Name: _____
Broker Code: _____ Broker Contact: _____
Broker Phone: _____ Broker FAX: _____

If loan is locked – provide Loan Number: _____

Borrower's Name: _____

Co-Borrower's Name: _____

Purchase Price: $_____ LTV: _____% CLTV: _____%

Appraised Value: $_____ _ Loan Amount: $_____

LOAN PRODUCT	PURPOSE	OCCUPANCY	PROPERTY TYPE
__30 Yr Fixed	__ Purchase	__ Primary Residence	__ SFR
__15 Yr Fixed	__ Refi No Cash	__ Second Home	__ 2 Family
__ FHA/VA	__ Refi Cash out	__ Investment	__ 3-4 Family
__ FNMA Fallout			__ Condo/PUD
__ Lite Doc			
__ Other _____			

DOCUMENTATION
__ Signed 1003
__ Signed Good Faith
__ Pre-qualification 1003
__ Consent for Credit Check
__ Credit Report
__ VOR/VOM
__ W2/Tax Returns
__ Pay Stubs
__ Source of Funds
__ Other _____

_____

REQUEST INFORMATION: _____ _____

_____

_____

_____

Figure 13:2 Sample Form - Underwriting Submittal Summary

Submission Sheet

DATE SUBMITTED: _____ ACCOUNT EXECUTIVE: _____
BROKER: _____
ADDRESS: _____
CONTACT: _____ PHONE: _____ FAX: _____

BORROWER/LOAN INFORMATION

BORROWER: _____ SSN: _____
CO-BORROWER: _____ SSN: _____
PROPERTY ADDRESS: _____

( ) Owner Occupied   ( ) Purchase   ( ) Full Doc   ( ) SFR
( ) 2nd Home   ( ) Refinance   ( ) Lite Doc   ( ) Townhouse
( ) Non-owner Occupied   ( ) Stated Doc   ( ) _____

LOAN AMOUNT: $_____   PROGRAM: _____
APPRAISED VALUE: $_____   RATE: _____ TERM: _____
SALES PRICE: $ _____   LTV: _____ CLTV: _____

BROKER'S FEES

ORIGINATION ____%   _____
REBATE   ____%   _____
PROCESSING   _____
APPRAISAL   _____
CREDIT REPORT   _____

_____   _____
_____   _____

FILE STACKING ORDER

__ SUBMISSION FORM	__ VOE'S
__ TYPED 1008	__ CURRENT PAYSTUBS
__ TYPED 1003	__ LAST 2 YEARS W-2'S/1099'S
__ HANDWRITTEN 1003	__ YTD PROFIT & LOSS STMT (SELF-EMP)
__ PURPOSE LETTER	__ LAST 2 YEARS 1040'2
__ CREDIT EXPLANATION	__ LAST 2 YEARS 1120/1065
__ CREDIT REPORT	__ APPRAISAL WITH ORIGINAL PHOTOS
__ VOM/12 MONTH RENT CKS	__ PRELIMINAY TITLE
__ BK SCHEDULE & DIS	__ COPY OF EXISTING NOTE
__ DIVORCE DECREE	__ EXECUTED SALES CONTRACT
__ VOD	__ BROKERS DISCLOSURES

ORIGINAL PACKAGE REQUIRED

Figure 13:3 Sample Form – Submission Summary

INCOME

A borrower must have adequate income to cover the repayment of their mortgage. Before a borrower can be approved for a loan, the stability of income and the probability of the continuance of that income must be shown. All of the income that will be used to qualify the borrower must be proven through acceptable sources including the borrower's employment record. Most loan programs will require that the employer confirm that the borrower will likely continue to be employed.

The stability of income is usually proven through the employment history.

> ➢ A two-year employment history is needed.

> ➢ It is preferable that the history is in the same line of work.

> ➢ The actual history can be comprised of multiple jobs if necessary.

> ➢ Education may be included as part of the 2 year history if it was education for the same profession.

You will gain information that details the two-year employment history when you complete the pre-qualification questionnaire. The borrower will inform you of the type of employment or income they will be using to qualify for the loan. You will obtain documentation that proves this history.

Salary or W-2 Income	You must obtain documentation that shows proof that a two-year history of receiving this income exists and proof that this income is likely to continue.
	The two-year history can be established by including the most recent 30-days pay stubs and the year-end Ww-2 for the prior two years.
	Continuance of employment will be established using a V. O. E. form.
Overtime or Bonus Income	The borrower must show proof that a two-year history of receiving this income exists.
	They must also show proof that this income is likely to continue.
	The borrower will need to provide documentation, such as pay stubs for the most recent 30-day period of the present year and the final W-2 for the prior 2 years.
	* Each of these documents must show the inclusion of the overtime or bonus income.
	The income will be factored as an average over the previous two years.
	You will need to obtain a V. O. E. from the employer confirming the history and future probability of continuance for this income.
Part-time Income	If the borrower will use part-time income, such as income from a second job or seasonal employment, a two-year history of receiving this income must also be proven.

The documentation must show that the borrower has a 2-year history of receiving this income without interruption

The V. O. E. will be used to show proof that the part-time income has a high probability of continuing

If the income cannot be used as qualifying income because of an interruption in receipt of the income, a lack of a two-year history or the inability to confirm the likelihood of the continuance of this income, you will still wish to document it. It may be considered as a compensating factor.

Commission Income

Commission income is based on the average of the previous 2 years income.

The borrower must provide their full Federal Tax Returns, including all schedules, covering the past two years and you must obtain a year to date income statement from the employer.

Any un-reimbursed business expenses must be subtracted from the gross income in order to gain the usable income figures.

Retirement, Social Security Income, Public Assistance, or Disability Income

If the borrower is using retirement or social security income as part of their qualification package, verification from the source of the income must be obtained.

An award letter from the social security administration or a statement of retirement income will be used for documentation purposes.

If the income will discontinue within 3 years, the income cannot be used to qualify the borrower and used only as a compensating factor.

Alimony, Child Support, or Income from Separate Maintenance

This income is not required for qualification, but a borrower may choose to use this income if they wish.

To use this income, the borrower will need to supply a 12-month payment history from the ex-spouse or the courts showing timely payment will be required.

Evidence that such payment will continue for at least 3 years must be provided.

A copy of the
- divorce decree
- settlement agreement
- other legal documents illustrating
  - amount of the income
  - history of the income
  - term for the continuance of this income

will be necessary.

Notes Receivable

In order to use income from a note, the borrower must provide a copy of the endorsed and binding note.

The borrower must also provide proof that payments have been received for a minimum of 12 months.

* This proof can be in the form of bank statements or copies of the cancelled payment checks.

If the note expires within 3 years, it cannot be used for qualifying but may be considered as a compensating factor.

Interest and Dividends

Interest and dividend income may be used if documentation, such as tax returns or account statements, illustrates a 2-year history or receiving this income.

Rental Income

Rent received from investment properties owned by the borrower may be used if the receipt of these rents can be documented.

Income from roommates and boarders is not acceptable.

Rental income is calculated from the borrower's Schedule E of the 10 40.

Depreciation can be added back in to the total received.

You should note that while positive rental income is considered as gross income, negative rental income must be treated as a recurring liability.

Copies of the leases must be provided to prove this income.

Self-Employment Income

A borrower with 25% or more ownership interest in a business can be considered self-employed.

A borrower must have more than a one-year history for income to be considered.

A two-year full tax return will be required.

Bank Statements

Some loan programs will allow the borrower to use the deposits shown on 12-months or 24-months bank must be sent statements as proof of income.

In order to qualify for a bank statement program, the borrower's position must validate the probability that their business is cash based business.

The deposits showing on 12 consecutive months' bank statements will be totaled and divided by the 12 months to arrive at an average income.

Keep in mind that this is considered a light documentation loan and may be penalized with higher interest rates or a higher down payment requirement.

THIRD PARTY VERIFICATION

Many factors of the loan require verification of information. This verification must be obtained from a third party who has access to specific details concerning a borrower's profile.

It is important to understand a borrower's right to financial privacy. Details concerning Financial Privacy and Authorization to Release/Obtain Information forms in are included in ethics and disclosure chapter. If you are unsure of the process and requirements for the completion of these forms, you will need to review the pertinent section of Chapter for additional information.

The following pages provide you with example forms for specific situations.

- Verification of Employment (VOE)

- Verification of Deposit (VOD)

- Verification of Rent (VOR)

- Verification of Mortgage (VOM)

Each of these verification forms will provide specific information concerning your borrower's situation, past, present and future.

You should forward these verification forms to the appropriate company or agency for completion. The forms should be accompanied by a copy of the borrowers consent to release information.

VERIFICATION OF EMPLOYMENT (VOE)

In addition to verifying the income of the borrower through acceptable documentation, underwriting will often require verification of the borrower's employment and the probability of continued employment before the closing of the loan.

Verification forms must be sent to the employer to confirm all vital facts regarding employment, income, and continued employment.

A **Verification of Employment (VOE)** is a form sent to past and present employers for last two years to verify income and time on the job. Some employers have an automated 900 number for employment verification.

Receiving a verification of employment typically takes 1 to 2 weeks so you will wish to send your request early in the loan process.

REQUEST FOR VERIFICATION OF EMPLOYMENT

Privacy Act Notice: This information is to be used by the agency collecting it or its assignees in determining whether you qualify as a prospective mortgagor under its program. It will not be disclosed outside the agency except as required and permitted by law. You do not have to provide this information, but if you do not your application for approval as a prospective mortgagor or borrower may be delayed or rejected. The information requested in this form is authorized by Title 38, USC. Chapter 37 (if VA); by 12 USC, Section 1701 et. Seq (if HUD/FHA); by 42 USC, Section 1452b (if HUD/CPD); and Title 42 USC, 1471 et. Seq., or 7 USC. 1971 et. Deq. (if USDA/FmHA).

Instructions   Lender – Complete items 1 through 7. Have applicant complete item 8. Forward directly to employer named in item 1.
                 Employer – Please complete either Part II or Part III as applicable. Complete Part IV and return directly to lender named in item 2.
                 This form is to be transmitted directly to the lender and is not to be transmitted through the applicant or any other party.

Part I – Request

1. To (Name and address of employer)	2. From (Name and address of Lender)		
I certify that this verification has been sent directly to the employer and ahs not passed through the hands of the applicant or any other interested party.			
2. Signature of Lender	4. Title	4. Date	6. Lender's Number (Optional)

I have applied for a mortgage loan and stated that I am now or was formerly employed by you. My signature below authorizes verification of this information.

7. Name and Address of Applicant (include employee or badge number)	8. Signature of Applicant

Part II – Verification of Present Employment

9. Applicant's Date of Employment	10. Present Position	11. Probability of Continued Employment

12A. Current Gross Base Pay (enter Amount and Check Period) __ Annual __ Hourly __ Monthly __ Other (specify) $ _____ __ Weekly	13 For Military Personnel Only		14. If Overtime or Bonus is Applicable Is Its Continuance Likely? Overtime __ Yes __ No Bonus __ Yes __ No
	Pay Grade		
	Type	Monthly Amount	
	Base Pay	$	15. If paid hourly – average hours per week

Type	Year to Date	Past Year 20_	Past Year 20_	Rations	$	
Base Pay	$	$	$	Flight or Hazard	$	16. Date of applicant's next pay increase
Overtime	$	$	$	Clothing	$	17. Projected amount of next pay increase
				Quarters	$	
Commissions	$	$	$	Pro Pay	$	18. Date of applicant's last pay increase
Bonus	$	$	$	Overseas or Combat	$	19. Amount of last pay increase
Total	$	$	$	Variable Housing Allowance	$	

20. Remarks (If employee was off work for any length of time, please indicate time period and reason)

Part III Verification of Previous Employment

21. Date Hired	23. Salary/Wage at Termination Per (Year) (Month) (Week)
22. Date Terminated	Base _____ Overtime _____ Commissions _____ Bonus _____
24. Reason for Leaving	25. Position Held

Part IV – Authorized Signature – Federal statutes provide severe penalties for any fraud, intentional misrepresentation, or criminal connivance or conspiracy purposed to influence the issuance of any guaranty or insurance by the VA Secretary, the U.S.D.A., FmHA/FHA Commissioner, or the HUD/CPD Assistant Secretary.

26. Signature of Employer	27. Title (please print or type)	28. Date
29. Print or type named signed in item 26	30. Phone No.	

Figure 13:4 Sample Form – Verification of Employment – HUD Release

You will complete sections 1 through 7 of the VOE request form.

➢ You will include the name of the employer and the applicable supervisor from whom the information is being requested.

➢ You should enter both your name and the company name as confirmation to the employer regarding the source of the request.

➢ Your full mailing address and any fax number that may be used for the return of the V. O. E. form should be included in the heading.

➢ You will sign the form as verification of the source of the request.

➢ Include your title and the date of the request.

➢ Section 7 allows you to include the information pertaining to the applicant so the employer has an easy reference when completing the form.

➢ The applicant should sign the form so that the employer knows that the release of the applicable employment data is authorized by the borrower.

* You may also attach the credit and information consent form that the borrower completed during the application process as additional verification that the borrower authorizes the release of the employment data.

The employer will complete PART 2 of the form and return it to your office.

When you receive the completed V. O. E., you should review all of the inclusions to ensure that they match the information contained within the borrower application.

If there is any discrepancy between the income information, employment data, or other inclusions of the forms, you should address this discrepancy and ensure that the incorrect information is corrected before submitting the verifications to underwriting for review.

MORTGAGE OR RENTAL HISTORY

The verification of mortgage or rental history is used to verify the payment history of the borrower relating to their previous housing obligations.

Mortgage or rental history is often used to project the probability of a borrower repaying their new mortgage in a timely manner. The theory behind this is that the manner that the borrower paid previous housing obligations reflects the seriousness with which they will approach the new housing payment obligations.

Mortgage histories are frequently included in a credit report.

If the mortgage or rental history is not included in the credit report, it must be verified in another manner.

V. O. M. stands for Verification of Mortgage

V. O. R. stands for Verification of Rent

These Verification forms are sent to a mortgage holder or a rental management company to verify the history of an account.

➢ Many lenders will not accept verification forms from a private party as these can easily be falsified. In that instance, you will need to acquire alternate documentation.

The borrower may supply copies of the most recent 12 months cancelled housing payment checks or money orders.

If these are not available,

The most recent 12 months bank statements can be obtained from either the borrower or the landlord showing 12 months concurrent withdrawals or deposits for the monthly housing payments.

More and more lenders are placing equal or greater weights on verification of rent or mortgages payments as on credit scores. It is a common belief that the history of payment of a mortgage or rent in the borrowers past reflects the probable payment performance in the borrower's future.

REQUEST FOR VERIFICATION OF RENT OR MORTGAGE

Privacy Act Notice: This information is to be used by the agency collecting it or its assignees in determining whether you qualify as a prospective mortgagor under its program. It will not be disclosed outside the agency except as required and permitted by law. You do not have to provide this information, but if you do not your application for approval as a prospective mortgagor or borrower may be delayed or rejected. The information requested in this form is authorized by Title 38, USC, Chapter 37 (if VA); by 12 USC, Section 1701 et. Seq (if HUD/FHA); by 42 USC, Section 1452b (if HUD/CPD); and Title 42 USC, 1471 et. Seq., or 7 USC. 1971 et. Deq. (if USDA/FmHA).

Instructions   Lender – Complete items 1 through 8. Have applicant complete item 9. Forward directly to landlord named in item 1.
Landlord Creditor – Please complete Items 10 through 18 and return directly to lender named in item 2.
This form is to be transmitted directly to the lender and is not to be transmitted through the applicant or any other party.

Part I – Request

1. To (Name and address of Landlord Creditor) | 2. From (Name and address of Lender)

I certify that this verification has been sent directly to the landlord/creditor and ahs not passed through the hands of the applicant or any other interested party.

2. Signature of Lender | 4. Title | 4. Date | 6. Lender's Number (Optional)

7. Information To Be Verified

Property Address | Account in the Name of   __ Mortgage __ Rental __ Land Contract | Account Number

I have applied for a mortgage loan. My signature below authorizes verification of mortgage or rent information.

8. Name and Address of Applicant(s) | 9. Signature of Applicant(s) X   X

Part II – To Be Completed by the Landlord/Creditor

We have received an application for a loan from the above, to whom we understand you rent or have extended a loan. In addition to the information requested below, please furnish us with any information you might have that will assist us in processing the loan.

__ Rental Account | __ Mortgage Account | __ Land Contract

10. Tenant Rented from _____ to _____ Amount of rent $_____ per _____ Number of late payments _____ Is account satisfactory? __ Yes __ No | 11. Date account opened _____ Original contract amount $_____ Current account balance $_____ Monthly Payment (P&I) $_____ Payment with T&I $_____ Is account current? __ Yes __ No Was loan assumed? __ Yes __ No Satisfactory account? __ Yes __ No | 12. Interest Rate _____ % __ Fixed __ ARM __ FHA __ VA __ CONV __ Other Next pay date _____ No. of late payments _____ No. of late charges _____ Owner of First Mortgage _____

Payment History for the previous 12 months must be provided n order to comply with secondary mortgage market requirements.

13. Additional information which may be of assistance in determination of credit worthiness

14. Signature of Landlord/Creditor Representative | 15. Title (please print or type) | Date

17. Please print or type name signed in Item 14

Figure 13:5 Sample Form – Verification of Rent / Mortgage – HUD Release

The completion of the verification of rent or mortgage form is similar to the completion and remittal of the verification of employment.

➤ You will again enter the applicable information into section 1 and 2 of the form.

➤ You should sign and date the form and include your title to illustrate to the mortgage holder or landlord that you are an authorized representative of the lending institution and therefore privy to this data.

➢ You will enter the borrowers PRESENT or PAST housing address into the field property address.

* The address entered should be the one whose payment history you are verifying, not necessarily the borrower's present address. You should have the borrower sign the authorization so that the individual knows that they have approved the release of their personal history.

➢ The landlord or mortgage holder will complete part two of the form and return it to your office.

➢ Upon receipt of the completed document, you should verify that the payment history, payment amount, and term of occupancy equate to the information entered into the ten oh three.

* If there is any discrepancy between the information contained on the form and the information in the borrowers file, you should have the incorrect forms corrected before submitting the file to underwriting for review.

SOURCE OF FUNDS

You will need to verify the source of the funds that the borrower will use for the transaction. Oftentimes, the source of funds will actually be a combination of sources used to arrive at the total figure that the borrower will use to total the amount of money needed to pay the down payment, closing costs, and other costs associated with the transaction.

➢ Each approval will come with a Loan to Value shortened as L. T. V.

The LTV is the amount the lender is willing to finance as opposed to the overall cost of the property.

➢ Some loans will come with a C. L. T. V. meaning Combined Loan to Value.

The combined loan to value is the additional amount the borrower may finance through subordinate financing with the seller of the property or an outside lending source.

➢ The balance between the LTV or CLTV and the total price of the property including the sales price and all closings costs, must be sourced, often as the borrowers own funds.

Borrowers are often required to invest their own funds in the property to aid in securing the loan against default. Generally, the higher the credit risks the higher the percent of the borrowers required investment. The premise behind this requirement is that a borrower is less likely to default on a loan if they are losing their own personal funds through the default.

The borrower's cash investment in the property must be equal to the difference between the amount of the mortgage, excluding any up front fees, and the total costs to acquire the property. All funds must be verified through acceptable methods.

Savings and Checking   Some lending guidelines will require that the borrower have saved funds to close in a savings or checking account while others will accept that the borrower has saved the funds for close in cash.

* You will want to confirm the specific holding requirements of the loan program you will be documenting.

Seasoning

Those lending programs that require the funds be kept in a savings or checking account may also require that the funds be seasoned.

The premise behind requiring seasoning of funds is that the time necessary to season funds helps to prove that the funds are the borrowers own money and not a result of a loan or gift from another entity or individual.

Seasoning means that the funds have been in the borrowers account a specific length of time. Often 90 days.

To prove seasoned funds, you will obtain a bank statement or a verification of deposit that covers the required seasoned term.

Certain loan programs do not require seasoned funds. These are often non-conventional programs.

➢ The underwriter will review the bank statements or verification of deposit form to insure that the funds have been in the borrower's possession for the required length of time.

➢ The underwriter will also use these statements to determine if the borrower is balancing and managing their bills properly.

You will wish to review the bank statements before remittal.

If the bank statement contains non-sufficient funds notations, the underwriter will require an explanation for the poor financial management and may place a hold on the approval.

➢ The underwriter may also use the bank statements to ensure that the debts illustrated on the credit report match up to the monthly payments shown on the statement.

They will review the deposits showing on the statements to determine if they are close to what the borrower is netting on their paycheck.

➢ If there are any large deposits, recurring debt not illustrated in the borrowers debt listing or other unusual entry on the bank statement, they will need to be explained.

* An occasional "N. S. F." may be cleared by underwriting if there is proper explanation as to why it occurred.

Cash saved at home

A borrower who has saved their money saved at home, can still purchase a home using this money.

The borrower must provide a written explanation of how the money was saved and the length of time taken to do so.

The lender will review the explanation to determine the creditability of these savings.

They will compare the statements to the borrowers

> Income

> Spending Habits

> History of using Financial Institutions for savings purposes

Many loan programs have limitations on the amount of cash saved at home, also termed mattress money that may be used for a transaction.

You will wish to check the specific underwriting guidelines for the specific program before allocating this mattress money to the transaction.

> If the amount of mattress money exceeds the limitations of the loan program, an alternate source of funds may be needed to gain underwriting approval for the transaction.

> If an alternate source of funds is not available, the funds may need to be deposited into a financial institution and the transaction placed on hold until the seasoning term requirements have been met.

The underwriter may request additional documentation relating to a mattress money transaction, including

o additional bank statements

o borrower statements

o details regarding non-debt to income related expenses

o other documentation specific to the situation

Gift Funds

Many loan programs will allow a homebuyer to receive all or some of the down payment for the purchase of a home as a "Gift".

A gift means that the borrower does not have to pay the funds received back. There are many acceptable sources of gift funds including.

> a relative

> the borrower's employer or labor union

> a charitable organization

> a governmental agency or public entity that has a program or established to provide homeownership assistance to low and moderate income families

NO REPAYMENT OF THIS GIFT MAY BE EXPECTED OR IMPLIED.

To use gift funds for the purchase a gift letter must be submitted to Underwriting.

This letter must be signed by both parties and state that there is no requirement to repay the funds received.

The gift letter must specify

- the dollar amount given

- be signed by the donor and the borrower

- state that no repayment is required

- show the donor's name, address, telephone number, and relationship to the borrower

- It must also contain language asserting that the funds given to the homebuyer were not made available to the donor from any person or entity with an interest in the sale of the property including the seller, real estate agent, broker, builder, loan processor, or any entity associated with any of these individuals or entities.

If the gift funds are already in the homebuyer's account

- You must document the transfer of the funds from the donor to the homebuyer by obtaining a copy of the canceled check or other withdrawal document showing that the withdrawal is from the donor's personal account along with the homebuyer's deposit slip or bank statement that shows the deposit.

If the gift funds are to be provided at closing by certified check, the check must be from the donors account.

- You must obtain a bank statement showing the withdrawal from the donor's personal account as well as a copy of the certified check.

If the donor purchased a cashier's check, money order, official check or any other type of bank check as a means of transferring the gift funds, then the donor must provide a withdrawal document or canceled check for the gift showing the funds came from the donor's personal account.

If the donor borrowed the gift funds and, thus, cannot provide the documentation from his or her bank or other savings account, the donor must provide evidence that those funds were borrowed from an acceptable source.

- The donor cannot borrow the funds from a party to the transaction including the mortgage lender.

- "Cash on hand" is often not an acceptable source of the donor's gift funds.

- Example: A retirement account would be an acceptable source of gift funds.

There may be limitations on the amount of closing funds that may be received as a gift.

You will want to check the specific guidelines for the loan program to confirm the gift fund limits and ensure that the source of funds necessary does not exceed these limits.

If the money that the borrower needs exceeds the gift fund maximum limits, you will need to assist the borrower in sourcing the necessary money from one of the approved source of funds items on the list.

Gift Equity

If the sale of a property is between immediate relatives, gift equity may be given as a seller concession toward the overall cost of the loan.

- Gift Equity is simply a reduction in the dollar amount the seller of the property expects to receive from the sale of the property.

- The reduction is given in the form of equity rather than a monetary gift or a subordinate loan.

The amount of equity that can be given as a gift between relatives is subject to maximum limitations and you will need to review the underwriting guidelines for the particular loan program to determine this maximum.

Gift Equity can only be given between immediate relative.

Earnest Money Deposit

Upon making an offer on a property, most Real Estate Agents require the buyer to remit an Earnest Money Deposit.

This deposit protects the agency and the seller in the event the buyer's change their minds and cancels the deal.

- Once an offer has been accepted, the property is removed from the market.

- If the buyer backs out of a deal once the property has been removed from the market, the earnest money deposit is retained between the sellers and the real estate agent.

- These funds are used as payment for the loss of time involved and any costs incurred.

If the transaction progresses as expected, the earnest money deposit is held in escrow, typically by the real estate agent and is used towards the borrower's funds necessary to close the deal.

In most cases, the source of the earnest money deposit will not need to be confirmed.

- If the amount of earnest money exceeds 2% of the sales price or appears to be excessive based on the borrower's history of accumulating savings, the deposit amount, and the source of funds may require verification.

Otherwise, satisfactory documentation includes a copy of the borrower's cancelled check or verification from the bank.

Seller Concession

Most loan programs allow the seller to allocate a portion of their funds toward the payment of the borrower's non-recurring closing costs and possibly towards the borrower's necessary pre-paids.

- This amount is vary by loan program but typically ranges from 3 to 6 percent of the sale price of the property.

169

Kenney

Seller's concessions must be agreed upon in the Sales Agreement to count as source of funds.

You will document the seller concession by remitting the sales agreement to the underwriter.

You should also confirm that the seller concessions are allocated on the HUD 1 in the correct location.

Example: Some loan programs will not allow seller concession toward recurring closing costs and the closing department will reject the closing documents if the HUD 1 illustrates that the seller concession is being used to pay these bills.

Prepaid Charges

Any cost involved with the loan that the borrower has paid in advance of closing can be considered funds to close the loan.

Example: Many borrowers will pay the appraisal fee, application fee, or credit report fee at some time during the loan process.

You will document these payments through copies of the bill and corresponding checks.

These amounts may then be allocated as a source of funds to close the loan.

Prepaid charges will need to be documented in the form a copy of the check written to the lender or service provider.

401K or Retirement

Borrowers may draw or borrow from a 401K or Retirement Account and use the funds received toward the closing.

o If the borrower must borrow against an account, they must be able to qualify with the monthly repayment amount resulting from this advance.

o You will need to obtain a statement illustrating the monthly repayment amount required on the loan from the account.

o This amount must be factored as a recurring liability and the borrower must be able to meet the debt to income qualification requirements of the program.

Sales Proceeds

The sale of an asset is considered an acceptable source of funds for most programs.

The borrower must provide adequate documentation of the value of the item sold, the amount received from the sale, and proof that the sale occurred.

Documentation may include

o a copy of the bill of sale or the HUD-1 Settlement Statement if the property sold was real estate

- o a copy of the check or verification of transfer of funds for the buyer to the borrower

- o a copy of the borrower's deposit slip or bank statement showing the deposit of the funds

In some cases when the value of an item is in question, the borrower may need to prove that the sale price of the property was fair market value. This may be accomplished using appraisals, market condition proof, or other source of proof of value.

Rent Credit and Option Premium

At times, you may be working on a transaction where the buyer has agreed to purchase the property from the seller under another transaction known as the lease option.

Under a lease option agreement, the buyer will typically give the seller a specific amount of money at the beginning of the transaction.

- o This money is termed an option payment.

   It is similar to a down payment or earnest money deposit in that it is money credited by the seller to the buyer in the event the buyer chooses to purchase the property.

   In exchange for the option premium, the seller agrees to sell the property to the buyer on or before a certain future date, at an agreed upon sum of money.

   The buyer will occupy the property as a tenant until the purchase date.

   If the buyer does not follow through with the purchase of the property, the seller retains the option premium in consideration of their removing the property from the sales market and holding any sale in abeyance for the buyer.

   If the buyer follows through with the agreed upon purchase, the option premium is credited toward the purchase price and may be used as a source of funds.

- o You will document this source by remitting a copy of the original agreement between the buyer and the seller along with a copy of the check used to make the option payment.

   Some lenders have set limitations on the amount of option payment that may be used toward a purchase.

   If the option payment exceeds the limitations set by underwriting, a new agreement may be required that lowers the purchase price to enable a credit to the borrower for the excess amount paid.

- o Under a lease option, many sellers will agree to credit a portion of the borrower's current rental payment toward the purchase of the property the borrower.

171

The sellers will typically charge an amount for the monthly payment that is in excess of the fair market rent for similar property in the area.

This excess amount is typically considered an allowable source of funds for the purchase

o   The borrower will need to provide a copy of the rental/lease agreement showing the option to purchase with the clause stating how much of the rental payment is to be used toward the purchase.

o   You may also need to show proof that the rent payment is above the estimated fair market rent for other, similar properties in the area.

Fair market rent may be established by illustrating the rental income from similar rental properties of similar size and similar locations in the area.

o   Underwriting will often allow only those portions of the rental payment that exceed the fair market rent for the area to be credited as a source of funds for close regardless of the agreement between the buyer and the seller..

Example   If the borrower has rented a home with a fair market rent of $750 a month the borrower may only use monies from payments that total above $750 per month.

If the borrower pays $1,000 a month, then $250 of each payment may be credited toward down payment funds.

If the borrower pays only $750 a month for this property then it is likely underwriting will allow none of the payment amount to be credited as down payment.

These are the most common source of funds acceptable to most Underwriting Teams. There are as many possibilities available as there will be borrowers in your office. Each situation is different and it is up to you to use your creativity in aiding your borrower in the sourcing of funds to close the loan.

Remember, any time you have a questionable source, run it past your Underwriting Team. They may have a method of documentation they will be willing to accept to consider this source as borrower funds toward closing.

Many of the sources of funds illustrated will require additional verification for documentation purposes. Some of this verification may be obtained from the borrower. Other verification documentation must be obtained from a third party source. The most common third party verification you will encounter is the Verifications of Deposit

The Verification of Deposit is a form sent to the borrower's banking institutions to verify average bank account balances for past 3 months.

Some banks will charge borrower a fee of up to $20 for this verification.

REQUEST FOR VERIFICATION OF DEPOSIT

Privacy Act Notice: This information is to be used by the agency collecting it or its assignees in determining whether you qualify as a prospective mortgagor under its program. It will not be disclosed outside the agency except as required and permitted by law. You do not have to provide this information, but if you do not your application for approval as a prospective mortgagor or borrower may be delayed or rejected. The information requested in this form is authorized by Title 38, USC. Chapter 37 (if VA); by 12 USC, Section 1701 et. Seq (if HUD/FHA); by 42 USC, Section 1452b (if HUD/CPD); and Title 42 USC, 1471 et. Seq., or 7 USC. 1971 et. Deq. (if USDA/FmHA).

Instructions	Lender – Complete items 1 through 8. Have applicant complete item 9. Forward directly to depository named in item 1.
	Depository – Please complete Items 10 through 18 and return DIRECTLY to lender named in item 2.
	This form is to be transmitted directly to the lender and is not to be transmitted through the applicant or any other party.

PART I - REQUEST

1. To (Name and address of depository)	2. From (Name and address of Lender)

I certify that this verification has been sent directly to the bank or depository and ahs not passed through the hands of the applicant or any other interested party.

2. Signature of Lender	4. Title	4. Date	6. Lender's Number (Optional)

7. Information To Be Verified

Type of Account	Account in Name of	Account Number	Balance
			$
			$
			$

To Depository: I/We have applied for a mortgage loan and stated in my financial statement that the balance on deposit with you is as shown above. You are authorized to verify this information and to supply the lender identified above with the information requested in Items 10 through 13. Your response is solely a matter of courtesy for which no responsibility is attached to your institution or any of your officers.

8. Name and Address of Applicant(s)	9. Signature of Applicant(s)

PART II – VERIFICATION OF DEPOSITORY To Be Completed By Depository

10. Deposit Accounts of Applicant(s)

Type of Account	Account in Name of	Account Number	Balance
			$
			$
			$

11. Loans Outstanding To Applicants

Loan Number	Date of Loan	Original Amount	Current Balance	Installments (Monthly/Quarterly)		Secured By	Number of Late Payments
		$	$	$	per		
		$	$	$	per		
		$	$	$	per		

12. Please include any additional information which may be of assistance in determination of credit worthiness. (Please include information on loans paid-in-full in Item 11 above)

13. If the name(s) on the account(s) differ from those listed in Item 7, please supply the name(s) on the account(s) as reflected by your records.

PART III – Authorized Signature – Federal statutes provide severe penalty for any fraud, intentional misrepresentation, or criminal connivance or conspiracy purposed to influence the issuance of any guaranty or insurance by the VA Secretary, the U.S.D.A., FmHA/FHA Commissioner, or the HUD/CPD Assistant Secretary.

14. Signature of Depository Representative	15. Title (please print or type)	16. Date
17. Please print or type name signed in item 14	18. Phone No.	

Figure 13:6 Sample Form – Verification of Deposit – HUD Release

Credit Report

You will order a preliminary credit report when the initial application is completed.

You may be required to order an updated credit report if the loan process takes longer than underwriting allocates for a credit report.

o   Underwriting will set the standards for the age of the report.

o   It is important to meet or exceed these standards and to caution the borrower not to take any action that may alter the credit report during the loan process.

o Any changes in the borrower's credit profile may create issues or changes to the loan approval status, causing delays in the closing of the loan.

Some underwriting teams require what is known as a tri-merge credit report or a full-factual credit report.

   o A tri-merge report is one that uses the data from all three major credit report bureaus and blends it onto a single report.

   o If the underwriting requests a full factual credit report, the credit bureau will verify all of the accounts and balances on the report prior to issuing the report to your office.

   A full factual report typically takes 2 - 5 business days for completion.

Credit Supplements

You may need to acquire additional supplements regarding specific credit issues.

These supplements can be obtained from the credit bureau by completing and submitting the request.

Request forms can typically be found on the last page of the credit report.

These credit supplements will serve to verify or clarify a specific matter found on the credit report and can usually be obtained within 2 to 5 business days of the request.

Purchase Contract, Addendums, Counter Offers

You will need to obtain a copy of the Purchase Contract, Addendums to the Sales Agreement and documentation related to counter offers for purchase transactions.

These are the original contracts regarding the terms of the purchase of the property.

All of the completed and signed forms will be needed for the loan file.

You should obtain these forms before ordering the appraisal, as appraiser requires a copy of the contract to complete their functions.

The realtor estate agent will typically provide these documents to you as soon as an agreement has been reached between the buyer and the seller. T

The negotiation process between the buyer and seller typically takes between 2 and 10 days but may take longer depending on the complexity of the transaction.

Explanation Letters

You may need to obtain Letters of Explanation from the borrower.

A letter of explanation is a letter written and signed by the borrower that explains any issues on the credit report, work history, bank account deposits, source of funds discrepancy, or other unusual matters relating to the file.

Appraisal

The Appraisal will be ordered from an underwriting approved appraiser. The appraiser will

- go to the property

- measure square footage

- verify required conditions

- check other recent comparable home sales

- determine value of the home

You will need to verify that the appraiser you choose to complete the appraisal process is one that is approved by underwriting.

You may also wish to discuss the appraiser you will use with the loan officer, as an appraiser is an affinity service provider who sometimes works with potential inbound referrals.

- The loan officer may wish to build a better referral relationship with a specific appraiser.

Appraisals usually take 1 week to complete but may take longer depending on your market.

- You will wish to request a timeline from the appraiser.

- You must ensure that the seller or real estate agent is aware that the appraisal has been ordered so that they can make themselves available to provide the appraiser with entry into the property. .

When you request the completion of the appraisal, you should provide the appraiser with all of the details and documentation that they will need to speed their activity.

- The appraiser can obtain this information from other sources, but you have it available and ensuring that the necessary details and documents are in the hands of the appraiser immediately upon receipt of the request helps to build stronger affinity service relationships and assists in speeding the appraisal completion time aiding you in processing faster closings.

You should fill in the appraisal request form completely.

- The branch or appraiser may have a different form that they prefer using for the request.

Kenney

- o We have included a sample form to assist you in gaining an understanding of the actions that you must take when ordering an appraisal.

- o You may use this form if your branch or appraiser does not have a preferred form available for your use.

Appraisal Request Form

DATE: _____   FROM: _____

TO: _____   FAX: _____

PURCHASE/REFINANCE/OTHER   FHA/VA/RURAL HOUSING/CONVENTIONAL

APPLICANT/BORROWERS: _____ PHONE: _____

REAL ESTATE AGENT: _____ PHONE: _____

CONTACT INFORMATION: _____

PROPERTY INFORMATION: _____

_____

ESTIMATED VALUE _____   SALES PRICE: _____

LENDER'S NAME: _____

PAYMENT OPTION: _____

ADDITIONAL COMMENTS: _____

_____

ITEMS ATTACHED: ___ Sales Agreement Page 1
                    ___ Sales Agreement Page 2
                    ___ Original Purchase Document
                    ___ Previous Appraisal
                    ___ Other: _____

Figure 13:7 Sample Form – Appraisal Request

1. You should include all of the contact information that the appraiser may need including the telephone numbers for the individuals the appraiser may need to contact.

   These include the real estate agent, the seller, and the closing company.

176

2. You should send the appropriate pages of a Sales Agreement.

    The appraiser will need to see the details included within page one of the sales agreement, and any addendums that relate to additional inclusions incorporated into the transfer.

    You should note in the comments section of the appraisal request that page one of the sales agreement is attached.

3. If you remit the appraisal request by fax, you should place the confirmation page that shows the date and time that the request was sent in the file.

    If you remit the appraisal request by mail or in person, you should include a copy of the dated request cover sheet in the file so that you have documentation of the actions taken on the file.

4. You should always note exactly how the appraisal bill is to be paid under the Bill Payment field of the request form. Common choices include

    "Collect from Customer at door"

    "Bill Office"

    "Bill Customer"

    "At closing"

    You should remember that the ordering loan office is ultimately responsible for the payment of the appraisal bill. If the appraiser does not obtain the payment via another method, the appraiser sends the bill to your office. This is the reason that many lenders now require the appraisal fees to be paid in advance.

5. You should log the request date on the file tracking form.

    Seventy-two hours after you have sent the request, you should contact the appraiser to determine the status of the appraisal.

    o If any issue exists that is prohibiting the appraiser from completing the appraisal, such as an inability to gain access to the property, you can address the matter and ensure that the appraisal is completed in time to complete the remaining tasks on the loan package.

    o It is your job to assist the appraiser in the process whenever possible.

6. If for some reason the appraisal is not complete after 72 hours, call appraiser every 24 hours until appraisal is complete.

    o If appraisal order is outstanding for more than one week, you need to begin searching for another appraiser partner.

    This is an excellent example of the reason it is vital that your office develops a "relationship" with your affinity providers.

    An appraisal that takes a week to complete can drastically slow your loan process.

    Many lending professionals and real estate agents fail to remember the fact that the property is as important to the security of the loan being made as the borrower profile.

Ensuring that appraisals are remitted to underwriting promptly helps to speed the loan process, leads to better quality loan files, and enables your office to gain a reputation as the office that can get the job done smoothly, efficiently, and with fewer surprises.

Preliminary Title Reports come from the Title Company who will insure the title of the home.

They research the property, seller, and borrower for any legal items, liens, or loans that may affect title to the property.

The completion of the preliminary title report typically takes between 1 and 2 weeks but you will wish to confirm the time requirements with the title company your office chooses to complete the abstract of title.

The title or settlement company may be chosen by

o   the real estate agent

o   the borrower

o   the seller

o   or your office

You may wish to ask the loan officer on the file if they have a title company preference.

A title company is an affinity service provider who sometimes refers potential borrowers to lending institutions.

The loan officer may have a specific title company with whom they are trying to build or strengthen a relationship.

In many areas, the title company and closing company are blended into one office.

Requesting title to a property from the company that will close the transaction requires the submittal of all of the transaction details, transaction documents, and loan program instructions.

The submittal of all of the necessary details and documents ensures that the company has all of the information that they need to complete the necessary title and closing functions within the timeline set on the sales agreement.

Title Request Form

DATE: _____ FROM: _____

TO: _____ FAX: _____

Borrower Name: _____

Phone Number: _____ SS#_____ SS#_____

Mailing Address: _____

Property Address: _____

Proposed Lender: _____ Loan Amount: _____

Purchase ____ Refinance ____ 2nd Mortgage ____ Prepared by: _____

Current Owners: _____

Address: _____

Phone Number: _____ SS#_____ SS#_____

Estimated Close Date: _____

Purchase Price: $_____ Loan Amount: $_____

Attachments:

      1003
      Sales Agreement

      _____
      _____

Figure 13:8 Sample Form – Title Request

TITLE REQUEST PROCESS

In general, you will want to use a closing company with whom you have a comfortable working relationship. You will want to check with your branch manager to determine if the branch has established affinity relationships already in place that can benefit you when ordering Title Work.

When ordering title and closing services, you should use a form that incorporates all of the necessary information and details related to the title and closing functions. Your branch or closing company may have preferred forms available for your use. We have included a sample form that you may use to request closing and title services.

1.   You should fill out Title Request form completely.

      Completing all entries will speed the process since the Title Company will not need to contact you for additional information.

2.   You should include all of the contact information and phone numbers for every individual concerned with the transaction. .You should include all of the contact details for

      o   Yourself

      o   The real estate agent

  o The buyer

  o The seller

  o The closing department at the lenders offices

  o Any inspection companies involved in the transaction

  o Any other individual specific to the transaction

3. When you send the title and closing request, you should also include the

  o 1003

  o sales agreement

  o any additional documentation specified by the closing company

You should confirm the documents that the company commonly requires before submitting any request.

4. You should include any additional information such as the application of seller concessions that are specific to your transaction under the comments section of the request form.

Additional information included with the request should include any detail that is vital to the completion of the title work or closing.

You should always define any special loan characteristics that apply to your loan and define the closing costs concession and second mortgage information to ensure that the closing package is prepared correctly.

5. You should log the date that you sent the request on the file tracking form.

Logging activity ensures proper documentation of all actions on a file and enables you to conduct follow-up activity if a delay or another issue arises at a later point in the transaction.

6. Twenty-four hours after request has been sent you should receive a confirmation of the request from the company.

You should note this confirmation within the file tracking form and place the confirmation form in the file.

If you do not receive a confirmation, you should follow up with the closing company and note the follow up action and any information you receive from the company on the file tracking form.

7. One week to 10 days before closing, you should request the Title Commitment.

 You may request the commitment verbally or with a fax request.

8. Upon receipt of the title commitment, you should contact the individual who will prepare the loan-closing package and confirm all of the transaction details. This confirmation helps to avoid calculations errors in the preparation of the closing documents. Some details to confirm include.

  o Sales Price
  o Loan Amount
  o Seller Concession

- o   Estimated closing costs
- o   Subordinate financing

9.   Within 48 hours, the Title Commitment should be provided to you for submittal to underwriting.

When you receive the commitment, you should verify that there is a closing protection letter included.

10.   You will place a copy of the wiring instructions for the closing company with the commitment.

If you use the same closing company for multiple transactions, they will typically provide you with a wiring instruction sheet that you can copy and attach to each file.

If you do not have a wiring instruction sheet for the closing company, contact the company offices to obtain one and then keep it for future use.

11.   You will add the title commitment and wiring instructions to any remaining stipulations and submit the final file to underwriting for review.

12.   Underwriting should clear any final conditions on the file at this time. If any stipulations remain outstanding, you will need to obtain the necessary documents to clear them.

You should log all contacts and conversations on the file tracking form so that any individual who accesses the file can immediately see the status of the processing activity relating to the transaction. This log also assist you in remember the actions that you have taken on a file and the date of the activity if an issue arises that creates a loan process delay.

Homeowners Insurance

Your most important product is customer service. As an added service to customers, offices offer the service of obtaining Homeowner's Insurance quotes.

Many borrowers, especially the first time homebuyer, are uncertain of the process and information required to receive an Insurance quote and a binder. While this is not a typical part of your job, it is an added service that you can provide to the borrower that enhances their overall experience and satisfaction with your office.

Requesting an insurance quote for the borrower also enables you to build an additional affinity service relationship with the Insurance Agent.

Referring insurance quote requests to the Insurance Agent provides them with a possible source of business that they did not have previously. In providing this business source, you are setting the groundwork for a cross-referral program where they will refer borrowers to your office for their home lending needs.

It is important to remember to tell your borrower that you are performing this service on their behalf.

You MUST also tell the borrower that you are obtaining the quote for comparison purposes only and that they are under no obligation to use the service provider for their home insurance needs.

A sample of the Homeowner's Insurance requirements that might be set by underwriting is included to provide you with a better understanding of what homeowner's insurance stipulations may be required for the file.

A binder is required either before or at the closing.

Often the borrower will not have the time available to secure the entire homeowner's insurance policy. A binder showing proof that coverage has been obtained and a receipt showing proof the policy has been paid in full is sufficient to satisfy most underwriting requirements and enable the loan to proceed to closing.

Request for Homeowners Insurance Quote

Borrower : _____ Co-Borrower Name: _____

DOB: _____ DOB:_____

SSN: _____ SSN: _____

Mailing Address: _____

Home Phone: _____ Best Time to Call: _____

Property Address: _____

Value: _____ Sales Price: _____

Payment to be made: _____ Prior to Close _____ At Close

Expected Close Date: _____ Binder Needed By: _____

Proposed Lender: _____

Additional Comments: _____

Attachments:

_____1003
_____Credit Report
_____Sales Agreement
_____Appraisal
_____
_____

Figure 13:9 Sample Form – Homeowner's Insurance Quote Request

---

HAZARD INSURANCE REQUIREMENTS

Lender:

To: Escrow Officer   Date:
                                                     Escrow #:
                                                     Loan #:

Listed below are our Lenders policies, procedures and minimum requirements for Hazard Insurance, which must be provided covering the subject property. We will require that the insurance premium has been paid and date when renewal is due if property is a refinance.

1. Coverage required must be the lesser of the principal balance or the insurable value of the improvements. The coverage amount must fully compensate for any damage or loss on a replacement cost basis. If the loan program allows for potential negative amortization, the lender may require that the amount of coverage be increased to protect the amount of potential negative amortization.
2. The insurance company providing coverage must have an "A" rating or better in the latest edition of "Best's Insurance Guide", must be licensed in the State in which the property described above is located, and must be licensed to transact the lines of insurance required in the transaction.
3. Coverage shall provide at least Broad Form on one to four units, and at least "Vandalism and Malicious Mischief" over four units, with no deviation. Homeowner's policies must be equal to HO2 form.
4. Policies may contain deductibles on any peril as follows: Maximum deductible is the great of $1,000.00 or 1% of the coverage amount.
5. Policy must provide coverage for a term of at least one year. Premiums may be paid on an annual installment basis only if the policy provides the Lender will be notified in writing of cancellation 30 days prior to expiration of coverage, for any cause. Purchases: One year must be paid through escrow.
6. If an existing policy is provided and will expire within three months from recording, it must be renewed for the required term as noted above. These policies will be acceptable if they are current.
7. All forms and endorsements pertaining to the company requirements must appear on the Declaration page of the policy.
8. New policies must be accompanied by signed Broker of Record Authorization if borrower has recently changed insurance agents.
9. Verification of renewal of insurance policies must be in the Lenders office at least thirty days prior to the expiration date of the existing policy. If this requirement is not met, the LENDER OR ITS SUCCESSORS OR ASSIGNS MAY AT THEIR OPTION, BUT WITHOUT OBLIATION TO DO SO, PROVIDE COVERAGE TO REPLACE ANY EXPIRING POLIIES WHICH HAVE NOT BEEN PROPERLY RENEWED. The premium for such coverage will be remitted promptly by the undersigned, or Lender may charge borrower's account for the cost thereof.
10. Insurance agent's name, mailing address, and phone number must be on or attached to Binder/Policy.
11. Lender's Loss Payable Endorsement 438 BFU to be affixed in favor of:

12. Property address and insurance names to be designated as per ALTA Policy.
13. Our loan number must be shown on the policy and any subsequent endorsements.
14. Effective date of new policies, endorsements, and/or assignments shall be as of, or prior to, date of recording.
15. Please notify your agent to forward future premium notices directly to you.
16. If the security property is a condominium, larger than twenty units a fidelity bond in a minimum amount of at least equal to the sum of three months assessments on all units in the project for Directors and Officers is required. A copy of the master policy must be submitted to the Lender prior to funding.
17. The minimum amount of Flood Insurance required is the lesser of the outstanding principal balance of the loan, the full insurable value of the property, or the maximum amount of flood insurance available.

All policies, assignments, and or endorsements, for completion of our loan escrow are to be mailed to this lending office.

Figure 13:10 Sample Form – Hazard Insurance Requirements

Additional supporting documents	Additional paperwork may be needed on a case-by-case scenario.
	The need for additional documents will vary by borrower's individual scenario and is one of the areas where you will await the stipulation list before requesting the documents.
	As you gain in experience, you will become better able to anticipate what unusual documents underwriting may request, but for now, you will likely need to rely on the stipulation list.
Any Documents missing from initial loan application	You must also review the file package to ensure that you have requested and obtained **any** paperwork or documentation item that was missing from original loan application.
	If the buyer or the seller is slow in providing the necessary documents, you may enlist the aid of the real estate agent in obtaining these items.
	If an affinity service partner is slow in providing you with a necessary stipulation, you may need to discuss the services of the affinity service provider with your branch manager so that the speed of affinity services can be addressed and any issues resolved.
Escrow / Closing Instructions	Escrow or closing instructions are drawn up by the Escrow or settlement Company and they define the transaction and settlement details.
	An Escrow or settlement company is an independent third party of the transaction that acts as the accountant. Some states call this the settlement company.
	In California and some other states, a closing attorney or title company acts as the escrow or settlement agent.
	The process of drawing up escrow instructions usually takes 2 to 7 days.

Since all of these documents are secured from various companies and individuals, this is most often, where there are delays. This portion of the loan process will normally take 1 to 3 weeks.

Developing relationships with your various affinity providers is essential in speeding this process. It is also very important to have an effective pipeline management system and loan process follow up system in place. This allows you to easily order items from service providers. This will also enable you to follow up on missing items with Real Estate Agents and borrowers efficiently.

A typical Real Estate Transaction involves the timely cooperation of many different parties. Due to the number of people involved, there can be problems.

Since no loan is closed until it is closed, this list of items is potential roadblocks. It is very important for you to bear in mind that you are ultimately responsible for organizing the loan process and ensuring that it moves along in a timely manner.

Some of the delays are easily avoided with an adequate loan process follow up and reminder system and others will require you to build strong relationships with affinity service providers.

The Real Estate Agents could create delays in the loan process and closing if they

- do not get all documents signed promptly
- Did not structure the transaction properly
- Did not pre-qualify the borrower for motivation
- Misunderstand the borrowers needs or your instructions due to a lack of real estate experience
- Won't return phone calls
- Transfer to another office
- Goes on vacation leaving no one to handle the file
- Has poor people skills with the borrower
- Gets the borrower upset over minor points
- Does not communicate with their borrower, your office, the appraiser or the settlement company

The Escrow or Closing Company may cause delays if they

- Fail to notify the real estate agent or lender of unsigned or un-returned documents so that they can contact the individual responsible for the document and cure the problem
- Fails to obtain information from beneficiaries, lien holders, title companies, insurance companies, or lenders in a timely manner
- Incorrectly prepares paperwork
- Is incorrect at interpreting aspects of the transaction
- Passes incorrect assumptions about the transaction to other parties
- Lets the principals of the transaction leave town without getting all necessary signatures
- Is too busy or overscheduled
- Loses the paperwork related to the transaction
- Does not pass on valuable information fast enough
- Does not coordinate well so that many items can be done simultaneously
- Do not find liens or problems until last minute

The Inspection Company or The Appraiser can cause delays if they

- Are overly picky during the inspection
- Infuriates the seller
- Makes mistakes when preparing the documents or completing the inspection
- Delays completing their report

The Seller may create delays if they

- Lose motivation for the sale

- Nets less money from sale than they originally believed that they would

- Cannot find another home to purchase

- Has an unexpected occurrence such as an illness or divorce

- Fails to disclose or does not know about defects in the property

- Receive a Home inspection that reveals defects that the seller is unwilling to repair

- Removes property from the premises that the buyer believed was included in the sale

- Is unable to clear up problems or liens against the property

- Did not own 100% of property as disclosed

- Thought that the obtainment of partners signatures were "no problem" but they were

- Leaves town without giving power of attorney to another individual who can finalize the transaction on their behalf

- Uses a notary that did not make a clear stamp when notarizing their signatures

- Delays the projected move-out date

By building strong affinity service provider relationships, providing clear instructions to each party involved in the transaction, and carefully coordinating and following up on each aspect of the loan process, you can minimize many of these delays. It is vital that you maintain a constant awareness of the status of each loan package so that you can ensure that each party completes all of the steps necessary to move the package to a smooth closing meeting.

Once the Underwriting department has determined that all of the stipulations are acceptable and issued a satisfaction status, you will need to schedule the closing and request the closing documents.

The loan document process is the stage when the funding agent is preparing the loan documents. These loan documents are the legal binding documents to finalize the transaction.

They will include important items to be signed. Nearly every transaction will require the completion of the

Promissory Note	defining the amount borrowed, the interest rate charged, and the terms or repayment method applied to the loan, and the monthly payment amount.
Deed of Trust	that places the property as security to the loan and note
HUD 1	that provides an itemized breakdown of all fees incurred for obtaining the loan, all costs related to the transfer of the property and any other financial matter related to the sale.

The lender will typically also require that the borrower complete additional legal forms to help to confirm that the borrower understands the transaction, verify the borrower's statements during the loan process, and promote the security of the transaction.

Occupancy Declaration	An occupancy declaration is a statement by the borrower that defines the use they intend to make of the property.

When a mortgage lender provides a mortgage loan, one aspect that will affect the approval is the use that the borrower intends to make of the property.

It is commonly believed that a borrower will make payments against their primary residence better than they will against a second home, investment property or other form of residence. As such, the entry that you make on the application form pertaining to occupancy plans of the property will change many aspects of the loan including interest rate, percentage of the value they will lend against and documentation requirements based on the occupancy plans of the borrower.

During the loan application process, the borrower will have provided information pertaining to the intended occupancy status of the property being transferred.

It is a common practice to request that the borrower complete a statement that confirming these occupancy plans during the settlement meeting.

This occupancy declaration will be included in nearly every closing package and it is essential that you have confirmed the occupancy plans of the borrower prior to remitting the initial application to the underwriting department for review.

A closing could be stopped if the borrower arrives and refuses to sign an occupancy declaration.

If you have conducted an adequate interview and completed the application forms properly, this document will have a limited impact on your closing.

MAILING ADDRESS CONFIRMATION / PAYMENT LETTER

From:

Re: Loan #   *** IMPORTANT, PLEASE READ THROUGHOULY ***
          Property Address

To:

Dear Homeowner:

A.   All mortgage servicing correspondence will be mailed to the above referenced property address. In order to ensure proper receipt of all mortgage servicing notifications (i.e. monthly statement, Q&A booklets, etc.) please indicate the correct mailing address if it is different from the property address. The address to mail payments and the phone number to call for customer service are listed below.

     Please indicate (X):

     ( )   The property address is correct as referenced above and should be used for correspondence.

     ( )   The proper mailing address is: _____

                                             _____

B.   The monthly payments on the above loan are to begin on   , and will continue monthly until

     Your monthly payment will consist of the following:

     MONTHLY PAYMENT ....$ _____
     MMI/PMI INSRUANCE .... _____
     RESERVE FOR COUNTY TAXES .... _____
     RESERVE FOR HAXARD INSURANCE....................... _____
     RESERVE FOR FLOOD INSURANCE.......................... _____
     RESERVE FOR CITY TAXES..................................... _____
     RESERVE FOR ANNUAL ASSESSMENT................... _____
     RESERVE FOR SCHOOL TAXES............................... _____
     _____ .... _____
             TOTAL MONTHLY PAYMENTS.........$_____

*** Please be aware that if you have an impound account, you may see a change in your initial monthly payment figure due to information available after the closing of your loan.

                        Engages the services of   as its servicer. You will be receiving a billing notice from   within two weeks of your loan funding.   has the right to collect your payments and this in no way affects the terms and conditions of the mortgage instruments, other than the terms directly related to the servicing of your loan. If you do not receive a payment booklet or have other questions about the servicing of your loan, please call:

Please send your payments to:

Any correspondence, or calls, in reference to your loan, please refer to the above loan number. However, your loan number will be changed for servicing purposes.

Copy received and acknowledged.

Figure 13:11 Sample Form – Mailing Address Confirmation / Payment Letter – HUD Release

FEE DISCLOSURE	
APPLICANT(S) NAME AND ADDRESS	MORTGAGE BANKER/BROKER NAME AND ADDRESS
PROPERTY ADDRESS	TYPE OF LOAN

Today you have submitted a mortgage loan application to the Mortgage Banker or Broker listed above. All fees paid by you are nonrefundable. State law (   ) requires that the following information be disclosed to you.

The Mortgage Banker or Broker is required to refund all fees paid by an applicant borrower, other than those fees paid by the Mortgage Banker or Broker to a third party, when a mortgage loan is not produced within the time specified by the Mortgage Banker or Broker at the rate, term and overall cost agreed to by the borrower.

However, this provision shall not apply when the failure to produce a loan is due solely to the borrower's negligence, borrower's refusal to accept and close on a loan commitment or borrower's refusal or inability to provide information necessary for processing the loan, including, but not limited to, employment verifications and verifications of deposit.

This disclosure does not constitute approval of your loan or a commitment to make a loan to you.

Figure 13:12 Sample Form – Fee Disclosure – HUD Release

Fee Disclosure	Many lenders now require that the payment for certain fees be given to the lender by the buyer. These funds are held by the lender to pay for services that will be ordered in relationship to documenting the loan.
	Other fees may be paid directly to service providers during the transaction processing stage or paid out of the proceeds at the closing table.
Rate Lock	If the interest rate has already been locked-in, the document person draws the loan documents.
	If the interest rate has not been locked in, you should ensure that the form is completed at this time.
Document Prep	Once the loan documents are printed, they are then over-nighted to the Escrow Company or Settlement Company.
Schedule Meeting	The settlement agent then contacts the borrower with the final figures for the scheduled closing.
	This process from document order to signing will normally take 2-5 days.
Settlement	After the loan documents have been prepared, signed, dated, notarized, and returned, they will go into funding.

Funding   Funding is the time when all of the signed documents are reviewed by the lender to insure that everything is signed correctly.

At this point, they will also do a final back-up quality control check of your borrower's credit and employment to insure nothing has changed since the loan was approved.

Once everything has been verified and checked, the lender will fund the loan.

The funding of the loan is the time when the monies borrowed are wired to the closing company, escrow office, or the closing attorney for disbursement.

o   This is when the actual exchange of money is completed.

This funding is usually completed through an electronic wire transfer.

o   Some lenders do dry closings in which the funds are not sent until all the review activity is complete.

In this case, the funding will usually take place 2 to 4 days after the loan documents have been returned to the lender by the closer.

o   In other cases, lenders send the funds to the escrow or closing company before the settlement meeting. If the funds are available at the settlement meeting, the escrow or closing agent will cut the checks and have them available for dispersal at the settlement table.

Recording   The recording process is the time that the legal, binding loan documents that were signed and notarized are taken to the county recorder office for recording.

The actual recording is simply, the time when the documents are time and date stamped by the county recorder office, recognized, and filed as an official public document.

The recording process usually takes place 24 to 48 hours after the loan has been funded and the electronic wire confirmed.

In some places a "special recording" or a same day recording may occur.

At this point, the loan is finalized and closed.

GLOSSARY OF MORTGAGE TERMS

1-year ARM: An adjustable-rate mortgage (ARM) that has an initial interest rate for one year, and thereafter has an adjustment interval of one year. The adjustment is based on comparison interest caps and the indexed rate

3/1 ARM: An adjustable-rate mortgage (ARM) that has an initial interest rate for three years, and thereafter has an adjustment interval of one year. The adjustment is based on comparison interest caps and the indexed rate.

5/1 ARM: An adjustable-rate mortgage (ARM) that has an initial interest rate for five years, and thereafter has an adjustment interval of one year. The adjustment is based on comparison interest caps and the indexed rate

7/1 ARM: An adjustable-rate mortgage (ARM) that has an initial interest rate for seven years, and thereafter has an adjustment interval of one year. The adjustment is based on comparison interest caps and the indexed rate

10/1 ARM: An adjustable-rate mortgage (ARM) that has an initial interest rate for ten years, and thereafter has an adjustment interval of one year. The adjustment is based on comparison interest caps and the indexed rate

Abstract of Title: A written history of all the transactions that bear on the title to a specific piece of land. An abstract of title covers the time from when the property was first sold to the present. Used by the Title Company to produce a title binder

Acceleration Clause: The section of a mortgage document that allows the lender to speed up the payment date in the event of default, making the entire principal amount due

Acre: An area of land 43.560 square feet

Adjustable Rate Mortgage: Mortgage in which the rate of interest is adjusted based on a standard rate index. Most ARM's have caps on how much the interest rate may increase

Adjustment Interval: How often the loan's rate can be changed

Alternative Mortgage: 7/23 and 5/25 mortgages with a one-time rate adjustment after seven years and five years respectively Also known as a hybrid mortgage or a two-step mortgage

Amortization Schedule: A timetable for the gradual repayment of a mortgage loan. An amortization schedule indicates the amount of each payment applied to interest and principal, and the remaining balance after each payment is made

Amortization Term: The amount of time required to amortize (repay) a mortgage loan. The amortization term is usually expressed in months. A 30-year fixed rate mortgage, for example, has an amortization term of 360 months

Annual Percentage Rate (APR): A standardized method of calculating the cost of a mortgage, stated as a yearly rate which includes such items as interest, mortgage insurance, and certain points or credit costs

Appraisal: A written report by a qualified appraiser estimating the value of the property

Appraised Value: An opinion of a property's fair market value, based on an appraiser's inspection and analysis of the property

Appraiser: A person qualified by education, training, and experience to estimate the value of real property

Appreciation: An increase in the value of a property due to changes in market conditions or improvements to the property

ARM: See Adjustable Rate Mortgage

Assessed Value: The value of a property as determined by a public tax assessor for the purpose of taxation

Assumable: A mortgage that a buyer can assume, or take over, from the seller of the property

Balloon Mortgage: A loan that has regular monthly payments, which amortize over a stated term but call for a final lump sum (balloon payment) at the end of a specified term, or maturity date such as 10 years

Basis Points: 1/100th of 1 percent. If an interest rate changes 50 basis points, for example, it has move ½ of 1 percent

Binder: See title binder

Biweekly Mortgage: A mortgage that schedules payments every two weeks instead of the standard monthly payment. The 26 biweekly payments are each equal to one-half of the monthly payment. The result for the borrower is a substantial reduction in interest payments because the mortgage is paid off sooner. See also prepayment plan

Bridge loan: A loan that "bridges" the gap between the purchase of a new home and the sale of the borrower's current home. The borrower's current home is used as collateral and the money is used to close on the new home before the current home is sold. Some are structured so they completely pay off the old home's first mortgage at the bridge loan's closing. Others pile the new debt on top of the old. They usually run for a term of six months

Broker: See mortgage broker

Broker Premium: A premium paid to the mortgage broker as the "middleman" in the mortgage process between the lender and the borrower

Built-ins: Cabinets, ranges, ceiling fans and other items permanently attached to the structure, and which a buyer may assume will remain with the structure

Buy down: The process of trading money for a lower mortgage rate. The borrower "buys down" the interest rate on a mortgage by paying discount points up front. It can also be a mortgage in which an initial lump sum payment is made to reduce a borrower's monthly payments during the first few years of a mortgage

Caps: The maximum amount the interest rate can change annually or cumulatively over the life of an adjustable rate mortgage. F or example, if the caps are 2 percent annual and 6 percent life of loan, a mortgage with a first-year rate of 10 percent could rise to no more than 12 percent the second year, and no more than 16 percent over the entire life of the loan

Certificate of Title: A statement provided by the Title Company or attorney stating that the title to the real estate is legally held by the current owner

Chattel: Personal property

Clear title: A title that is free of liens or legal questions as to ownership of a piece of property

Closing: The meeting at which the sale of a property is finalized. The buyer signs the lender agreement for the mortgage and pays' closing costs and escrow amounts. The buyer and seller sign documents to transfer the ownership of the property. Also known as the settlement

Closing costs: Expenses incurred by buyers and sellers in transferring ownership of a property. Closing costs normally include an origination fee, an attorney's fee, taxes, escrow payments, and charges for title insurance. Lenders or Real Estate Agents provide estimates of closing costs to prospective homebuyers

Closing Statement: A financial disclosure accounting for all funds changing hands at the closing. See also HUD-1 Statement

Cloud on title: Any fact or condition that could adversely affect the title

Commission: In real estate, the broker, or mortgage associates fee for assisting in the transaction. Usually expressed as a percentage of the total paid by the buyer

Commitment: A formal offer by a lender stating the approved terms for lending money to a homebuyer

Common Area Assessment: A levy against individual unit owners in a condominium or planned unit development to pay for upkeep, repairs, and improvements to the property's common areas, such as corridors, elevators, parking lots, swimming pools and tennis courts

Comparables: Refers to "comparable properties" which are used for comparative purposes in the appraisal process. Comps are recently sold properties that are similar in size, location, and amenities to the home for sale. Comps help an appraiser determine the fair market value of a property

Condominium: A real estate project in which each unit owner has title to a unit of the project, and sometimes and undivided interest in the common areas

Conforming Loan: A loan that conforms to the standard rules for purchase by Freddie Mac or Fannie Mae

Contingency: A condition that must be met before a contract is legally binding. For example, homebuyers often include a contingency that specifies that the contract is not binding until after a satisfactory report from a home inspector

Contract: In real estate parlance, the contract is the legal document by which buyer and seller make offers and counteroffers. The real estate contract describes the property, includes or excludes items in the property, names the price, apportions the closing costs between the parties and sets forth a closing date. When a buyer and seller agree on the terms and sign the same document the property is said to be "under contract". More formally known as the agreement for the sale, purchase agreement, or earnest money contract

Conventional Mortgage: Usually refers to a fixed-rate, 30-year mortgage that is not insured by FHA, Farmers Home Administration, or Veterans Administration

Convertible Mortgage: An adjustable rate mortgage ARM that can be converted to a fixed mortgage under specific conditions

Cooperative: A type of multiple ownership in which the residents of a multiunit housing complex own shares in the cooperative corporation

that owns the property, giving each resident the right to occupy a specific apartment or unit

Cost-of-funds: A yield index based upon the cost of funds to savings & loan institution in the San Francisco Federal Home Loan Bank District. It is one of the indexes commonly used to set the rate of adjustable rate mortgages

Covenant: A written restriction on the use of land, most commonly in use today in homeowners associations

Credit report: A report on a person's credit history prepared by a credit bureau and used by a lender in determining a loan applicant's record for paying debts in a timely manner

Debt-to-Income Ratio: The percentage of a person's monthly earnings used to pay off all debt obligations. Lenders consider two ratios, constructed in slightly different ways. The first called the front-end ratio, the ratio of the monthly housing expenses – including principal, interest, property taxes, and insurance, (PITI) is compared to the borrower's gross, pretax monthly income. In the back-end ratio, a borrower's other debts such as auto loans and credit cards are figured in. Lenders usually consider both and set an acceptable ratio. Some lenders and some lending qualifying agencies only consider the back-end ratio

Deed: The legal document conveying title to the property

Depreciation: A decline in the value of a property as opposed to appreciation

Discount Points: A type of point (1 percent of the loan) paid by the borrower to reduce the interest rate

Down payment: The amount of a property's purchase price that the buyer pays in cash and does not finance with a mortgage

Earnest money: A deposit made by potential homebuyers during negotiations with the seller. The sum shows a seller that the buyer is serious about purchasing a property

Easement: The right of another to use a property. The most common easements are for utility lines

80-10-10 Loan: A combination of an 80 percent loan-to-value first mortgage, a 10 percent down payment and a 10 percent home equity loan. This is also sometimes referred to as a CLTV (Combined Loan-to-Value)

Encumbrance: A lien, charge, or liability against a property

Equal Credit: A federal law that requires lenders and other creditors to make credit equally available with out discrimination based on race, color, religion, national origin, age, sex, marital status, or receipt of income from public assistance programs

Equity: The value of a homeowner's unencumbered interest in real estate. Equity is the difference between the homes fair market value and the unpaid balance of the mortgage and any outstanding liens. Equity increases as the mortgage is paid down or as the property enjoys appreciation

Escrow Payment: The portion of a homeowner's monthly mortgage payment that is held by the loan servicer to pay for taxes and insurance Also known as reserves. The loan servicer holds the escrow funds separately from money meant to pay principal and interest

Fair Credit Reporting Act: A consumer protection law that regulates the disclosure of consumer credit reports by credit reporting agencies and establishes procedures for correcting mistakes on a person's credit record

Fannie Mae: Nickname for Federal National Mortgage Association. It is a government-chartered non-bank financial services company and the nation's largest source of financing for home mortgages. It was started to make sure mortgage money is available in all areas of the country

FHA Mortgage: A mortgage insured by the Federal Housing Administration

First mortgage: A mortgage that is the primary lien against a property

Fixed-rate Mortgage: A mortgage in which the interest rate does not change during the entire term of the loan, most often 15, or 30 years

Flood Insurance   Insurance that compensates for the physical property damage resulting from rising water. It is required for properties located in federally designated flood areas

Foreclosure: The legal process by which a homeowner in default on a mortgage is deprived of interest in the property. This usually involves a forced sale of the property at public auction with the proceeds of the sale being applied to the mortgage debt

Freddie Mac: Nickname for Federal Home Loan Mortgage Corp. A financial corporation chartered by the federal government to buy pools of mortgages from lenders and sell securities backed by these mortgages

Ginnie Mae: Nickname for the Government National Mortgage Association

Good Faith Estimate: A written estimate of closing costs that the lender must provide to prospective homebuyers within three days of submitting a mortgage loan application

Government National Mortgage Association (Ginnie Mae) A government-owned corporation within the US Department of Housing and Urban Development (HUD) Created by Congress in 1968, GNMA has responsibility for the special assistance loan program known as Ginnie Mae

Hazard Insurance: Insurance coverage that compensates for physical damage to property from natural disasters such as fire and other hazards. Depending on where a piece of property is located, lenders may also require flood insurance or policies covering windstorms (hurricanes) or earthquakes

Home Inspection: An inspection by a building professional that evaluates the structural and mechanical condition of a property

Homeowners Association: A nonprofit association that manages the common areas of a condominium or PUD Unit owners pays the association a fee to maintain areas owned jointly

Homeowner's Insurance: An insurance policy that combines personal liability insurance and hazard insurance coverage for a residence and its contents

Housing Expense: The percentage of gross monthly income that goes toward paying a Ratio mortgage or rent on a home

HUD-1: The document with an itemized listing of closing costs payable at the closing or settlement meeting when buying property The closing costs can include a commission, loan fees, and points, and sums set aside for escrow payments, taxes, and insurance. It is signed by both the buyer and the seller, who may be paying some of the closing costs. The statement form is published by HUD

Hybrid Mortgage: See alternative mortgage products.

Index: A published measure of the cost of money that lenders use to calculate the rate on an ARM. The most common indexes are the one-year Treasury Constant Maturity Yield and the FHLB 11th District Cost of Funds

Indexed Rate: The sum of the published index plus the margin. For example, if the index were 9 percent and the margin 2.75 percent, the indexed rate would be 11.75 percent. Often, lenders charge less than the indexed rate the first year of an ARM

Initial Interest Rate: Starting rate of an ARM

Interest Tax Deduction: Most mortgage holders can deduct all the interest paid on the loan in filing income tax The deduction applies to people with just on mortgage on a primary residence, as well as those with a combination of loans. Within certain time limits set by the IRS, points paid up front on a mortgage are usually deductible in the year the house was purchased

Jumbo Mortgage: Mortgages larger than the limits set by Fannie Mae and Freddie Mac. A jumbo mortgage will carry a higher interest rate than a conventional mortgage

Lease-purchase A financing option that allows a potential homebuyer to lease a property with the option to buy. Often constructed so the monthly rent payment covers the owner's first mortgage payment, plus an additional amount as a savings deposit to accumulate cash for a down payment. A seller may agree to a lease-purchase option if the housing market is saturated and the seller is having a difficult time selling the property

Lien: A legal hold or claim from one person on the property of another. The lien placed by a first mortgage is special. It is called a first lien and takes precedence over others

Lifetime Rate Cap: In an ARM, it limits the amount that the interest rate can increase or decrease over the life of the loan. See also caps

Lis Pendens: A pending lawsuit; in real estate, the constructive notice filed in public records that a legal dispute exists over a piece of property

Livery of Seizin: Under common law, the process of transferring title

Loan Origination: The process by which a mortgage lender obtains a mortgage secured by real property. An origination fee is charged by the lender to process all forms involved in obtaining a mortgage

Loan-to-value (LTV) Ratio: The ratio of a mortgage loan amount to the property's appraised value or selling price, whichever is less For example, if a home is sold for $100,000 and the mortgage amount is $80,000 the LTV is 80%

Lock: Lender's guarantee that the mortgage rate quoted will be good for a specific amount of time. The homebuyer usually wants the lock to stay in effect until the date of the closing

Lock-and-Float: Rate programs offered by companies that allow borrowers to lock in the current interest rate on a mortgage for a specified period, while also letting them "float" the rate down if market conditions improve before closing

Low-down Mortgages: Mortgages with a low down payment, usually less than 10 percent. Frannie Mae and Freddie Mac design loan programs that spell out a set of standards for lenders. In recent years, these government-chartered agencies have made low-down mortgages more available

Margin: The number of percentage points added to the index on a one-year ARM

Maturity   : The date on which the principal balance of a loan becomes due and payable

Mortgage: A legal document that uses property as collateral to secure payment of a debt

Mortgage Banker: The lender that originates a mortgage loan, the one making the loan directly, and closing the loan

Mortgage Broker: An individual or company that brings borrowers and lenders together for the purpose of loan origination   Unlike a mortgage banker, brokers do not fund the loan but work on behalf of several lenders. Brokers typically require a fee or a commission for their service. See broker premium

Mortgage Insurance: A policy that insures the lender against loss should the homeowner default on a mortgage. Depending on the loan, the insurance can be issued by government agencies such as the FHA or a private company. It is part of the monthly mortgage payment. (See also private mortgage insurance PMI)

Negative Amortization: A gradual increase in mortgage debt that happens when a monthly payment does not cover the entire principal and interest due. The shortfall is added to the remaining balance to create "negative" amortization

No-doc or low-doc Loan: These no-documentation or low-documentation loans are designed for the entrepreneur or self-employed, for recent immigrants with money in foreign countries or for borrowers who cannot or choose not to reveal information about their incomes

Note: The document giving evidence of mortgage indebtedness, including the amount and terms of repayment

Origination Fee: A fee paid to the lender for processing a loan application

Owner financing A transaction in which the seller of a house provides all or part of the financing Sellers may provide financing because they need to sell the property right away or they are having difficulty selling the house and want to provide financing as an incentive to a buyer

Periodic rate cap: In an ARM, it limits how much an interest rate can increase or decrease during any one-adjustment period. See also caps

PITI: Stands for principal, interest, taxes and insurance that are the usual components of a monthly mortgage payment

PITI Reserves: A cash amount that a homebuyer must have on hand after making a down payment and paying all closing costs. The reserves required by a lender must equal the amount a buyer would pay for PITI for a specific number of months

Plat: A map that shows a parcel of land and how it is subdivided into individual lots. Plat maps also show the locations of streets and easements

PMI: See private mortgage insurance

Points: A point equals 1 percent of a mortgage loan. Lenders charge points as a way to make a profit. Borrowers may pay discount points to reduce the loan interest rate. Buyers are prohibited from paying points on HUD or VA guaranteed loans

Pre-approval: This process goes a step further than pre-qualification. It means the lender has contacted the borrower's employer, bank, and other places to verify all claims of earnings and assets. In return, the borrower receives a letter stating the lender is willing to grant a mortgage for a specific amount within a limited period with the stipulation that there are no material changes to the borrower's situation

Prepayment Penalty: A fee imposed by certain lenders if the first mortgage is paid off early

Prepayment Plan: Similar to biweekly mortgage, but operated by a third party   In it, the borrower pays to the third party, half the monthly mortgage payment every two weeks   At the end of the year, the plan operators typically take the extra money that results from the process and sends lump sum payment to the participants' lenders

Pre-qualification: An early evaluation by a lender of a potential homebuyer's credit report, plus earnings, savings, and debt information   The homebuyer gets a non-binding estimate of the mortgage amount the borrower would qualify for, or how much house the borrower can afford. Buyers who pre-qualify can go a step further and seek a pre-approval

Rate Lock: A commitment issued by a lender to the homebuyer or the mortgage broker guaranteeing a specific interest rate for a specified amount of time. See also lock

Real Estate Agent: A person licensed to negotiate and transact the sale of real estate on behalf of the property owner

RESPA: Real Estate Settlement Procedures Act. A consumer protection law that requires lenders to give homebuyers advance notice of closing costs, which are payable at the closing or settlement meeting

Realtor: A real estate broker or an associate who holds an active membership in a local real estate board that is affiliated with the National Association of Realtors

Refinancing: Securing a new loan in order to pay off the existing mortgage or to gain access to the existing equity in the home

Roll-in Loan: A refinance loan that rolls any closing costs or fees into the loan. These programs best serve people who have a reasonable amount of equity, want to reduce their overall interest expense, and plan to stay in their homes

Rural Housing Service (RHS): The agency in the US Department of Agriculture providing financing to farmers and other qualified borrowers buying property in rural areas who are unable to obtain loans elsewhere. It offers low-interest-rate loans with no down payment to borrowers with low-to-moderate incomes who live in rural areas or small towns

Sales Agreement: A written contract signed by the buyer and the seller of a house stating the terms and conditions under which the property will be sold

Second Mortgage: A mortgage on the property that has a lien position behind the first mortgage

Servicer: An organization that collects monthly mortgage principal and interest payments from homeowners and manages escrow accounts for paying taxes and homeowners' insurance premiums The servicer often services mortgages that have been purchased by an investor in the secondary mortgage market

Settlement: See closing

Sub-prime Mortgage: A mortgage granted to a borrower considered sub-prime, that is, a person with a less-than perfect credit report. Sub-prime borrowers either have missed payments on a debt or have been late with payments. Lenders charge a higher interest rate to compensate for potential losses from customers who may run into trouble and default

Time is of the Essence: A phrase inserted in contracts to require a punctual performance

Title: A legal document proving a person's right to claim entitlement to a property, including the history of the property's ownership

Title Binder: Written evidence of temporary title insurance coverage

Title Company: A company that specializes in examining and insuring titles to real estate

Title insurance: Insurance that protects against loss from disputes over ownership of a property. A policy may protect the mortgage lender and/or the homebuyer

Title search: A check of title records to ensure that the seller is the legal owner of a property and that there are no liens or other claims against the property

Transfer Tax: State or local tax levied when title passes from one owner to another

Treasury Index: An index used to determine interest rate changes for certain ARM mortgages. It is based on the results of auctions that the US Treasury holds for its Treasury bills and securities or is derived from the US Treasury's daily yield curve, which is based on the closing market bid yields on actively traded Treasury securities in the over-the-counter market

Truth-in-Lending Act (TILA): A federal law that requires lenders to disclose, in writing, the terms and conditions of a mortgage, including the annual percentage rate APR and other charges

Underwriter   A company or person undertaking the responsibility for issuing a mortgage. Underwriters analyze a borrower's credit worthiness and set the loan amount

VA Mortgage: A loan backed by the Veterans Administration. It requires very low or no down payments and has less stringent requirements for qualification. Members of the US armed forces are eligible for the loans under certain qualifying conditions

Wraparound Mortgage: A new mortgage that includes the remaining balance on the old mortgage plus a new amount

Chapter 1 - The Lending Process

1.   What are the two classifications within the mortgage market?

2.   What is an investing pool?

3.   What are the three most common employment opportunities for a Loan Processor?

4.   What is the purpose of a mortgage brokerage?

5.   What are the most common entities within the secondary mortgage market

6.   Which is not a common entity within the primary mortgage market?

    a. Mortgage Brokerage Office
    b. Mutual Savings Bank
    c. Credit Union
    d. Insurance Company

Chapter 2 - Borrower Prequalification

1. What is the primary reason that many Loan Processors fail to obtain the information that will be needed for a pre-qualification?

2. What is the essential element to gaining the information you need from a borrower?

3. Why is the initial contact with any potential borrower important?

4. Why should you request referral information of each pre-qualification?

5. Why do you ask if the applicant has chosen a home to purchase during the pre-qualification interview?

6. What is your most important product?

7. Most loan inquiries are taken

    a. by the underwriter
    b. by the Loan Processor
    c. over the telephone
    d. both b & c

8. Your most valuable tool in planning a loan strategy is

    a. customer service skills
    b. information
    c. qualification skills
    d. loan knowledge

9. The pre-approval questionnaire contains

   a. all of the information you will need from the borrower
   b. most of the information you will need for the loan application
   c. all of the information the underwriting team will require
   d. most of the information necessary to close the loan

10. The initial contact

    a. sets the tone for your relationship with the borrower
    b. is the most essential information-gathering period
    c. sets the loan program you will use for the borrower
    d. none of the above

11. You will request a credit authorization verbally before pulling borrower credit.

    a. True
    b. False

12. You may enter common nicknames for the borrower

    a. True
    b. False

13. You must always have a co-borrower for the loan

    a. True
    b. False

14. You should complete the pre-qualification questionnaire as soon as the borrower locates the home they wish to purchase

    a. True
    b. False

15. The most important lending product is

    a. low rate loans and fixed products
    b. professionalism and responsiveness
    c. varied products with low down payment
    d. none of the above

16. The pre-qualification questionnaire will provide you with

    a. answers to every question on the questionnaire
    b. information that will be noted in the explanation of credit section
    c. all of the required documentation
    d. none of the above

Chapter 4 – Reading the Credit Report

1.   What does a credit report show about a borrower?

2.   What is your primary concern when reviewing a borrower's credit report?

3.   Explain the premise of debt-to-income ratios.

4.   What is the score range you can expect to see on a credit report?

5.   What are the three credit bureaus you will encounter?

6.   What is a FICO?

7.   How is the FICO generated?

8.   Fair, Isaac credit bureau scores do NOT use what as predictive characteristics:

9.   What do credit bureau scores provide to a lender?

10.   How can you gain information to assist you in understanding why a credit report scored the way it did?

11.	Credit Reports are:

	A. A great way to see how many things people buy
	B. A way to get to know a borrower's likes and dislikes
	C. An overview of a person's entire history of spending and payment
	D. None of the above

12	Credit reports are an overview of a person's entire history of spending and payment habits.

	A. True
	B. False

13.	The ability to borrow more money is affected by

	A. How much debt potential a borrower currently carries
	B. How many things a borrower has in his house
	C. How a borrower treats you and your company
	D. All of the above

14.	A bankruptcy can remain on a credit report for

	A. 3 years
	B. 7 years
	C. 10 years
	D. Life

15.	Accounts to medical services that a borrower has failed to pay as agreed are

	A. Often treated differently
	B. Never a concern
	C. An underwriting condition
	D. Always to be paid in full

16.	Repeatedly requesting a borrower's credit report may

	A. Adversely effect the credit score
	B. Show the borrower's can obtain further credit
	C. Cause an underwriting condition
	D. All of the above

17.	Debt to Income is

	A. The amount of debt a borrower carries
	B. The amount of income a borrower brings home
	C. The amount of income a borrower makes before taxes
	D. None of the above

18.   A late payment is any payment paid past the due date even when within the grace period

        A. True
        B. False

19.   Credit bureau scores are based upon

        A. Every action taken by a borrower with regard to debt
        B. The data contained within the credit bureau
        C. All information contained within the loan application
        D. None of the above

20   A credit bureau score will rank order potential borrowers based upon the number of good loans to bad loans.

        A. True
        B. False

Chapter 5 – Compensating Factors and DTI

1. What is a compensating factor?

2. Why do you use compensating factors?

3. Name three potential compensating factors:

4. What does a debt ratio tell you about a file?

5. What is a front-end ratio?

6. Which ratio is defined as the gross income divided by the new PITI mortgage payment and the minimum monthly payment from all other liabilities?

7. Name three items not commonly factored into the debt ratio:

8. What are three methods that you might employ to assist in adjusting debt ratios?

9. How many times do you factor each debt when calculating debt ratios?

10. Whose income and credit history do you use when calculating debt-to-income ratio for married applicants?

11   When a borrower falls just below or on the edge of a credit tier, you may

A. Bump them up to the next level
B. Request an exception
C. Submit every document possible
D. None of the above

12.   The debt ratio will determine

A. What loan programs the borrower may obtain
B. If the borrower has sufficient monthly income
C. How much additional debt a borrower can afford
D. All of the above

13.   Which monthly liability will not be used to calculate the debt ratio

A. Car Payment
B. Child Support
C. Utilities
D. None of the above

14.   The Debt-to-Income Ratio can be adjusted if

A. There are items that can be paid off
B. The interest rate can be lowered
C. There are items that will be paid in full within 4 months
D. All of the above

15.   A compensating factor would be

A. Larger than minimum down payment
B. Credit scores within a few points of the next highest level
C. Excellent savings history
D. All of the above

16.   A compensating factor is used to

A. Exceed normal guidelines
B. Subvert normal guidelines
C. Coerce the underwriter
D. None of the above

17.   You will calculate the debt ratio using

A. Gross Income
B. Net Income
C. Additional Income
D. None of the above

Chapter 6 – The Loan Application

1. Why is it important to include the amortization method planned for a loan package on the initial application?

2. What is the appropriate entry on the application if a borrower is applying for a pre-approval with no property in mind?

3. Why is it important to enter information regarding the use the borrower plans to make of the property?

4. What factors may alter the source of funds information entered as the loan process moves toward completion?

5. What action should you take if you need additional space to reference residence history, employment history, debt information or other borrower specific information that needs to be included in the application?

6. Why would you include borrower income that cannot be used for qualifying purposes on the application?

7. What monthly payment amount will you enter for a revolving liability that currently has not balance?

8. What is the premise behind requesting the highest loan amount that a borrower will be eligible to receive when submitting for a pre-approval that has no actual subject property?

9. Why should you include any information you have regarding possible subordinate financing early in the approval process?

10. If you do not use the space provided on the continuation sheet page what action should you take?

11.   The method of amortization should be included on the loan application because

A. It dictates the monthly payment
B. It will affect the debt ratios
C. It affects the required disclosures
D. All of the above

12.   You must always have the subject property address prior to completing the loan application.

A. True
B. False

13.   Federal Housing Acts have differing guidelines for

A. Single Family Houses
B. Multiple unit property
C. Second Homes
D. All of the above

14.   Occupancy Status will effect

A. Approval Levels
B. Underwriting Schedule
C. Appraised Value
D. All of the above

15.   It is a portion of your job function to assist borrowers in determining the source of funds to be used in a transaction.

A. True
B. False

16.   Non-qualifying income should be disclosed

A. Always
B. Only in compensating factor requests
C. Only at the request of the borrower
D. Never

17.   Pre-paid items are dictated by

A. the sales agreement
B. underwriting guidelines
C. available funds
D. none of the above

18.   Seller concession toward closing costs must appear

        A. on the sales agreement
        B. within the loan application
        C. on the settlement statement
        D. all of the above

Kenney

Chapter 9 – Appraisals

1. Why is an appraisal vital to the loan process?

2. What is a red flag?

3. What is URAR?

4. What is your goal when reviewing an appraisal?

5. What action should you take if you discover an error in a loan document?

6. Why is it important to locate red flags early in the process?

7. What alterations should you make to a completed appraisal if you discover an issue during your review?

8. What does the sales comparison valuation approach consider?

9. The property in a loan process is as important a factor as borrower history

    A. True
    B. False

10. The appraisal will be used for

    A. Equity assessment
    B. Title insurance
    C. LTV Assessment
    D. All of the above

208

11. URAR is an abbreviation for

A. The Uniform Residential Appraisal Report
B. The 1004
C. The most common appraisal you will encounter
D. All of the above

12. The appraiser will note Red Flags during the appraisal process

A. True
B. False

13. The appraiser will assess

A. The property
B. The neighborhood
C. Recently sold property
D. All of the above

14. You should never read the appraisal before underwriting

A. True
B. False

15. If you note a discrepancy, error or issue on the appraisal report you should

A. Notify underwriting
B. Influence the appraiser to alter the item
C. Notify the appraiser of the issue
D. Request a field review appraisal

16. Property Valuation will be determined by

A. Comparison with other property
B. Sales price of other property
C. Proximity to recently sold property
D. All of the above

Chapter 10 – Guideline Matrix

1.   Why is it important to become familiar with the guidelines of the various loan products available through your branch?

2.   What is a product matrix?

3.   What is the first step in grading a package for loan placement?

4.   What factor may alter the pricing you initially plan for a loan placement?

5.   What are some steps you might take if the new loan causes the borrower to exceed the ratio limitations set by the loan guidelines?

6.   You must place each loan carefully because there are a limited number of loan products to choose from

A. True
B. False

7.   A product matrix is

A. The final underwriting guideline manual
B. A snapshot of minimum requirements
C. A snapshot of final requirements
D None of the above

8.   A product matrix will allow you to assess a loan's suitability for your borrower.

A. True
B. False

9.   You will begin grading using

       A. The loan application
       B. The pre-qualification questionnaire
       C. The credit-scoring key
       D The borrower history

10.   You will need to compare

       A. At least one decisioning factor
       B. All decisioning factors
       C. Specific decisioning factors
       D. None of the above

11.   You should begin grading

       A. At the lowest approval tier
       B. At the highest approval tier
       C. At the highest paying approval level
       D At the bottom of the matrix

12.   You may exceed an approval level by

       A. Changing the credit report
       B. Speaking to underwriting
       C. Supplying adequate compensating factors
       D. Never

13.   If the housing expense exceeds the loan criteria, you must

       A. Move on to the next loan matrix
       B. Suggest alternative options to the borrower
       C. Request underwriting change the matrix
       D None of the above

Chapter 11 – Pricing the Loan

1.   What is a pricing restriction?

2.   What is the second step in loan pricing?

3.   What three items must you determine prior to beginning the actual pricing?

4.   Who is the best candidate for a fixed rate program?

5.   What is a prepayment penalty?

6.   What common pre-pay terms do most lenders offer?

7.   What benefit does the pre-payment penalty offer to a lender?

8.   What is the primary benefit to the use of a pre-pay penalty for the borrower?

9.   What does it mean to price at PAR?

10.   When do you use the Margin?

11.   When pricing a loan you should use

A. The rate sheet that generates the most income for your branch
B. The most current rate sheet
C. The rate sheet provided by your branch manager
D. None of the above

12.   Pricing restrictions may occur as a result of

A. Internal requirements
B. Applicable laws
C. Pre-payment penalty
D. All of the above

13.   All rate sheets will include qualifying information for you to review

A. True
B. False

14.   You will determine the interest rate offered using

A. The loan term
B. The LTV
C. The branch income
D. All of the above

15.   The pre-payment requirements may

A. Impact the final rate
B. Generate additional branch income
C. Violate regulations
D. All of the above

Chapter 13 – File Documentation

1.   Why is it important to document each loan package you submit?

2.   Why should you note any missing information on the loan cover letter that you submit with the package?

3.   Why should you include compensating factor information at the time of the initial submittal even when an exception request is not expected?

4.   Why should you include information regarding the approval and transaction specifics you are requesting as part of your loan cover sheet?

5.   What is the purpose of a stipulation list?

6.   What are the three common written decisions you will see from underwriting?

7.   What is an affinity provider?

8.   Who is ultimately responsible for the smooth process and timely closing of the loan?

9.   How can you avoid loan process delays?

10.   How can you foster positive relationships with affinity service providers?

11.   The Loan Processor is the liaison between

        a. the borrower and the loan funder
        b. the borrower and underwriting
        c. the broker and underwriting
        d. the lender and the broker

12.   Each time you submit a stipulation the underwriter will

        a. review the entire loan file
        b. request additional documentation
        c. complain about the documentation
        d. request a different stipulation

13.   If you must repeatedly return to the borrower for additional documentation, you will gain

        a. borrower loyalty
        b. a poor reputation
        c. underwriting approval
        d. all of the above

14.   The underwriting summary is a form of

        a. checklist of inclusions
        b. guideline
        c. application overview
        d. none of the above

15.   When requesting an appraisal you should note

        a. the borrowers approval rating
        b. the method of billing and payment
        c. the title company who will close the loan
        d. the possibility of a field review

16.   The most important product a Loan Processor has available is

        a. low interest rates
        b. fast underwriting approvals
        c. customer service skills
        d. the ability to relate well to borrowers

17.   The first act you will take on a loan package is to

        a. pull the credit report
        b. review the application
        c. complete the pre-qualification
        d. send VOE/VOR/VOM forms

18.   You should revise the good faith estimate

a. frequently throughout the loan process
b. upon altering any borrower credit specifics
c. upon receipt of the sales agreement
d. upon receipt of the initial loan approval

19.   The borrower should be informed of the final loan specifics

a. before the closing
b. the day of closing
c. at the closing table
d. none of the above

20.   The Loan Processor should take gifts to the closing

a. True
b. False

21.   The underwriter will review all aspects of the file including:

a. Source of down payment
b. The borrower's personal recommendations
c. The borrower's professional references
d. All of the above

22.   The underwriter will review the file and issue an

a. approval
b. denial
c. conditional approval
d. Any of the above

23.   Prior to closing documents must be provided to the underwriter before the loan documents can be requested.

a. True
b. False

24.   The processing stage is a stage where

a. all information is verified and submitted
b. missing documentation is requested
c. data is transferred to the underwriter
d. all of the above

25. A verification of deposit is a form sent

    a. To the closing or settlement agent to verify the funds to close
    b. To the bank to verify the average bank account balance of the borrower
    c. to the real estate agent to verify the earnest money deposit
    d. none of the above

26. The funding is when

    a. the underwriter completes a final loan review
    b. the monies borrowed are wired or sent to the closing agent
    c. the monies borrowed are disbursed to the proper individuals
    d. none of the above

27. Delays in the loan process can be avoided by

    a. implementing a loan process follow-up and reminder system
    b. creating strong relationships with affinity service providers
    c. efficient pipeline management
    d. all of the above

28. Many Loan Processors forget to create

    a. a good closing team
    b. an adequate filing system
    c. positive service relationships
    d. borrower commitment

29. An affinity service provider includes any individual who must accomplish tasks in a timely and professional manner in order for you to accomplish your goal of closed loans.

    a. True
    b. False

30. You should treat your affinity service providers

    a. Respectfully
    b. Friendly
    c. With Consideration
    d. All of the above

Chapter 1 - The Lending Process
1. Primary Mortgage Market
Secondary Mortgage Market
2. A group of smaller investors seeking a low risk, long term investment and having capital available to purchase packaged loan products
3. Bank Brokerage Office E Commute
4. To act as a liaison between the borrowers seeking mortgage funds and multiple funding sources.
5. Insurance Companies Pension funds Individual investors
Primary Lenders with excess deposits
6. d. Insurance Company

Chapter 2 – Borrower Prequalification
1. Because they are afraid to ask for information
2. You must ask for the information
3. The initial contact sets the tone for the entire relationship with that borrower. Most people will make decisions concerning your professionalism and character within the first 30 seconds of contact.
4. To assist in tracking referral source information, assessing marketing and advertising effectiveness and to provide follow-up information regarding the applicant to the referral source
5. This question enables you to assess the urgency of the query and determine if the borrower thus enabling you to prioritize the flow of work within your office.
You will also be able to determine if the borrower is working with an agent thereby strengthening referral relationships.
If the borrower has chosen a home, you will be able to use real purchase numbers to assess DTI and borrower expectations prior to the first face-to-face meeting.
6. The professionalism, attentiveness, and responsiveness you provide to your borrowers.
7. D 8. B 9. B 10. A 11. B 12. B
13. B 14. B 15. B 16. B

Chapter 4 – Reading the Credit Report
1. Credit reports are an overview of a person's history of spending and payment habits.
2. Any action that had a negative or derogatory impact on a borrower's credit history.
3. Debt-to-income ratio's are the amount of open debt a borrower carries weighed against the borrower's monthly income and in general, the higher the DTI the greater the potential risk of borrower default on a loan.
4. 450 to 850
5. Beacon at Equifax Empirica at Transunion TRW/Fair Isaac at TRW
6. The Fair, Isaac Credit Bureau Score
7. The FICO is generated using a system of scorecards created by compiling the credit data from millions of consumers and then applying complex mathematical methods and extensive research to note credit patterns that predict probable credit performance.
8. Race, color, religion, national origin, sex, marital status, age, occupation, length of time at present housing, or any information not contained within the credit file
9. A means of rank ordering potential borrowers based on the likelihood that they would pay their obligations as agreed
10. By reviewing the score factor reason codes included on the report
11. C. 12 A 13. A. 14. B. 15. A.
16. A. 17. D. 18. B. 19. B. 20 A.

Chapter 5 – Compensating Factors and DTI
1. Any items that exist in the borrower's profile that may exceed the normal circumstances commonly encountered and reflect favorably on the borrower
2. To provide underwriting with a solid reason to approve a borrower at a higher level when that borrower falls on the edge of a credit tier or approval level
3. Less than 10% increase from the old rent/housing payments to the new housing expense.
A decrease from the old rent/housing payments to the new housing expense.
A borrower's excellent savings ability (as shown by savings accounts, etc.).
Income that is not qualifying income.
Larger than minimum down payment.
Residual income (excess after expense) of $500 per adult and $250 per child.
Time at current residence exceeds 5 years.
Time at current employment exceeds 5 years.
Debt-to-income ratios below maximum guidelines as set forth for that approval level.
Credit scores fall within a few points of next highest level.
A perfect mortgage or rental history, as proven through the credit bureau.
4. How much loan borrowers can afford
5. The gross income divided by the new PITI mortgage payment
6. The back end ratio
7. Utility Bills Car Insurance Health Insurance Cell Phone Bills
8. Pay off certain items Lower the interest rate of the new loan Lower the loan amount offered to the borrower
9. One time, regardless of the number of times the debt appears in the report(s).
10. Both parties' income and credit history is considered, but you factor each debt only once even if it appears on both credit reports.

11 B. 12. C. 13. C. 14. D. 15. D. 16. A. 17. A.

Chapter 6 – The Loan Application

1. The amortization method dictates the monthly payment, debt load, and types of disclosures required on an application.
2. To be decided
3. Approval levels will vary depending on the occupancy status of the property.
4. Subordinate finance negotiated Seller assistance toward closing costs Sales price
Other possible factors not yet visible
5. You should include additional information on the last page of the application.
6. To bring this information to the attention of the underwriter early in the process in order to set the stage for compensating factors in the event an exception is required.
7. A standard figure is $15.00 for each revolving line the applicant has available if the balance is zero but the specific underwriting guidelines for the loan program you are planning should be consulted.
8. You can easily lower the loan amount later but an increase in the loan amount requested will require the underwriting department to recalculate all numbers and issue a new approval.
9. Including the terms of a subordinate finance agreement early in the process allows the underwriter to approve or decline the terms of subordinate financing before the deal has progressed.
10. If the space available for additional information is not used you should cross through the blank area. This crossing through assures the borrower that you will not alter or add any items to their application after their signature is affixed.
11. D. 12 B. 13. D. 14. A. 15. A.
16. C. 17. B. 18. D.

Chapter 9 - Appraisals

1. A borrower is responsible for repaying the loan but the property acts as collateral in the event the borrower does not fulfill their obligations.
2. Any information that appears regarding issues that will stand in the way of the completion of the loan.
3. Uniform Residential Appraisal Report
4. To scrutinize any item that appears to vary between documents in the file and the entries on the appraisal to determine which document contains the error and to note any item that is below the minimum requirements of the loan guideline, which you are planning for the loan file.
5. You should have the person responsible for the errors address them in writing.
6. Because it is sometimes more effective and a faster process to request the necessary correction items or additional information immediately rather than waiting for the underwriter to generate a stipulation regarding the matter.
7. You should only request alterations arising because of an error or omission not an alteration to the opinion or decision of the appraiser.
8. The sales comparison approach assesses the characteristics of the subject property as compared to other similar properties sold within a given time period.
9. A. 10. D. 11. A. 12. A. 13. D. 14. B.
15. C. 16. D.

Chapter 10 – Guideline Matrix

1. The more familiar with loan guidelines you become the more capable you will be at moving the loan package through the loan process and to a successful closing. Familiarity allows you to locate and address any red flag issues that may be apparent before an issue inhibits the closing of the loan.
2. A snapshot of the minimum requirements needed to place a loan in a particular program and approval level.
3. Rate the credit report scoring key elements against the product matrix levels.
4. The debt ratio may change after you price the loan because of interest rate and subsequent monthly payment. If this ratio becomes excessive, you may need to re-price the loan.
5. Obtain an exception to the ratio limitations with compensating factors.
Reduce the maximum sales price/loan amount the borrower may obtain.
Reduce the points wrapped in the interest rate and allow the borrower to make payment for the services of your office on the front end.
Pay off consumer debt in an attempt to reduce overall debt load.
Obtain seller assistance toward closing costs or additional borrower funds to buy down the interest rate to a level that generates a payment that fits within the borrower debt-ratio guidelines.
Search for a different program that allows the borrower to approve at the levels needed to close the loan under the present circumstances.
6. B. 7. B. 8. A. 9. C. 10. B. 11. B.
12. C. 13. B.

Chapter 11 – Pricing the Loan

1. An internal limitation or requirement and applicable laws regarding loan pricing.
2. Review the minimum qualifying guidelines included on the rate sheet to confirm that your borrower meets the current criteria.
3. Preferred loan terms The LTV required Pricing including office payment
4. Perpetual high-risk borrower Long-term purchaser Cautious borrower
5. A monetary penalty which is assessed for the early payoff of a loan containing a prepay clause.
6. 0, 2, 3, and 5-year penalties
7. Security that the borrower will retain the loan for a certain period thereby securing the expected interest payments for the lender or that if the borrower pays the loan off early the interest loss to the lender will be offset by the penalty.
8. Lenders will often offer a reduction of the initial interest rate in exchange for the pre-payment clause because of the added longevity of loans on the books.

9. There are no points included in the interest rate and you must obtain payment for the branch as points charged on the good faith estimate and HUD Settlement Statement.

10. When you use an ARM option in the loan, you will note the margin that refers to the rate of adjustment that may occur

11. B. 12. D. 13. B. 14. D 15. D.

Chapter 13 – File Documentation

1. Without proper documentation, the underwriter cannot make a valid decision on the loan package and will request additional items or stipulations prior to issuing an approval or conditional approval.

2. To assure the underwriter that you are aware of the lacking information and are working to obtain all necessary documentation.

3. To set a positive tone for the loan package

To bring the compensating factors to the attention of the underwriter before they initially review the borrower profile

To set the stage if something occurs later in the process that requires a positive decision or exception from the underwriter

4. This inclusion allows the underwriter to review the material and is a courtesy action that will smooth the underwriter's workload.

5. To allow the underwriter to request information required for loan decision, closing or secondary market sale and to provide clarification information regarding any file item that is unclear to the underwriter.

6. Approved Everything contained within the file meets the guidelines for final approval

Conditional Additional documentation will be needed to ensure final loan approval

Denied Aspects of the file do not conform to the guidelines

7. Any individual who must complete their tasks in a timely, professional manner in order for you to accomplish your goal of closing the loan

8. The Loan Processor

9. By maintaining an organized flow process, using an adequate loan process follow-up and affinity service provider reminder-system.

10. By treating these providers in a respectful, friendly, and considerate manner to foster positive relationships, build rapport and create an overall good relationship.

11. B 12. A 13. B 14. A 15. B

16. C 17. C 18. C 19. A 20. B

21. D 22. D 23. B 24. D 25. B

26. B 27. D 28. C 29. A 30. D

Appendix C
Lending Mathematics

DEBT-TO-INCOME RATIO EXCERCISES

To calculate a borrower's debt to income take the total monthly debt load and divide it by the total monthly income. For example:

A borrower who earns $2800.00 monthly and has installment debt of $750.00 monthly has a debt-to-income ratio of 26.78%.

D   I   R
750 / 2800 = 26.78%

1. Income $6200
    Debt $1900
    _____
    Ratio   %

2. Income $3000
    Debt $1350
    _____
    Ratio   %

3. Income $3750
    Debt $ 970
    _____
    Ratio   %

4. Income $1600
    Debt $ 340
    _____
    Ratio   %

5. Income $2000
    Debt $ 420
    _____
    Ratio   %

6. Income $2480
    Debt $ 920
    _____
    Ratio   %

7. Income $4200
    Debt $1850
    _____
    Ratio   %

8. Income $4800
    Debt $2175
    _____
    Ratio   %

9. Income $5100
    Debt $1950
    _____
    Ratio   %

10. Income $5500
    Debt $1775
    _____
    Ratio   %

11. Income $5750
    Debt $1900
    _____
    Ratio   %

12. Income $3425
    Debt $1350
    _____
    Ratio   %

13. Income $4387
    Debt $1218
    Ratio   %

14. Income $2330
    Debt $ 961
    Ratio   %

CALCULATING LOAN-TO-VALUE

When calculating loan to value, assuming the Value and the LTV Percentage are given the formula is Value multiplied by percentage.

Assume a house with a value (sales price) of $112,000 with a LTV of 95% would have a loan amount of $106,400.

Sales Price	x LTV Percentage	= Loan Amount
$112,000	**x .95**	**= $106,400**

1. Sales Price $99,000
   LTV 85%

   Loan $ _____

2. Sales Price $110,000
   LTV 90%

   Loan $ _____

3. Sales Price $144,900
   LTV 95%

   Loan $ _____

4. Sales Price $75,000
   LTV 80%

   Loan $ _____

5. Sales Price $69,900
   LTV 70%

   Loan $ _____

6. Sales Price $104,900
   LTV 75%

   Loan $ _____

CALCULATING COMBINED LOAN TO VALUE

When a Combined Loan-to-Value is offered, you will calculate the secondary financing figure using the same formula above.

Sales Price   x CLTV Percentage   = Subordinate/Secondary Financing Loan Amount
$112,000   **x .05**   **= $5600 maximum second mortgage**

1. Sales Price $99,000

   LTV 85%   CLTV 95%

   Loan $ _____

2. Sales Price $110,000

   LTV 90% CLTV 95%

   Loan $ _____

3. Sales Price $144,900
   LTV 90%   CLTV 95%

   Loan $ _____

4. Sales Price $75,000
   LTV 80% CLTV 90%

   Loan $ _____

5. Sales Price $69,900
   LTV 70%   CLTV 80%

   Loan $ _____

6. Sales Price $104,900
   LTV 75% CLTV 85%

   Loan $ _____

SELLER CONCESSION

When calculating seller concession toward borrower's non-recurring closing costs you will want to use the SALES PRICE of the property as your base number. The seller concession figure is negotiated in the sales agreement and can be a fixed dollar amount or it may be a percentage. For these exercises, assume the seller is willing to grant 6% of the sales price toward borrower's non-recurring closing costs.

Sales Price   **x Concession Percentage**   **= Dollar Concession Amount**
$112,000 x 6%   = $6720

1.   Sales Price $99,000   2.   Sales Price $110,000

3.   Sales Price $144,900   4.   Sales Price $75,000

5.   Sales Price $69,900   6.   Sales Price $104,900

7.   Sales Price $49,500   8.   Sales Price $219,900

9.   Sales Price $53,350   10.   Sales Price $189,000

SELLER CONCESSION

For additional exercise in calculating maximum seller concession, you can calculate using a maximum seller concession toward buyer's non-recurring closing costs of 3% of the sales price. (6% and 3% are the most commonly allowed maximum seller concessions under most underwriting guidelines.)

Sales Price   **x Concession Percentage**   **= Dollar Concession Amount**
$112,000 x 3%   = $3360

1.   Sales Price $99,000   2.   Sales Price $110,000

3.   Sales Price $144,900   4.   Sales Price $75,000

5.   Sales Price $69,900   6.   Sales Price $104,900

7.   Sales Price $49,500   8.   Sales Price $219,900

9.   Sales Price $53,350   10.   Sales Price $189,000

Kenney

MAXIMUM HOUSING EXPENSE (PITI)

It is important to be able to calculate the maximum monthly housing expense (PITI – Principal, Interest, Taxes, and Insurance) your borrower could afford under any loan program approval. This allows you to set borrowers and Agents expectations as to the cost range of properties that the borrowers should be shopping.

Begin with the maximum DTI as per the approval level. Subtract the borrowers current DTI (excluding any housing expense from the ratio). The total is the percentage of income available to spend on PITI. This percentage should be multiplied by the borrower's total monthly income to achieve a maximum dollar amount that may be spent toward PITI.

The formula for calculating Maximum PITI payments is as follows:

Maximum DTI %   **– Current DTI %**   **= % Income Available for Housing Costs**
41%   **- 22%**   **= 19%**

Monthly Income   X % of Income Available for PITI   = Maximum Mthly PITI
$3200   **X 19%**   **= $608 maximum PITI**

For the following problems, assume a maximum DTI of 45%

1. Current DTI 29%
   Income $3750

2. Current DTI 18%
   Income $2100

3. Current DTI 22%
   Income $2880

4. Current DTI 31%
   Income $4195

5. Current DTI 24%
   Income $2655

6. Current DTI 12%
   Income $3875

7. Current DTI 19%
   Income $3150

8. Current DTI 26%
   Income $1775

9. Current DTI 14%
   Income $1980

10. Current DTI 36%
    Income $3650